KT-450-817

David Mitchell
Back Story

A Memoir

HARPER

HARPER

An imprint of HarperCollins*Publishers*
77–85 Fulham Palace Road,
Hammersmith, London W6 8JB

www.harpercollins.co.uk

First published by HarperCollins*Publishers* 2012
This edition published 2013

1 3 5 7 9 10 8 6 4 2

© David Mitchell 2012

David Mitchell asserts the moral right to
be identified as the author of this work

A catalogue record of this book is
available from the British Library

PB ISBN 978-0-00-735174-9
EB ISBN 978-0-00-738294-1

All photographs are courtesy of the author, his friends or family, with the
exception of the following: p12 (bottom) cutting reproduced from the *Hampstead
& Highgate Express*; p13 (lower centre) Objective Productions; p15 (bottom)
Intermedia Productions; p16 (top) Janie Airey

While every effort has been made to trace the owners of copyright
material reproduced herein and secure permissions, the publishers
would like to apologise for any omissions and will be pleased
to incorporate missing acknowledgements in any
future edition of this book.

All rights reserved. No part of this publication may be
reproduced, stored in a retrieval system, or transmitted,
in any form or by any means, electronic, mechanical,
photocopying, recording or otherwise, without the prior
written permission of the publishers.

Printed and bound in Great Britain by Clays Ltd, St Ives plc

MIX
Paper from
responsible sources
FSC® C007454

FSC™ is a non-profit international organisation established to promote
the responsible management of the world's forests. Products carrying the
FSC label are independently certified to assure consumers that they come
from forests that are managed to meet the social, economic and
ecological needs of present and future generations,
and other controlled sources.

Find out more about HarperCollins and the environment at
www.harpercollins.co.uk/green

For VC (M)

TOWER HAMLETS LIBRARIES	
91000001976901	
Bertrams	07/06/2013
BIO791.45	£7.99
THISWM	TH13000213

Contents

Introduction

This is one of those misery memoirs. And it's one of those celebrity memoirs. It's also a very personal journey, a manual for urban ramblers and a weight-loss guide. Surely it'll sell?

I realise the whole 'Let me tell you about my pain' thing is a classic envy-avoidance technique. What it's saying is: if you envy me my interesting job, my relative affluence and moderate fame, then don't. Because I struggle daily with a dark and terrible problem. With some it's drugs, abuse, depression, the loss of loved ones, the terrible illness of a child – well, you can't have it all, I suppose, and so I've made do with a bad back.

What do you reckon to that then, enviers!? Eh? You want to swap!? Ow, my back! You want to swap places!? Well go ahead, if you like terrible pain and misery, hardly assuaged at all by getting to be on TV! Eek, my poor spine! You want to take my place in the horror dome!? Ow, it's creaking and spasming! Well, make my day! By which I mean life!

I'm assuming here that my life is enviable enough to require this mitigating strategy. Well, I admit it – I think it is. Aside from being born into the free and affluent West and never having had to worry about food, shelter and warmth, I do basically think I'm a jammy sod. I'm not saying there aren't things that worry and upset me a lot, but I reckon everyone gets that. And I make a very good living doing something I love, a state of affairs that tends to be envied by those who don't share it. Of course there will be loads of people who don't envy me at all. I probably envy *them*. I expect they'll have all yachts and kids and stuff.

What this book isn't is one of those novels by David Mitchell. You know, David Mitchell the novelist. I'm sure he would never allow a sentence with 'isn't is' in it like that. Everyone says he's a very good novelist but I've never checked, partly because I resent him for sharing my name without asking and partly because I do a lot of my novel reading on the Tube and it would feel weird to be reading a book with my name on it in public. If one of the people who conflate me and the novelist saw that, they'd think I was sitting there *reading my own book*. 'He might as well spend the whole journey admiring his own reflection in a hand mirror,' such a person might think.

David Miliband is such a person (although he might take a less than averagely dim view of narcissism). I was once in a London park, on a crisp winter afternoon, feeding some bread to the ducks with a girl, when David Miliband wandered up with his kids. He stood there, a couple of yards behind us, for what felt like minutes. He was playing with his children in the park at the weekend, like a perfectly normal husband and father, who is being portrayed by a power-crazed Martian.

The woman I was with urgently wanted us to say hello. She was all interested, I don't know why. I couldn't see the point in bothering him. I thought it would be embarrassing. I was right.

'Oh, you're David Mitchell,' said David Miliband, adding politely to my companion: 'I love his books.'

This was nice of him. But it was a complicated moment. He can't have known that there were a comedian and a novelist both called David Mitchell and mistaken me for the other one, because he recognised my face. He must have just assumed we were the same person.

Or he knew perfectly well I was only the comedian, and had particularly enjoyed *This Mitchell and Webb Book*, my most recent publication at the time. In fact, my only publication at the time. But he'd said 'books'. Perhaps he was looking ahead? Yes, that must be it. He was so confident he'd enjoy my future volumes, he was already able to say he loves them. Thinking about it, I'd have been quite justified in putting that quote on the cover.

But I'm not the novelist, I'm the one who's a bit known from TV. And of course there are millions of other David Mitchells who are neither. Was it the pain of my slightly problem back that gave me the need, the will and the focus to become one of the David Mitchells that potential Prime Ministers mistake for one of the others? Was it because I was maddened yet driven by a constant sciatic throb that I was able to conceive of sketches and characters that were marginally more amusing than those of people who didn't end up on TV? Is it the desire to get up and stretch that inspires my trademark panel show 'rants'? Would I happily exchange all the success for a less problematic spine? Or is my aching back so completely a part of me that, metaphorically bitter and literally twisted though it makes me, I wouldn't change it if I could? Do I, as Captain Kirk said in *Star Trek V*, 'need my pain'?

You will find the answers to all those questions in this book. Indeed in this section. On this very page. In this paragraph. In fact, in two words' time. It is 'No.' To all of them.

I know what you're thinking. Why didn't BBC Four snap this up? It would make a cracking documentary. Good point. It would be gold dust. Me moaning about my back, pottering around stiffly, interviewing other people about their niggles, talking to specialists, shaking my head with concern as I'm told about the annual man-hours lost nationally, before suddenly putting an anguished hand to a cricked neck. They could even have clips of *The Simpsons*, for God's sake. That episode where Homer goes to the chiropractor.

But no, when it comes to celebrities moaning about their problems, they only want to hear about depression and madness. The liberal media have a tremendous bias in favour of disorders of the nervous system's cerebral centre rather than its provincial offshoots.

It's London-centricity made anatomical and there was no shifting any TV commissioner to the Salford that is my spine.

Yet, let me tell you, back pain is a fascinating topic – as long as it's your own. It may not be *fun* to think about, largely because it happens in the context of nagging back pain – it's like trying to solve an engrossing country house murder while gradually being murdered yourself – but it's never boring.

That was my situation in 2007. It was really worrying me. I tried everything. By which I mean, I tried some things. You can't try everything. The world is full of evangelists – people who are convinced the answer lies in acupuncture, chiropractic, osteopathy, physiotherapy, cod liver oil or changing the pocket you keep your wallet in. I tried some remedies, and felt guilty that I wasn't trying more, but also tired because the condition stopped me sleeping properly. Even Poirot's little grey cells might have misfired if he was being occasionally bonked on the head by an invisible candlestick as he tried to address the suspects.

I took note of the things that I wanted to hear (such as 'you can fix it by sitting on a ball') and not the things I didn't (such as 'you might need a major operation') – like you do when you're infatuated with someone and can't yet bring yourself to draw the dispiriting conclusion that they don't fancy you. That would mean you'd have to start the incredibly unpleasant process of getting over them. In those circumstances – and I feel this gives an insight into the mentality of the stalker – you treasure any sign of affection or kindness and build great castles of reason around them in your mind: how could they possibly have said that, smiled then, noticed this, if they didn't on some level return your feelings? Meanwhile you ignore the overwhelming body of evidence of their indifference and the fact that they're often really quite pleasant to a wide range of people without that meaning they'd ever be willing to have sex with them. (More of this later.)

It's a sign of how deep my despair became, and yet how stubbornly I avoided dealing with the subject via official medical channels because of my weird fear of doctors and hospitals, that I started sitting on a ball – and indeed that I still sit on a ball, that I'm sitting on a ball as I write this. A giant inflatable yoga ball. Apologies if that's shattered your image of me lounging in a Jacuzzi smoking a cigar while dictating these words to an impatient and topless Hungarian supermodel. But, no, I'm perched alone on a preposterous piece of back-strengthening furniture in my bedroom in Kilburn surrounded by dusty piles of books and old souvenirs from the Cambridge Footlights.

You have no idea how greatly sitting on a ball offends me aesthetically and challenges my sense of who I am. Or maybe you do. After all, you have bought a book written by me – you're probably aware of my tweedy image. You've probably guessed that all things 'new age' tend to make me raise a sceptical eyebrow. And a sceptical fist, which I bang sceptically on the table while wryly starting a sceptical chant of 'Fuck off! Fuck off! Fuck off!' before starting sceptically to throw stuff and scream: 'You can shove your trendy scientifically unsubstantiated bullshit up your uncynical anuses!'

To me, sitting on a ball feels a bit wind chimes. It's got a touch of the homeopathic about it. In homeopathic terms: a massive overdose. It smacks of wheat intolerance. Which, to me, smacks of intolerance. And I'm very intolerant of it.

The other major lifestyle change I adopted was walking. That was the only thing about which there appeared to be any consensus among the people offering me advice: that walking, even if it hurt, always helped. Resting, oddly, did not. Resting oddly certainly didn't. (Take that, Lynne Truss!) Walking was something I could do. This was so much more approachable as a solution than either the conventional medicine route (doctors, painkillers, scans, scalpels, unconsciousness) or any of the trendier alternatives, a lot of which – yoga and pilates, for example – seemed to involve going to classes.

I don't think men can really go to yoga classes, can they? I mean, it would be weird. All the women would just think you were there in the hope of a covert ogle or to hit on them afterwards. This is what I had always suspected until I was talking to a female friend about yoga. It was a group conversation in the pub. She was extolling the virtues of her yoga classes and saying how everyone should go until one of the men present asked: 'But wouldn't it be weird for a man?'

She seemed surprised. She thought for a moment. Then she said: 'Yes, you're right. It would be really weird. I was just recommending it because I go and I like it. But, no, of course if a man turned up, we'd all assume he was a pervert.'

But you seldom get called a pervert just for walking, unless you're naked and circling a primary school. So I started to walk, first for half an hour and then for an hour every day, and let me tell you it has cured my back. I get the occasional niggle, but then, who doesn't? But it doesn't feel fragile any more and I can bend down without having to take a few minutes to plan.

That's the main advantage. There's a secret other one, which is that I've lost about two stone in weight. But that's incidental. I refuse to let myself be pleased about it. Or rather I'm in total denial of how pleased I am about it. I don't want to think of myself as that vain – or to admit that I'd even noticed the lamentable chubbiness that encroached over successive *Peep Show* series. If it made me a bit trimmer, that's a happy accident. Not even that, an irrelevant accident. I'm not the sort of person to care about that sort of thing: I don't go to gyms or diet. I fear that calorie counting, if I ever tried it, would be a short hop from powdering my wig, dousing myself in scent and speaking French to passers-by. I just take a daily constitutional. In a British sort of way.

And it turns out that I like walking. I find it relaxing – differently from, if not necessarily more than, watching television. It gives me some time to think, without the self-consciousness of having set aside some time to think. I find I'm more aware of the weather and the seasons and I have a much greater knowledge of the city I live in. If ignorance of one-way systems and not having a driving licence weren't a handicap, I'd be able to qualify as a taxi driver.

In this book, I'll take you on one of my walks – and I promise I won't go on about my back. It's a walk through my life, really, but I'll try to point out some of the notable London landmarks along the way so you can use it as a travel guide if you prefer. But it's basically a weight-loss manual.

-1-

The *Fawlty Towers* Years

Anyone watching me lock my front door would think that I was trying to break in: frantically yanking the handle up and down, pulling it hard towards me and then pushing against the frame with a firmness that's just short of a shoulder barge. Then running round to the kitchen window and furtively peering in. In fact I'm checking that the door's properly locked and then that the gas is off. This is the wrong way round but I'm relatively new to having gas and so the neuroticism about it kicks in marginally later than my door doubts, which date from having a locker at school.

I never had anything of any value in my locker – not so much as a Twix. But the fact that it was lockable meant it should be locked, meant that I had to remember to lock it, meant that I had to check that it was locked, meant that I had to remember if I'd checked that it was locked.

That was the advent of my school-leaving dance (by which I mean the odd routine I put myself through every day before going home, not a sort of prom; my school didn't have a prom, it was in Britain – in fact it had a ball; I didn't go). The steps were: locking my locker, checking it absent-mindedly, walking out of the room, pausing unsure whether I'd checked it, returning to the locker, annoyed the whole way about the time I was almost certainly wasting; approaching the locker with such a complete expectation that it was locked that my mind wandered and I barely noticed myself check it so that when, moments later, I was leaving the school again, I wasn't one hundred per cent sure that I'd checked it or that, in that moment of complacent absent-mindedness, I'd have noticed if it wasn't locked; turning back again.

To say that this could go on for hours would be an exaggeration but it could take a quarter of an hour. In time I learned that the key was to concentrate when checking the locker. Take a mental photograph of the moment. Say to myself: 'Here I am, now, me, sane, with a locked locker. Remember this in the doubting moments to come.'

But the concentration is tiring so, having gone through it with the door today, I'm unwilling to unlock it to go and check the gas when, by peering through the window, I can probably check the alignment of the hob knobs. (I wonder if that's where the biscuit got its name. I'm suspicious about that biscuit's name. It's like Stinking Bishop: recent, yet quickly adopted as a go-to reference for those wishing to be cosily humorous. It got its Alan Bennett licence too early and easily. I suspect the advertising agency was involved.)

I adjust the collar of my jacket, massaging a slightly jarred wrist from my high-energy security check. It's a spring day and slightly too warm for a jacket really – certainly once I get walking. Unless the temperature is absolutely Siberian, a brisk walk always warms me up, especially when I've got a jacket on. Or at least warms up the middle of my back, which then sweats through my shirt. So I have to wear a jacket to hide that.

My walk begins on the exterior staircase from my flat, which I have to descend carefully in case there's sick or a used needle. Listen to me, glamorising the place! There's never sick or a needle! This is Kilburn, not Harlesden. I mean wee or a bit of cling-film from one of those little cannabis turds. Sometimes some kids are sitting at the bottom. One of them might say: 'Hey, are you the guy from *Peep Show*?' I am, so I nod.

I don't know how I ended up in Kilburn. I'm not from here – but then hardly anyone who lives in London is from there. I think it's slightly weird to be from London. As a child, London terrified me, largely because I considered it to be the British manifestation of New York which, on television, looked like a living hell. I think I'm largely basing this on Cagney and Lacey, who seemed to have a horrible time. It was all drugs and crowds and scruffy offices and huge locks on the inside of apartment doors.

The size of those locks was unnerving. Who or what were locks that sturdy and that numerous meant to keep out? And by the time such a gang or monster, or drug-addled gang made monstrous by their craving, was bashing on the door, you might as well just open it and hope they kill you quickly, because what's the alternative? Escape via the garden? Oh no, no one has a garden. There's a park you can get to on a frightening underground train full of junkies, and where you can maybe play a bit of frisbee while old ladies are raped in the bushes around you, but this is a world without gardens, without swingball and where it certainly isn't safe to ride your bike with attached stabilisers along the pavement.

That's what I assumed London was like. My childhood self would hate where I live now. He would also be disappointed that I'm not ruler of the world or at least Prime Minister or a wizard. But the fact that, far from a castle, mansion or cave complex, I don't even live in a normal house with a garden and an attic and a spare room would basically make me indistinguishable, to his eyes, from a tramp.

Growing up, there were metaphorical stabilisers attached to my whole life. Born in Salisbury, brought up in Oxford and a student in Cambridge, I was 22 before I had to deal on a daily basis with anywhere other than affluent, ancient, chocolate-box cities where murders never happen but murder stories are often set. I was cosseted in deep suburban security and probably fretted about the outside world all the more as a result.

I have often suffered from the fact that warnings are calibrated for the reckless. Very sensibly, parents, teachers and people at TV filming locations who provide you with blank-firing guns for action sequences (to pick three random types of authority figure) design their remarks to prevent the fearless from accidentally killing themselves. 'Don't look at the sun or you'll go blind' ... 'A blank-firing gun is an incredibly dangerous weapon' ... 'Verrucas can kill.'

The collateral damage is every last scrap of more timorous people's peace of mind; the sum of their warnings makes people like me view life as a minefield. So my childhood, as I remember it, was laced with fear.

But, before I can remember, there was definitely a moment of recklessness – when I pushed at the stabilising boundaries that my doting parents had set for me. This was in Salisbury – in fact a little village just outside called Stapleford where we lived in a bungalow. I couldn't walk but I did have a sort of walker – a small vehicle with a seat and wheels, but no engine, that I could propel along, Flintstones-style, with my bare feet. Having mastered this contraption, I apparently became unwilling to learn to walk properly but would career around in it at high speeds.

One day I took a corner too fast and smacked my head on a skirting board. There was blood everywhere. I was scarred for life. Literally. I still bear a tiny scar in between my eyebrows of which I was immensely proud as a child. And now I don't drive. Can that be a coincidence? No, I say it CANNOT be a coincidence. Before that crash I was a fearless speed junky. I was destined for Formula One greatness. Also I was brimming with infant brain cells of which the crash must have led to a holocaust. My timorousness, my lack of a driving licence, the tiny mark on my face, my B in GCSE Biology all stem from that moment. If you don't like this book, blame the corporate child abusers who made that deathtrap walker.

Maybe everyone is fearless in infancy and what marks us apart is our ability to absorb fears – some of us are made of sponge and soak them up while others are resistant willows that have to be repeatedly painted with the linseed oils of caution to prevent cracking from the dehydrating effect of their own imprudence. And, before you ask, no I haven't lost control of that metaphor: I'm saying some people are thoughtful, sensitive types like me while others are wooden-headed idiots as a result of whom every foodstuff has to carry an over-cautious 'Use by' date. I think I should bloody sue.

I carry on along my road towards the Kilburn High Road. In many ways the Kilburn High Road isn't very nice – it's messy, often crowded, usually gridlocked, has a large number of terrible shops selling cheap crap, lots of places selling dodgy kebabs, about two others selling kebabs that are probably okay, pawnbrokers, pay-day loan sharks, old Irish pubs, closed old Irish pubs, closed old Irish pubs that have tried and failed to go gastro, closed old Irish clubs that have tried to go a bit nightclubby, the worst branch of Marks & Spencer in Britain and a little paved area which was almost certainly designed by '60s planners to give the place a sense of community but is primarily used by people trying to encourage you to become Christian or Muslim with the use of leaflets, megaphones and sometimes both. There's also an Argos.

But I like it. You probably saw that coming. I expect you're expecting me to say that it's vibrant next. Well it is. And also, I'm used to it and I tend to like what I'm used to. I'm not going to be here much longer but I expect I'll come back and visit. (I expect I won't.)

Oh, and also it's on a Roman road, which I like. I get a sense that there's something genuinely ancient about Kilburn as a scuzzy little strip development along the Roman road into London: that London needs, and has always needed, these little pockets of grubby prosperity. And so, as well as liking the vibrancy and familiarity, I'm comforted by the thought that Kilburn is a constant in a changing world. When the recession hit in 2008, a lot of Kilburn's pound shops and garage-sale-style outlets closed, like weeds knocked back by a harsh frost. But they grew back in the next few months, with different names but the same displays of stuff which I can't imagine anyone ever wanting to buy. I found that cheering.

My parents like Kilburn – they liked it as soon as I moved in, despite making the mistake of eating in the greasy spoon café at the end of my road. They're not fussy eaters but they hate bad service. They used to be hotel managers – in the 1970s, the era of *Fawlty Towers* and of a Britvic orange juice being an acceptable starter. But I think they were good hotel managers, for the time. That's what they've always led me to believe, and they're not, in general, boastful people.

When I was born they were joint managers of the White Hart hotel in Salisbury. They weren't from Salisbury – my mother grew up in Swansea and my father in Liverpool – but they'd met on a degree course in Glasgow, where they were studying hotel management. And then they got married and became hotel managers and got a job working for a hotel chain and were posted to Salisbury. Posted in the military sense. I think they probably went by car.

So: Ian and Kathy Mitchell, a husband and wife running a West Country hotel in the 1970s. But instead of a Spanish waiter, they had a baby, who they kept in the cleaners' cupboard when they were working. This was primarily because it was a large enough cupboard to have a phone in it. By which I mean, it actually had a phone in it. Almost every cupboard is large enough to have a phone in it, otherwise it'd barely be more than a box attached to a wall. I mean large enough to warrant the fitting of a phone line. So it was really a sort of terrible room. Or an amazing cupboard.

Anyway, it was where they kept the cleaning equipment for the hotel. The first word I ever said was 'Hoover'. I didn't even know that other brands of vacuum cleaner were available.

And the relevance of the phone? It was so I could order stuff on room service. And also so that it could be put on 'baby monitor', which meant that someone on reception could listen in and hear if I was crying, rather than asleep or dead, which very different states share the attribute of not requiring immediate action.

They stopped being hotel managers when I was two and we moved to Oxford, where my dad got a teaching job at the polytechnic. The decision was always explained as being to do with me – that running a hotel and family life were incompatible – which I suppose makes sense. Then again, thinking about it, my friends with children seem to find the first two years of childcare the most onerous and it always seems the impact on their careers is lessened thereafter. So maybe my parents were sick of running hotels for other reasons and rationalised it as a family decision, or just very wisely expressed it to me that way so I'd feel grateful at their sacrifice rather than irritated that they no longer had interesting jobs.

I was a bit sorry, as a child, that they didn't run a hotel any more. And that when they had, I'd been too young to notice anything more than an industrial Hoover. (My first adjective was 'industrial'.) (It wasn't.) I love hotels – they're fun and fascinating – and having one to run around in, albeit carefully and with a beady eye fixed on sharp skirting boards, would have been brilliant.

And I wanted there to be a place of which my parents were in charge. I'm hierarchical like that. I wanted them to have people working for them rather than just lots of 'colleagues'. That makes me sound like a bit of a megalomaniac. But my hunch is that most children are like that. Ideally, my parents would have been a king and queen. Failing that, hotel manager seemed to me a bit higher up the scale than 'people who teach hotel management at a polytechnic'. When I got older, a different snobbery came to bear: the polytechnic became a university and 'university lecturer' seemed better than 'hotel manager' – more to do with learning and less with trade. So my view changed over the period of my minority as I changed from one kind of little shit to another.

This will be grist to the mill of people who think I'm a posh twat. 'Listen to him, nasty little snob,' they will be thinking. They will also probably be wondering why they've bought a copy of his book. Or maybe not. Perhaps there's a constituency of people – the most rabid online commenters, for example – who actually seek out the work of people they loathe. They may be skimming each page with a sneer before wiping their arse on it and flushing it down the loo. Or attempting to post it to me. If so, I'd like to say to those people: 'Welcome! Your money is as good as anyone else's.'

But of course being a snob and being posh are different things. Being a snob, a conventional snob, involves wanting to be posh whether you are or not, and thinking less of people who aren't. Wanting to be posher, usually – which is why the very poshest people are seldom snobs: they know they can't be any posher so it's no good wishing for it.

I plead guilty to being a snob when I was a child. I definitely valued poshness, jealously guarded it to the extent that I felt I possessed it, and wanted more. My instinct was not to despise the social hierarchy but to want to climb it. So maybe it serves me right that I now get called posh all the time, when I'm not really and I've long since realised that it's a worthless commodity. In fact, career-wise, it would have been more fashionable to aspire in the other direction. But I didn't have the nous to realise that there would be any advantage in playing the 'ordinary background' card – or that, as a child of underpaid polytechnic lecturers, albeit one sent to minor independent schools thanks to massive financial sacrifices on those parents' part, I completely qualified for playing it.

Had I guarded my t's less jealously and embraced the glottal stop, I could have styled myself a person 'with an ordinary back-ground who nevertheless got to Cambridge and became a com-edian' rather than 'an ex-Cambridge ex-public schoolboy doing well in comedy like you'd expect'. Both descriptions are sort of true, but people like to polarise and these days I might have been better off touting the former.

Still, I'd have been giving a hostage to fortune. The estuary-accent-affecting middle classters always get hoist by their own petard in the end, when it turns out that Ben Elton is the nephew of a knight or Guy Ritchie was brought up in the ancestral home of his baronet stepfather.

The thing is, I find the idea that my life has followed an unre-markable path of privilege rather comforting. I wanted to think I was posh because I felt, not entirely without justification, that bad things didn't happen to posh people. If other people thought I'd be all right – even in a resentful way – I could believe it too.

So, in the binary world of popular opinion, I got dumped on the posh side of the fence – which is sometimes annoying as it denies me the credit for any dragging myself up by my bootstraps that I might have done (it's not much but, you know, we never had a Sodastream). It also leaves me worrying that people will think I'm claiming to be properly posh – when proper posh people know I'm not. My blood is red and unremarkable. (Although I always remark when I see it, as my scant knowledge of medicine leads me to believe that it's not really supposed to come out.)

This is a roundabout way of saying that my background was neither that of a Little Lord Fauntleroy, as the people who write the links for *Would I Lie to You?* would have it; nor was it the opposite.

But who, in the public eye, is really the opposite? Very few people who come to prominence, other than through lucrative and talent-hungry sports, genuinely come from the most disadvantaged sections of society – we just don't live in a country with that amount of social mobility. Which is why famous people who went to a comprehensive and can sustain a regional accent do themselves a lot of favours by letting those facts come to the fore, so that journalists can infer a tin bath in front of the fire and an outside loo rather than civil servant parents who were enthusiastic theatre-goers.

Perhaps you think I'm thinking of Lee Mack. Well, I am now, obviously. But I don't think his parents were civil servants and I wouldn't say Lee has ever seriously pretended to be anything he's not, any more than I have (which is quite an indictment of both our acting powers). That said, on *Would I Lie to You?* we're very happy to milk comedy from people's assumptions that he keeps whippets and I've got a beagle pack. And we're both amused by the underlying truth that, in terms of our values and attitude, we're incredibly similar. We're middle class. We're property owners who would gravitate towards a Carluccio's over a Pizza Hut. I bet he's got a pension. I know he's got a conservatory. He used to have a boat on the bloody Thames! I live in an ex-council flat, for fuck's sake!

But he's got a regional accent, so the audience makes certain assumptions and I'll happily play to them. If he doesn't claim to be working class, I'll do it for him. So – in spite of everything I've said about people's instinct to polarise, and worrying about appearing to be something I'm really not – I'm also quite happy to accept a cheque for telling Lee not to get coal dust all over the studio while he wonders whether I shouldn't offer a glass of water to the foot-man he claims I'm sitting on.

It's a lot easier than going on TV with the premise that you're basically normal.

2

Inventing
Fleet Street

I'm not taking a direct route because I want the walk to last over an hour. It's the brisk continuous walking that seems to be the best back medicine. So I turn left down Quex Road. Some of the road names round here are brilliant: just off Quex are Mutrix Road and Mazenod Avenue. Quex, Mutrix and Mazenod! They sound like robots. I wish I'd ever written anything that needed three names for robots so I could have used those. In fact, what am I doing writing this? It should be a sci-fi epic about Quex, Mutrix and Mazenod, three evil cyborgs blasting their way around the galaxy and seeing who can destroy the most planets.

I think the main reason I associate those names with robots is that I've always had a feeling that 'x' and 'z' are the most futuristic letters. I don't really think they are. In fact I'm pretty sure 'x' in particular is about as ancient as a letter can be – it's just two lines, after all. Anything less than that and it's not really writing. It's just a mark. But, because they're not very useful letters, they somehow feel like the alphabetical equivalent of shiny silver jumpsuits.

Sadly those three street names have nothing to do with space or the future and everything to do with places in Kent. The family who owned the estate on which that bit of Kilburn was built also owned a Quex House in Kent. Mutrix and Mazenod are nearby villages. It's a bit of a dull explanation for the names, really. Of course I've no idea why those villages are called that. I expect it's because some space robots once attacked Kent. Yawn.

The first street name I was aware of was Staunton Road, which is where we moved to in Oxford. The second was Fleet Street. That's because my parents were constantly being hassled by paps. Not really. I became aware of Fleet Street at the point when I thought it was a phrase I'd invented. It was a road name I came up with for my toy cars to drive along. I was so sure it had originated in my brain that when I came across it again, in a story about Gumdrop the vintage car (I was terribly interested in cars at the time but managed to get it out of my system a decade before everyone else got a driving licence), as a name for an ancient and famous London thoroughfare, I was furious.

I was convinced that I'd thought of it entirely separately and it seemed so unfair to me that, having displayed the genius to come up with such a demonstrably successful name for a street (I think I assumed that Fleet Street's prominence and centuries of prosperity were somehow *because* of its name), I should go unrewarded. I felt like a victim of history. I could so easily have been born hundreds of years earlier and been the one to come up with the name in the first place. Surely this would have brought me great fame and fortune, I thought. I didn't seem to realise that the identity of the inventor of the name 'Fleet Street' is lost in the mists of the past and that whoever it was probably went to his or her grave unlauded and unremunerated for having named a street after the nearby Fleet river.

I don't know whether this means I was an imaginative child. I think that's how I thought of myself, though. I was an only child for the first seven and a half years of life and so I spent quite a lot of time on my own, inventing games and pretending to be other people. I loved dressing up but at the same time it made me ashamed – very much like masturbation a few years later.

In my special costume trunk (box of old clothes) I had a highly patterned lime green and brown jumper which was too small for me but was my outfit for being someone to do with *Star Trek* (not actually Captain Kirk – I think I styled myself his boss). In truth there was nothing remotely Star Trekky about it, but the way it clung to my arms reminded me very much of the way the shirts in *Star Trek* clung to people's arms. I also had an old pocket calculator which I could flip open in a way that was satisfyingly reminiscent of a communicator.

And then there was a black mac. I got tremendous use out of that black mac. It spent a while as the coat I wore as one of the versions of Doctor Who I pretended to be – I think I was essaying a slightly more rainproof version of the Peter Davidson incarnation. I definitely remember putting some foliage into the buttonhole at one point to represent the stick of celery he always had pinned to his. My mother was reluctant to provide actual celery for such trivial use, which is a shame because, as it turned out, that moment of asking was the only point in my life when I was ever going to see any point in celery.

But the mac's starring role was as the – what I now realise is called – 'frock coat' of an eighteenth-century king. At the time I didn't know he was eighteenth-century, but I've since worked out that this was the era of historical dress I was trying to emulate when I tucked my trousers into my socks and tied a bit of string round the tails of the coat.

This is the costume I most associate with shame. I remember one Saturday, when I was wearing this costume, some older children from next door rang the doorbell because they'd hit a ball into our garden and, as my parents let them in, I was immediately and forcibly struck with shame and humiliation at my appearance and ridiculous inner life. I couldn't have felt worse if I'd been caught wearing lipstick and a dress.

I don't think the ball-searchers noticed at all, but I remember going off to search for the ball at the opposite end of the garden to everyone else – in a place where it couldn't possibly have landed – just to be able to hide from them. Everyone was saying, 'It won't be there – what are you doing? Come and look over here!' while I mumbled that I was just going to check here down behind the garage where no one could see me. I could sense that, more than the costume, this behaviour was making me seem like a weirdo.

That feeling of being a weirdo oppressed me. Conventional to the core, I was keenly aware that my dressing-up-and-pretending-to-be-other-people games weren't as wholesome as climbing trees or playing football. I had a sense that there was something effeminate about dressing up – and certainly there was no worse accusation that could be levelled at me as a small child than that I was like a girl.

Maybe it was a forerunner of my early teenage fear that I might turn out to be gay. I don't mean that to sound homophobic, although I probably was homophobic at the age of thirteen – God knows my school was a homophobic environment – but there's no doubt that I didn't want to be gay. I thought that would be awful and would lead to a life of mockery and self-loathing. And, as a natural pessimist, I was quite sure that my eagerness not to be gay meant I definitely would be.

I'm not. As you must have guessed by now. I mean, they'd have put that on the cover. I think I had the odd crush on girlish-looking boys in my early teens but never to the extent that I'd do anything about it or in a way that registered on the same level as my feelings when I met real girls. I hope that doesn't disappoint anyone, by the way. Some people have speculated on the internet that I might be gay, which troubles me only in the implication that, if I were, I'd think there was something wrong with that or try to hide it.

In many ways, I think I might have been happier in my later teens if I had been gay. Certainly it would have been a difficult thing to come to terms with during puberty but, having done so, I would have had a justified sense of achievement at being brave enough to come out. Also my all-male educational history wouldn't have thrown up such a barrier to flirting. I was basically a bit afraid of girls and women for a long time, in a way I don't think I would have been about men even if those were the sort of human I had turned out to fancy.

Anyway these fears, doubts and thoughts were a long way ahead of me as I searched for a tennis ball where I knew there wouldn't be one, with my trousers tucked into my socks, a bit of string tied around the mac I was wearing in the sweltering sun and plastic sword at my side. The fact that I was not a king was never more bitterly apparent than at that moment. I was just a small boy and not quite as normal as I'd have liked.

I felt I should be more into Lego. I was conscious that I wasn't a keen reader – I much preferred television. I wanted to like porridge. It bothered me that I wasn't more focused on the acquisition of sweets and chocolate. I've never been a healthy eater – my palate perversely favours fats and alcohols while sending troubled if not protesting messages to the brain when confronted with vegetation or roughage – but I've never much liked sweets. I like puddings, but sweets – sweet-shop sweets, cola bottles, refreshers, stuff to do with sherbet – have never really been to my taste. Which presents a bit of a problem if you aspire to be a normal boy. It's like being a socialist on Wall Street: you find yourself not wanting the currency.

So I settled on chocolate as a respectable sort of sweet to aspire to owning. And I liked chocolate, just nowhere near as much as toast. At Christmas and Easter, therefore, I would be given quite a lot of chocolate. I would be aware that this was a good thing; that, in the economy of children, I was briefly rich. This was a state of affairs to be cherished, I reasoned. So I wouldn't eat it. I'd hoard it. This took very little self-control as the pleasure I took from eating chocolate was massively outweighed by the displeasure I endured from ceasing to own it.

What a natural miser, you might think. I hope not – and I don't think so. In general, I like what money buys more than the money itself. But I don't spend a lot on chocolate. Of course, my nest egg – or nest of chocolate eggs – was no good to me. When I returned to my stash weeks later, it had taken on the taste of the packaging and developed that horrible white layer. A poor reward for my prudence.

I have no idea whether these feelings of oddness and inadequacy are normal and, if so, whether I felt them to a greater or lesser than normal extent. Is it normal to feel you're not normal but want to be normal? I think it probably is.

I certainly don't think that those feelings drove me to comedy. Although it may explain some of the murders (see Book 2).

I'm always suspicious of that 'comedy comes from pain' reasoning. Trite magazine interviewers talk to comedians, tease a perfectly standard amount of doubt, fear and self-analysis out of them and infer therefrom that it's this phenomenon of not-feeling-perpetually-fine that allowed them to come up with that amusing routine about towels.

Well, correlation is not causation, as they say on Radio 4's statistics programme *More or Less*. Everyone's unhappy sometimes, and not everyone is funny. The interviewers may as well infer that the comedy comes from the inhalation of oxygen. Which of course it partly does. We have no evidence for any joke ever having emanated from a non-oxygen-breathing organism. At a sub-atomic level, oxygen is absolutely packed with hilarions.

What distinguishes the comedian from the non-comedian, I always want to scream at the interviewers, is not that they are sometimes unhappy, solemnly self-analyse or breathe oxygen but that they reflect upon these and other things in an amusing way. So stop passing this shit off as insight, interviewers. You've not really spotted anything about the people you're speaking to. You think you see unusual amounts of pain when it's just performers politely glumming up so as not to rub your noses in the fact that their job is more fun than yours. So they mention that they sometimes feel lonely and hope the article plugs the DVD.

I suspect that my levels of infantile self-doubt were no more remarkable than my year of birth – which is 1974, by the way. And

I certainly didn't feel inadequate all, or even most, of the time. I often felt special and clever and like I'd probably grow up to be a billionaire toy manufacturer or captain of the first intergalactic ship with a usable living room. In those moods I didn't want to be normal.

If I was a happy little four-, five- or six-year-old – and I think I probably was, for all my worries and doubts – it's thanks to my parents. They always gave me the impression that they were delighted by my very existence – that I rarely did anything wrong and, if I actually did anything right, then that was a tremendous cherry on the amazing cake. I was made to be well-behaved in front of other people, but I certainly felt I could say anything to them – scream, rage, cry, worry, speculate as to the presence of wasps, ask to be addressed in the manner of an eighteenth-century king, pretend to be in a spaceship or on television, suddenly need the loo – and all would still be well.

There is really only one thing I remember about their general parental shtick which irritates me now, and that was their attitude to Oxford. They were really quite down on it. I suppose they'd only just moved there and didn't particularly feel welcome or like they belonged there – in contrast, I think, to Salisbury with which they'd also had no previous connections but had immediately loved. My mother missed living by the sea – she still does – and my dad, who grew up in the north, has never had the accent but developed a little of the sixth sense for snootiness. And you don't need a sixth sense for snootiness to detect it in Oxford. It's undoubtedly a snooty place. But then it's got a fair bit to be snooty about. (It's also got a massive chip on its shoulder about Cambridge, which is understandable.)

I think my mum and dad imagined they'd move somewhere else before too long, so they discouraged me from getting attached to the place. You're not really from here, you were born in Salisbury, your mum's Welsh and your dad's a bit Scottish, so you're not even really English – you're British and not really from the only place you can remember ever being in. That was the message I was given. And I can understand why.

But that's not much use when you're four, when you're looking for the things that define you. You want a home town and you want to be able to bask in the illusion that it's the best place in the world. You might even consider supporting the football team.

Such securities were denied me because, while they never said Oxford was a dump and would always concede that it was a beautiful place with a famous university, I was never allowed to forget the city's failings – and indeed England's. England, I was given the impression, was the snootiest part of Britain and consequently undeserving of my allegiance.

My parents still live in Oxford and I'd be very surprised if they ever leave. They have lots of friends in the area and they've grown very fond of it. My brother, Daniel, was born there and our parents were already coming round to the place by then. Consequently he did support the football team for a while and feels tremendous allegiance to the city, to the extent that he has, up till now, neglected to move away.

So I've always felt a bit rootless, but without any of the cachet of most rootless people. You know the sort: Danish father, Trinidadian mother, live in Thame (I'm thinking of a specific boy in my class). For people like that, the fact that they have no single place of allegiance is part of what defines them – it's interesting and glamorous. Being definitely British but with your loyalties split between various unremarkable parts – Oxford, Swansea, Salisbury, the Scottish Borders – has no exotic upside to compensate for the absence of a one-word answer to the question: 'Where are you from?'

The Danish-Trinidadian boy had real candles on his Christmas tree, which necessitated having a fire extinguisher on stand-by. And he was called Sigurd Yokumsen. I bet no one ever mistakes him for a fucking novelist.

3

Light-houses,
My Boy!

I cross Quex Road to avoid a small crowd of people around the bus shelter. It's too cramped a bit of pavement to have a bus shelter really, and weaving through all the people standing there feels intimate and inappropriate, like stomping through a cocktail party with a bag of tools.

It's also quite a likely and awkward place to get recognised. I get recognised from the television quite a bit these days. It's increased gradually over the years from the very occasional occurrence, when I first did a TV show called *Bruiser* and then the first series of *Peep Show*, to the point where now it happens most times I leave the house. So I've been able to get used to it gradually, which I'm grateful for. It must be very difficult for people who have to cope with suddenly becoming famous, like *Big Brother* contestants or people the tabloids decide have done a murder.

I'm not complaining, by the way. I'm well aware that people knowing who I am helps me get work and God knows I'm grateful for that, so the loss of my ability to potter around unobserved is a side effect of a good thing. My feelings about it are complicated. In lots of ways, I like it. Most people who approach me say something nice or, at worst, neutral. The feeling that a stranger might be pleased to see you is a warming one. Also, like most performers, I have an unhealthy streak of megalomania and being recognised makes me feel important. Even at times when I'm embarrassed or annoyed about being spotted, there's still a nasty spiky joy underneath which a dark and hungry part of my soul is feasting on.

And there are times when it's not so nice. Places like this bus stop or a Tube train, where there are other people standing or sitting around observing the encounter – and, I always feel, resenting it – are among the worst. I can't escape the feeling that these observers think I've actively done something to make a stir or scene. It's as if they think that recognition in others' eyes is something that emanates from me, that I'm deliberately beaming it out. Essentially that, just by being there, I'm showing off.

I was once walking back down my road from the supermarket, carrying several heavy bags of shopping and therefore feeling slightly exposed – like a squirrel looking for somewhere to bury a huge nut. There's definitely something about carrying food that, on a deep evolutionary level, makes me feel defensive. I'm sure I'm not alone. Try catching the eye of someone returning from a buffet with a heaped plate: you'll see the shade of a Neanderthal, furtively dragging a mammoth carcass into his cave.

There was a small group of blokes on a corner. I think maybe they were builders or decorators, or perhaps they were planning a robbery. I'd be surprised to discover they were opposing counsel in a fraud case having a discreet chat during a recess, but who knows. Anyway, one of them said something like:

'Oi, there's that bloke off the telly!'

They all turned to look at me and I turned to look at them. We weren't that close to each other but I smiled and, as far as was possible with an arm weighed down by beer and ready meals, I waved. A beat passed.

'Twat!' one of them shouted.

I carried on walking home, feeling very much like a twat. Look at the twat who eats! There's that twat off the telly all weighed down with groceries – what a lame bastard!

Now, that was a very atypical encounter in one way – people are seldom rude. But typical in another. It made me feel very exposed and visible. It reminded me that all the things people normally do anonymously in a big city, in my case might have to be done while being observed and made to represent the innate twattiness of all mankind.

But even when strangers are very pleasant, I find it impossible to respond unselfconsciously. From the moment someone says 'Excuse me', I'm thinking about how I'm coming across. Do I seem like a nice person? Or do I seem annoyed? Or do I seem like a nice person who's rightly annoyed at being asked for a photo/autograph/ to say hi to their friend's voicemail under these awkward circumstances? Or do I seem like a nice person who's rightly thrilled? Or a horrible person who's wrongly thrilled? Or a horrible person who's wrongly annoyed? Or a nice normal person who's understandably surprised but the reality of whose goodwill shines through?

Sometimes I walk away buoyed up by the enthusiasm of someone who's said I'm funny. Other times I'm fretting about the embarrassing awkwardness of the encounter. But I almost always wish I'd been nicer or 'more genuine' – that the warmth I attempt to display didn't feel so forced. I can't avoid the conclusion that really nice people don't keep asking themselves if they seem nice. Smug bastards.

So I cross the road and walk north-east up the south-west side of Quex Road, past the junction with Mutrix and past a school on the corner with Abbey Road. I don't like the look of this school. It looks like a primary school. I don't like primary schools. It's also a modern building and, if we must have primary schools, I'd rather they weren't in modern buildings.

There's a bit in a Sherlock Holmes story where Holmes and Watson are coming back into London past Clapham Junction and Holmes says: 'It's a very cheery thing to come into London by any of these lines which run high and allow you to look down upon the houses like this.'

I agree with Holmes, it is. Watson didn't, as he tells the reader: 'I thought he was joking, for the view was sordid enough' – I suppose the Battersea area wasn't so gentrified in those days.

But Holmes is admiring something specific: 'Look at those big, isolated clumps of buildings rising up above the slates, like brick islands in a lead-coloured sea.'

'The board-schools.'

'Light-houses, my boy! Beacons of the future! Capsules with hundreds of bright little seeds in each, out of which will spring the wiser, better England of the future.'

When you travel into London on any of those raised lines, you can still see exactly what Holmes meant. At that time (this story was published in 1893) London itself was a fairly new phenomenon, the modern metropolis, the largest city there had ever been, Ripper London, a terrifying, blackened, smog-ridden, lawless place, a horrific vision of humanity's future lit by the guttering flames of coal gas: teeming, impoverished, disease-ridden millions crammed into a place of crime and death.

Until well into the second half of the nineteenth century, the life expectancy of those in urban areas was vastly lower than that of country-dwellers. Cities were very fertile breeding grounds for disease. But they were just as welcoming to business and industry as they were to bacteria. So people were drawn to the cities to get jobs, and went in the knowledge that they might consequently die. The commercial draw of the capital more than compensated for the deaths it caused, so London's population rose despite them. It was a bath with the plug out that was nevertheless filling up.

We rightly associate Victorian times with that sort of chaotic urban squalor. But we should also credit the people of that era with solving the problem. In the middle of the century, everything seemed to be getting worse: larger, more crowded, more inhabited yet less inhabitable. And, basically, they sorted it out. With sewers, epidemiology and schools. They coped with London's uncontrollable growth and they found magnificence in it. They taught the world that urban living could work; they showed it how. Frightening though the giant city must still have seemed – much more so than even my *Cagney and Lacey*-inspired vision of 1980s New York – Holmes, or rather Conan Doyle, spotted that by the 1890s things were moving decisively in the right direction and celebrated the fact.

However irrelevant, discredited or penurious Britain becomes, London will always have been the first modern city, the place where the method of life now favoured by most of mankind was devised. And the Victorian schools, the old board schools, are a symbol of that – a symbol of hope and pragmatism delivered in brick. It's inspiring that there are so many of them and that lots of them are still schools. (I get a bit depressed when I see one that's been converted into flats.) That's why I'm so proud to live here. London, more than any other city on earth, is the new Rome – so much so that Rome is in some ways just the old London.

So I make an exception for primary schools in Victorian buildings but, in general, I view them with distaste.

It's just a feeling. I don't want anything to be done about it. I know we need to have primary schools. I know some of them will have to be in modern buildings and that, broadly, that's a good sign as it suggests that money is being invested in education. So I'm not against this school I'm walking past, any more than I'm against sewage plants. And by making that comparison, I don't mean to liken children to sewage. But, as with a sewage plant, when I pass a primary school I acknowledge that it's an important facility without being particularly pleased to see it.

I wonder why. Is it because, despite the jolly colourful classrooms, the evidence of fun projects and well-motivated teachers, we all know what they really are: the means by which we introduce infants to the idea that their time is no longer their own? For your whole life, primary school is teaching them, you will have to go somewhere every day and obey other people's instructions. Today, painting or nature table, to lure you in. In twenty years' time: the company accounts, a Cornish pasty production line or an OHP presentation on 'Corporate Goals Going Forward'.

Or is it just because I hated primary school? I absolutely did. At the age of four I started to attend Napier House, the primary day school section of Headington School, a private girls' school in Oxford. They took boys only until they were six. Up to that age, they must have been convinced, there was little or no chance of a boy instigating any sort of sex incident. So, whether I'd have gone sex-crazy at eight if I hadn't been segregated from the girls for their own safety, we'll never know.

Now, this place wasn't Dotheboys Hall. The staff were probably trying their best. I'm sure many, if not most, of my contemporaries were perfectly happy. Also, the place improved markedly in the five years between my leaving and my brother starting there, because Dan seemed to have a very happy time and he's just as neurotic as I am. So, you know, perhaps it was a lovely school.

That said, I found Napier House a vicious, bitter, judgemental, cold, cruel, jealous and mediocre institution presided over by thoughtless, self-important, misandrist crones. It is one of my tragedies not to have known the word 'cunt' (as an expression for a very unpleasant person rather than a woman's genitals, you understand) at the time in my life when I would have had most use for it. I'm sure those cunts would have expelled me and it would have been a relief.

The key issue I had with them was over food. At lunch they had a rule, not uncommonly for the time, that you had to eat everything that was put in front of you. You were also not allowed to refuse anything that was on offer. Now, for most adults, eating something you don't like is easy – and far preferable to social awkwardness, on occasions when someone's well-meaning dinner party preparations have led to a plateful of soap-flavoured gravel. You just swallow it politely and say it's delicious. Any bishops or actresses reading will know what I mean.

But it's different for children. Their palates are more sensitive, their feelings of discomfort keener. When I had to eat one of the four things I found utterly disgusting from the school's rotation of dishes – macaroni cheese, gooseberry pie, rhubarb crumble and croquette potatoes – I found it horrific and I would always be sick.

That's not a disaster and you wouldn't think primary school teachers would be fazed by seeing pupils throw up after meals – particularly since this one was attached to an all-girls' secondary school. I wasn't fazed by it either. It had happened to me many times before, admittedly only when ill, but still: once it's over and the period of stomach-lightened commiseration begins, then all is well.

So it really came as a horrible shock to me that they were so angry about it. They thought I'd been sick on purpose, as an act of insolence. They weren't standing for it, let alone allowing me to change my clothes. I would spend the rest of the day in a state of disgrace – and caked in my own vomit.

Now, if that's the worst thing that ever happens to you, you're a lucky person. But you could say the same thing about being kicked in the balls by a sommelier and you'd still ask to see the manager. It just seems so unnecessarily unkind, such a failure in empathy on the part of those teachers. They made me *so* unhappy, and all they had to do to fix it was excuse me from eating things that made me throw up or (even if they couldn't bring themselves to so lower their standards) to be nice to me if I did throw up. My whole life, I have always been nice to people when they throw up.

And the thing that makes me even crosser and more uncomprehending is that I know I wasn't a difficult child to keep under discipline. I have always responded with slightly lamentable obedience in the face of authority. I am no rebel – I will do what I'm told when my gag reflex permits it. If I was to be unhappy at school, it should have been because of bullying from my peers, not because I came to blows, or rather heaves, with authority!

Neither am I, nor have I ever been, a fussy eater. There were just a few things I couldn't stand when I was tiny. I think that's normal. I don't know how the other children coped with this rule. Maybe some of them hid food they didn't like – which I would have been afraid to do because it was against the rules – and maybe some others threw up as well.

So, for my first three years at school, I thought I was one of the naughty children – it was something that I couldn't help. My stomach had ordained it. At school, it seemed, I was destined to spend a certain amount of time standing in the corner facing the wall, despite my sincere desire to do exactly as I was told. And I spent every day dreading the lunch hour and was only ever able to relax afterwards, if I'd been lucky enough to be given food I could keep down.

I moaned about all this to my parents, of course – and on several occasions, when they collected me, I'd be caked in sick. They complained too, but the school's response was very firm. I could be specifically excused certain foods in advance, but that was as far as they were willing to bend from their policy. But I wanted to be excused more things than my parents felt able to specify without embarrassment, so the problem continued.

I think they were swayed by the school's argument that this rigid approach to lunchtime discipline was important to a child's development. This was a fee-paying school, which was a stretch for my parents – I think my grandfather helped them out – and they probably felt that they should respect the educational judgements of the professionals they were paying, however counter-intuitive that must seem when your five-year-old son is stinking of his own stomach lining. To ignore the educational specialists would be like throwing away a doctor's prescription.

There's a dutiful middle-class approach for you! – laced with the Protestant notion that you have to be cruel to be kind. It's very different from the approach taken by those parents in the Jamie Oliver series about school food who protested at the school gates against fresh vegetables and passed bags of chips through the railings. The exact opposite, really. But my parents just didn't feel that sense of entitlement – they were paying too much money.

The school I went on to when I was seven – New College School, a small prep school originally established for the choristers of New College – was, by most standards, strict and old-fashioned. But their take on lunch was that, while you had to eat everything on your plate, you didn't have to put anything on your plate that you didn't want to eat. There were stricter lessons, lots of home-work and regular exams at that school, but to me, thanks to their liberal lunch policy, it was like escaping to the free West. I never had to stand in a corner again.

- 4 -

Summoning Servants

The houses round here don't contain enough servants for my liking. I've turned off Quex Road onto West End Lane, which is lined with large houses that have been converted into flats. The life that was lived in them when they were built would seem bizarre to us today – when every one of the hundreds of thousands of buildings like that, all over London, had a version of *Upstairs, Downstairs* going on inside. Not quite as grand as that perhaps, but along the same lines, with the presiding family on the middle floors and servants cooking in the basement and sleeping in the attics. Each building probably accommodated about the same number of people then as one household as it does now all divided up. In a way, it's a nice metaphor for how society has become comparatively more egalitarian – certainly the country's property is divided between many more people now.

That's not how I saw it as a child. I was aware of the concept of servants from an early age. In fact I can't remember a time when I didn't know what servants were, which is odd because I can remember when I didn't know what a tumble-dryer was. And we had a tumble-dryer while I've never even met a servant. Nobody is a servant these days – apart from a few anachronistically trained 'butlers' who wear fancy dress and work for Texans. Rich people might have cleaners, gardeners, nannies and au pairs, maybe the occasional housekeeper. But no one has maids, valets or footmen any more. The profession of servant has pretty much totally disappeared and it wasn't much more prevalent in the late 1970s and early 1980s when I was a small child.

Yet I was very servant-aware. I was growing up not long after the era of bells and butlers. Millions of Britons spent their lives 'in service' until the Second World War – and it must have remained a significant profession for much of the 1950s (I'm largely basing that assumption on what I gleaned from episodes of *Miss Marple*), which is only twenty or so years before I was running around Staunton Road pretending to be a king.

Perhaps it's Miss Marple's fault. Not just Miss Marple, but *Upstairs, Downstairs* and *Brideshead Revisited* and *Dynasty* and the dozens of other things on TV that seemed to be full of uniformed and obedient domestic staff. They definitely caught my imagination; I was disappointed that people with the twin dignities of wealth and 'being from the olden days' had servants while we did not. It didn't occur to me that a damned sight more people *were* servants than had them.

Don't get me wrong – I think if I'd actually lived in a house where you rang a bell and an adult employed by my parents appeared to do my bidding, I would have found that weird. (Although there was a time, at my grandparents' house in Swansea, when I did have a little bell which I'd ring if I wanted to be given more orange squash. This was humiliatingly revealed on *Would I Lie to You?* and, I must stress, was a temporary arrangement and basically just a game linked to all my dressing up and pretending to be other people. So I hope that goes some way to expunging the image you're forming in your head of me as a spoilt and snobbish little brat. That's what I hope, not what I expect.) I wasn't thinking about servants as individual people but about the overall concept, which seemed so smart, so grand, so *posh*.

At Napier House, which being a private school wasn't purpose-built by visionary Victorians but had once been someone's home, there were still bells on the wall for summoning servants. The fact that they no longer worked and, even if they did, no one was in the kitchen to hear them ring seemed to me a step backwards for civilisation. The world – and certainly Britain – was not what it used to be.

I know that, as economic analysis goes, this is a heady cocktail of the nonsensical and the heartless. But, in my defence, I was forming these ideas as a very small child and most very small children have in their psychological make-up many of the personality traits of the tyrant and the megalomaniac. And I had a natural liking for hierarchies. 'Who's in charge of who's in charge of who's in charge of who?' is what I always wanted to know. And of course I imagined my future self being in charge of everyone and everything.

Having said that, I think I wouldn't have minded the thought of only being in charge of some people while others were in charge of me. I found the thought of that sort of military-style order of precedence quite satisfying. It might even be worth being a servant, just to live in a world where some people had them.

Much as recalling these thought processes is quite embarrassing, I can still feel the attraction of the pyramid-shaped institution. I mean metaphorically pyramid-shaped – architecturally I prefer a nice Georgian square.

After all, complete meritocracy, complete social mobility, of the sort that we in the West sometimes flatter ourselves we live in, doesn't really exist or work. In Britain, most of us know that, while merit and application can help in life, a lot of people get on because of who they know, how much money they've already got and other pieces of luck: being born intelligent, talented or having the ability to apply yourself are also pieces of luck. We think society is probably more meritocratic than it was fifty years ago but that doesn't mean things are actually completely fair or ever likely to become so.

But some Americans seem genuinely to believe they're living the meritocratic dream. There are two problems with this: first, it's nonsense. While it's of course possible to transform your life by hard work and talent in the United States, there are millions who live in miserable circumstances with few chances of escape. Not none, but few. The ridiculousness of the notion that the United States, wonderful country though it basically is, is a level playing field for opportunity is demonstrated by their political system which, much like Britain's in the nineteenth century, is dominated by a small number of rich and influential families. We had the Russells, the Cecils and the Churchills – they have the Kennedys, the Bushes and the Gores. At least our Victorian leaders didn't claim to be egalitarian.

The second problem is that a proper meritocracy would be a heartless place. In such a society, those at the bottom of the heap not only have to cope with poverty, boring jobs or no jobs, they are also denied the solace of considering it unfair. This is such a hapless state of affairs to contemplate, it's actually funny. History has a recurrent theme of the down-trodden rising up and overthrowing their oppressors (or in Britain, gradually extracting concessions over hundreds of years), and of injustices which had kept people in penury being swept aside. In this scenario, people aren't kept in penury by injustice, but by justice. The poor sods deserve it – like Baldrick in *Blackadder*. And their chances of overthrowing their oppressors would be pretty slim because presumably they'd cock everything up. Their betters would run rings round them because – well, the clue's in the name. Those unhappy Baldricks would just have to hope that merit and kindness go hand in hand, just like aristocracy and kindness seem to in Julian Fellowes's vision of early twentieth-century England.

As a child, I was much of Fellowes's mind. I simply thought that servants were good because they came from 'the olden days' – and everything from the olden days was better and more glamorous than my own time.

I liked the thought of kings and emperors, kingdoms and empires; people in old-fashioned clothes being in charge of lots of other people. A mixed-up world of treasure and swords, steam engines and suits of armour, castles and wing collars – as cheesy and incoherent as a historically themed Las Vegas casino.

Cars used to be better, I thought, with shiny round headlamps on either side of the bonnet like eyes. Trains were better too: how could drab diesel boxes ever have been considered preferable to those brightly polished steaming metal tubes with massive and magnificent wheels?

The only thing that matched the olden days for style and excitement was the future, by which I basically meant space. If I were to trade in my hopes of crowns, castles, steam engines and servants, it would be for a spaceship – preferably a massive one like the *Starship Enterprise*, which must surely have had as many rooms as a palace – and a laser, a communicator and an opportunity to visit other planets.

Somehow my own time had managed to fall between those two glittering stools. We had neither penny-farthings nor matter transporters. NASA's rockets and shuttles were pitiful objects that could barely go as far as the moon. They didn't even have gravity inside them, for God's sake. The astronauts spent the whole time floating around in their pyjamas, eating disgusting liquidised food. In order to leave the ship, they seemed to have to don motorcycle helmets. It all looked extremely undignified.

Two school subjects, history and science, were poisoning my enjoyment of the universe by lacing it with regret. History made it seem as if the magical world of kingdoms and castles, although admittedly not dragons and wizards, had once existed and had only been eclipsed because humanity had collectively lost its sense of the aesthetic. Similarly, the word 'science' in science fiction made me consider that world to be attainable if only humankind got its shit together. I quietly blamed the people of my own era for its stolid, unmagical mediocrity.

I don't remember any of my friends sharing this frustration. I can't recall much of what I did when friends came round. I think there was an afternoon when Adam Bryant and I pretended to be

Superman and Batman who'd teamed up to fight crime, with a comparable disparity of actual capabilities to Angel-Summoner and the BMX Bandit.

Laurence Noble must have had a stronger personality than me because he managed to make me play 'The Professionals'. Laurence lived in a bungalow with a swimming pool. This was an unusual type of dwelling for a suburb of Oxford, but then his dad was a builder. I had no idea what 'The Professionals' was, but hoped that it was to do with space. Did the Professionals have a ship? I asked. No, they just had a car. Well, two of them did while the third stayed in the office. Did they have a transporter? Only the car. Did they have lasers even? No, even better, they had guns. Normal guns? Yes, normal guns.

This was not 'even better' in my view. Laurence was also a fan of James Bond who, as far as I could tell, had no superpowers at all and just drove around in a car trying to cuddle women. Soppy, if you asked me. Laurence would occasionally make noises like 'Berecca', 'Walkakeekeepay' or 'Smithywesso' which he explained were the names of guns.

'Normal guns, with bullets?'

'Yeah,' he'd say making shooting noises.

'Hmm.' Hardly phazers, were they?

But we played The Professionals. He had a poster in his room with 'CI5' written on it, as well as 'The Professionals'. CI5, it seemed, was where the Professionals worked instead of space. The silhouettes of three normal men were also on the poster and I was informed, to my suppressed distaste, that I was to be 'Bodie'.

'Bogie?'

'No, Bodie. I'm Doyle.'

Laurence favoured Doyle, which was fine by me as he seemed to be the one with a girl's hairdo.

Playing The Professionals involved hurling ourselves around the living room, on and behind sofas, pointing pretend normal guns at people, while Laurence attempted a spittle-spraying version of The

Professionals' signature tune, the accuracy of which, as I'd never seen the programme, I was unable to vouch for.

Pretending to be a glorified policeman who was unable to go five minutes without hurling himself to the ground failed to capture my imagination. But I was somehow embarrassed to suggest games based on my own TV preferences – *Star Trek* (which involved sitting in chairs, occasionally spasming around to demonstrate heavy Klingon fire, or standing on specific tiles on the kitchen floor in order to beam to places) or, my absolute favourite at the time, *Monkey*.

Monkey was a bizarre programme, dubbed into English from the Japanese, and based, I suspect, on some ancient and brutal Far Eastern myths. It featured a sort of half-human, half-simian superhero called Monkey, who travelled around on a magic cloud beating up bad guys. For me, it was the perfect mixture of the sci-fi, the mythical, the historical and the comic book. The BBC brought out a record of the signature tune called 'Monkey Magic' (this was in the age before videos or DVDs, so books and records were the limit of merchandising's reach), which my parents bought me. I would run round and round the dining-room table, swinging the extender pole to one of those dusters designed to get into the top corners of high rooms, which I considered to be uncannily similar to Monkey's magic staff.

The trouble with playing Monkey, though, was that only one person could be Monkey. Monkey's companion, Pigsy, who fought with a large garden rake, was less flattering casting even than Bogie, although he did have pointy ears a bit like Spock. So I was stuck with The Professionals: falling over and endlessly miming getting in and out of a Ford Capri. The kind of boring car that could only have existed in the rubbish present.

I wonder now if my sense of 1970s Britain as a second-rate or unexciting environment was partly a response to my parents' attitude. It wasn't a great time for British self-esteem, I've since realised. Mum and Dad must have had a sense of political or economic decline. Maybe I picked up on that. Maybe my instinctive attraction to a grandiose past was something they found hard to completely refute. I'm pretty sure they voted for Thatcher.

I don't remember the strikes but I do remember power cuts. It only occurred to me about six years ago, during a power cut, that you don't get power cuts any more. That might sound like a ridiculous thing to think as I blundered around in the dark. But I was thinking about it because I didn't have any candles. The absence of candles was much more compelling evidence of the absence of power cuts than any one power cut can be of their presence, if you see what I mean. I didn't have them in stock, like loo roll and bin liners, because power cuts used to be a thing and they've stopped being a thing.

Eventually, moving around by the light of my laptop screen and wondering how long the battery would last, I tripped over a goody bag and found a scented candle inside it. I'm in showbusiness, you know: an infantilised profession where, at the end of some awards dos, you get goody bags like after children's parties, except instead of a balloon and a slice of cake, there's different crap you don't want: moisturiser, expensive soap – or it would be expensive if it weren't free – and, in this case, a scented candle.

I know that doesn't sound great. This might be a good point to admit that I'm not the sort of man who owns a tool kit. I'm too feeble and disorganised to own hammers and drills, whereas I get issued with moisturiser and scented candles at work. It's not fair. I never had the chance to be a real man. I hope there aren't many like me or the country's fucked. If the French invade, all I'll do is stand on the box that my widescreen TV came in and pelt them with cherry liqueurs.

Incidentally I don't in general approve of scented candles. They strike me as a pointless fire hazard. My mother often leaves unattended scented candles on top of the television which has, in my view, nearly caused a fire on dozens of occasions. My use of the word 'nearly' is open to criticism here because it has never *actually* caused a fire and I've never had to visit my parents at the I Told You So Burns and Smoke Inhalation Clinic.

But I reckon our modern, non-power-cut-associated use of candles for fun, atmosphere, smell and a general aura of romantic pampering is a pretty shabby way to remember the countless thousands from history who died in candle-related house fires or lived their lives having to choose between darkness and a small but constant risk of conflagration. The idea that, when there's a much less risky way of lighting houses, we'd carry on using candles *for fun* would, I'm sure, make them turn in their barbecuey graves.

The candles I associate with childhood were much more utilitarian plain white emergency ones. In those days power cuts were, like thunderstorms, not things that happened every day but a constant possibility. They were certainly more common than trips to restaurants. Now, for my parents as well as me, it's the other way round. That shows how Britain's changed.

I'd say it's also quite a good way of judging the context in which you're living: if your life involves more meals out than power cuts, you can justifiably feel smug or grateful, according to your nature. The young middle-class family I grew up in during the late '70s and early '80s did not have that satisfaction.

I don't think the power cuts I remember were to do with strikes. The three-day week was before I was born, although not long enough before it to account for my conception, which is a shame. I'd like to think I was a product of industrial action.

The power cuts frightened me because I was unoriginal enough to be scared of the dark – and particularly scared of the sudden dark. One of my earliest memories is of eating bread and strawberry jam (bread, I assume, because, in a power cut, the toaster doesn't work) while sobbing. These weren't distressed sobs but the after-shock sobs that, when you're little, continue for minutes after you've been comforted. The shock of darkness had passed, candles had been lit, I'd been given a cuddle and now it was time for some bread and jam while we waited for the power to come back so we could make tea. It's a happy memory, of security and love. I know I'm very lucky to have childhood memories like that.

Back to the horrors of modern life: I've reached the corner of Abbey Road and Belsize Road, where there's a horrible example of 1960s architecture – all the more unsettling for the fact that it was probably well meant. Two huge and hideous tower blocks are joined by a bridge, so that the Londoners of the twenty-first century (the planners must have thought) would, like Ewoks, only have to touch the ground on special occasions. And, in the ground floor of one is a pub, the Lillie Langtry.

My guess is that there was always a pub on this corner and, when the area was bulldozed for redevelopment, they decided to incorporate it into the new estate – still on the corner but now with a dozen concrete floors on top of it. The old Victorian gin palace, or even Elizabethan alehouse, was recreated in utilitarian breezeblocks.

It's horrible and inhuman – they might as well have installed a vending machine for alcohol injections. It's a grim, doomed pub, architecturally immune to the gentrification of the area, incapable of going gastro. It looks dated in the way only the naïve prognostications of people in the past can. It's like watching an episode of *Space 1999*, a show made in 1975 which predicted habitable moonbases before the end of the millennium but showed no sign of expecting its star, Martin Landau, to win an Oscar five years earlier.

- 5 -

The Pianist and the Fisherman

I don't know whether the architects who designed this crossroads, their heads full of moonbases and a new, three-dimensional London where people travelled back from work by flying car, which they parked on top of their skyscrapers before going downstairs to bed, would have approved of the two shops in the ground floor of their monstrosity, next to the stricken pub. One sells fireworks and the other pianos. The most creative party planners go shopping round here.

I turn left up Belsize Road and walk towards Swiss Cottage, thinking of fireworks and pianos. Those are two things I became aware of as early as servants. Fireworks are the ultimate form of all-round family entertainment. They really are fun for everyone except the blind – and even some blind people probably like the noise. For most people the noise is the downside. Some, especially children, find it frightening. But the noise is like the cholesterol in a bacon sandwich. There's got to be a nasty or dangerous side to anything enjoyable or there's something wrong, something suspicious and hidden. If everything seems perfect, it means you're one of the Eloi and a Morlock is watching you with a napkin tucked under its chin. I always thought Disneyland might be like that but people tell me there are long queues so that's okay.

The downside of pianos is having to practise. I learned that young. I started having piano lessons aged six and I suppose that means I could have been a concert pianist. I had the opportunity to put in the ten thousand hours of practice that Malcolm Gladwell recommends. Although, like learning the details of how a magic trick is done, thinking about a musician in that way really undermines their art in my eyes. Suddenly one is more amazed by the massive faff that the attainment of their skill has involved than by the skill itself. It seems such a ridiculously obsessive, disproportionate act, like keeping all your wee in jars. You feel like saying they needn't have bothered.

I think I wanted to learn the piano because of my maternal grandfather, who played it beautifully. He was Welsh and, until he died in 1985, probably my favourite person in the world. He couldn't read music but he could make tunes from his head turn into tunes coming out of a piano. This was the closest to magic that I ever witnessed before I got an iPhone, and it meant he possessed a quality that the Welsh seem to value above all others: he was musical.

I am extremely proud of my Welsh heritage. My mother's parents were kind, interesting, funny, happy people and their house in Swansea was a wonderful place to be. I adored Swansea too; it is truly an 'ugly, lovely town' as Dylan Thomas said. It seemed to me in every way preferable to Oxford, and not just because the people were friendlier – which, according to my parents, it had in common with everywhere outside Stasi-controlled East Berlin.

I loved the weird and wrecked old industrial buildings – the huge warehouses near the largely disused docks with the names of defunct companies written in faded paint between dozens of smashed windows; the dark appearance and malevolent smell of the Carbon Black Factory which, as we drove from Oxford, signified that we were nearly there. I loved the graceful terraces of the Uplands where my grandparents ran a filling station; the shiny writing on the brand new 'Leisure Centre' which struck me as so much swankier than a mere 'public swimming pool' could ever be; the Victorian ironwork of Mumbles pier.

And the seaside – the amazing Gower coast, more beautiful than a thousand Radcliffe Cameras. Actually a thousand Radcliffe Cameras wouldn't be beautiful. It would be odd but also monotonous: a vast and weird expanse of limestone pimples. I think I mean a thousand times more beautiful than the Radcliffe Camera. (If you haven't heard of the Radcliffe Camera, this may be a baffling paragraph. I should explain that it's not a camera, it's a building – a very pretty building which doesn't even look like a camera. It looks more like the dome of St Paul's.)

I learned so many things through Swansea. What the Second World War was; that the Germans had tried to bomb British cities to bits but failed; that lights had been put on Clyne Common near my grandparents' house so the Luftwaffe would mistake it for the docks and unleash their payload harmlessly there. I thought this plan brilliant and was not yet sufficiently aware of the city's wrecked centre to realise how seldom it had worked.

I learned the difference between rugby and football: the fact that the latter required rigorous policing while the former would only have a couple of bobbies overseeing a crowd of tens of thousands; and that the Welsh were pre-eminent in the former and, largely, disdained the latter.

Where the world's best ice cream is made: Swansea. And by whom: Joe's ice cream parlour.

Where coal came from and how it was used. What a slagheap was. How coal had made Britain great but how there wasn't so much left now. How Welsh coal burned hotter.

I've never had a stronger sense of belonging to a place than I did about Swansea when I was sitting on my grandfather's knee, behind the counter of his filling station in the Uplands, being introduced to all the customers.

And then there were my evil grandparents: my father's mother and father, who lived in Scotland. 'Evil' is a terribly unfair way to refer to them but it was how I felt a lot of the time. I think that many children probably cast their grandparents in these contrasting roles, largely on the basis of one set of grandparents being marginally more easy-going than the other. But, as a small child, it felt to me that, while I could do no wrong in Grandpa and Grandma's eyes, to Grandad and Grannie I was trouble. Particularly to Grannie. To her, I think I represented all that was flawed in my father's personality for having chosen to marry my mother rather than someone stupider and more old-fashioned, plus the much greater flaws in the character of my mother, and all the consequent flaws in the disgracefully modern way they'd chosen to bring me up.

This is a familiar collection of attitudes for a disgruntled grandmother to have – I expect a lot of people will recognise it from their own families – but, looking back, it seems truly daft. By any objective reckoning, my parents were conventional. They weren't hippies; they believed that children should be, if not 'seen and not heard', well-behaved and obedient, and should, in public at least, defer to adults. They weren't as old-fashioned as they would have been if they'd been born in the 1910s instead of the 1940s but, since my grandmother didn't trouble to give birth to my father until 1946, I think that was more her fault than his.

I don't want to give an exaggerated impression of how difficult she was: she wasn't horrible all the time and she could be very kind. But she was tricky and inconsistent, and kept tricky and inconsistent dogs as pets.

My grandfather on that side was a remarkable man who died in 2011, three days after his 100th birthday. He was intelligent, witty, successful, quite rich and as financially generous as he was emotionally miserly. He loved fishing and shared many of the temperamental attributes of his prey.

This was not a man you hugged. I don't know how I knew this – maybe I'd been told or maybe I just felt it. But I only ever shook hands with him, as did my dad. He would kiss my mother on the cheek perfunctorily, like a chat show host with a difficult actress.

Icy judgement emanated from him. He abhorred being kept waiting and, if we were going out for lunch (something which happened when he was around because he was rich), we'd have to get to the restaurant early when it was deserted, cryptlike. If we didn't, his displeasure would manifest itself in my dad's rising stress levels. Grandad hardly needed to say anything himself; some unseen power would make my father squirm, like when Darth Vader uses the force to strangle someone.

He had a snooker table and I remember once, when very small, wandering into the snooker room where he and my dad were having a game. I was too young to know what snooker was but, seeing a red shiny ball on a table at about my eye level, I picked it up. The reaction was like an east wind as my dad quickly took the ball from me and replaced it. My grandfather showed no surprise, only quiet displeasure. My behaviour had merely been typically disappointing.

He loved comedy though and, while we were never close, I think he was proud that I became a comedian, even if *Peep Show* was probably never to his taste. He was more of a fan of Peter Sellers and I can't fault him there. I remember him wheezing and crying with laughter at the various *Pink Panther* films and I think such abandoned enjoyment of comedy from someone who was so controlled and controlling made me respect comedy even more. I concluded that everyone loved and admired comedy, however stern or important they might seem.

I was wrong about that. Lots of people don't particularly like comedy. Some really have no sense of humour at all – they genuinely don't find things funny. Consequently they often laugh a lot in the hope that they won't be found out – that, by the law of averages, they'll be laughing when a joke happens. I find that sort of person extremely unsettling.

And then there are people – and these don't unsettle but enrage me – who think comedy is trivial. They believe that serious, intelligent people should focus on worthy, momentous things and that jokes, levity, piss-taking, subverting and satirising are the pastimes of the second-rate. Words cannot express how second-rate I consider such people. In my experience the properly intelligent, whether they're astrophysicists, politicians, poets, lawyers, entrepreneurs, comedians, taxi drivers, plumbers or doctors, however serious or trivial their career aims, all *adore* jokes. And they have that in common with a lot of idiots.

For as long as I can remember, I have always thought that being funny is the cleverest thing you can do, that taking the piss out of something – parodying it, puncturing it – is at least as clever as making that thing in the first place. This view, which, I'm happy to say, will be most offensive to the people I want most to offend, was probably formed watching my cold grandfather, with all his financial acumen and preference for fish over humans, cry with laughter at a van being repeatedly driven into a swimming pool.

- 6 -

Death of a
Monster

My attempt to swerve round another bus stop is scuppered when I can't help stopping to stare at the advert on it – for Turkey. 'Bootiful!' declares a bronzed Bernard Matthews as the Aegean sparkles behind him. It must have been his last gig before he died – and a great piece of lateral thinking from the guys in Ankara.

Or it would have been, if they'd actually had Bernard Matthews. Sadly – and this is where I can't pretend ad executives are fools – the Turkey advert halts me in my tracks not with a great visual pun, but with a picture of a girl's arse. The arse is flecked with white sand and in the background are some Roman ruins. Now, that's pulling in two different marketing directions. You can get away with women in bikinis on holiday pictures because you're saying it's a sunny climate in which to go to the beach. If the woman looks sexy and men associate the destination with sexy thoughts, that's not your fault. You might even give the bikini woman a toned husband and small child to make it even more respectable. Although that reduces the subliminal sexiness.

But if you stick white sand on the arse of the bikini-clad woman, there's nothing incidental about it. You're in the realm of also showing a tantalising glimpse of the side of a breast. Really, you might as well at that stage. You absolutely *never* see that sort of bikini-clad woman with kids. You're overtly going for sexiness and taking the risk that you look a bit cheap as a result.

So putting a Roman ruin next to the sandy bottom is mixing your messages. It's too late to go all 'lecture tour of the Med' – that's like a Spearmint Rhino club saying it's got a library. It doesn't take the curse off the arse any more than if one of the adhering bits of sand turned out to be an interesting shell or fossil. An alliance between the history-liking parts of the brain and the bronzed and shapely woman-liking parts of the penis is unlikely to convince. It's a coalition without credibility.

Holidays were a big deal for my parents when I was little. Most of the year was spent planning the summer holiday, which puzzled me because I would have been just as happy spending the fortnight at home. It seemed nonsensical to be going somewhere we wouldn't have access to a television.

The first summer holiday I remember was in France when I was four. We went to a village called Benodet on the Brittany coast and stayed in a caravan. A British holiday company had put loads of them there, so that holiday-makers on a budget could soak up the Gallic atmosphere by living in France as trailer park trash for two weeks. I must say, I loved it.

It was a big financial stretch for my parents, largely because of the poor exchange rate. It may surprise you to learn that I wasn't aware of that at the time. But, no, I'm not that intelligent/tedious, I'm afraid/relieved to say. I think at that point I probably wasn't even aware of how money worked in my own country.

I remember shopping trips with my mother when I was very small. In those days, food shopping still involved going to lots of different places: baker's, butcher's, greengrocer's, fishmonger's, etc. All the old types of shop were present except for the grocer's, which had been supplanted by a supermarket. But my mother would only buy things like tinned food, sugar and flour there – nothing that needed to be fresh. I don't think she would have said so but I suspect she considered that 'common'.

The other 'shop' I was aware of was the bank, which, I had been told, was where you went to get money. I assumed that they just gave it to you and then you exchanged it for all the other things you needed. When you ran out, you went back for more. The relationship between work, earning and spending was lost on me. It was an attitude prescient of the boom conditions of the early 2000s. It came as a nasty shock when my mother explained to me that the bank only looked after your money – it didn't give it to you – and you had to work in order to get hold of it.

So my parents' reduced spending power, thanks to a weak pound and a strong franc, was beyond my understanding and I only know about it because it was mentioned on future holidays.

'It's a lot easier now you get ten francs to the pound,' my father would often say.

'Yes, it was terrible when we first came. Everything was so expensive,' my mother would reply.

That memory won't go away. When I'm befuddled and incontinent in a home, in anywhere between one and six decades' time, my last coherent remarks will be on the subject of exchange rates in the late 1970s. In the summer of 1978, all I knew was that French things were prohibitively expensive, as I wouldn't have put it at the time.

Eating out, for example – which didn't bother me but must have been a shame for my parents because it meant we largely ate food they'd brought with them. But I was introduced to French bread, Orangina and Boursin – all things that were then unobtainable in Britain. The fact that I liked the Boursin came as a massive surprise to my parents who, like most Britons at the time, thought garlic was a bit exotic. They liked it, but they thought of it as an adult or acquired taste, rather than a very basic ingredient that the British inexplicably decided to turn their nose up at for a few generations.

The other food which I was encouraged to try was lobster. At one point in the holiday, as a special treat and to make up for the fact that they couldn't afford to eat in any of the nice French restaurants, my parents decided to buy and cook a lobster. A lobster that was alive. I know that's the only way fresh lobsters come, but it seemed to me a perverse way to buy food. I was aware that much of what I ate had once roamed free and careless, but my instinctive response – and one that I stick to – was not to think about it: to avoid contemplating the fact that my dinner may once have been a lovable, cuddly, helpless thing.

I discovered that lobsters didn't fall into that category when my parents purchased what I can only describe as a small monster. I am not saying lobsters are evil. The fact that they are hard, cold, spiny and viciously armed, rather than large-eyed and soft-furred, is not, I realise, a moral failing. It is arbitrary, maybe even prejudiced, that humans tend to lavish affection on fellow warm-blooded mammals and quite right that those who choose to keep spiders, snakes and scorpions as pets should not be run out of town as twisted perverts but respected as animal-lovers.

But lobsters definitely look evil. And, while I admit that I have never met one under conditions likely to bring out the best in a crustacean, I have yet to see evidence of their goodwill. It is human nature to be repelled by such creatures – just as it is human nature to think, quite wrongly, that it might be a good idea to cuddle a lion cub.

As a four-year-old, I was even more hardline about this than I am now. In this weird country where no one could speak comprehensibly and we were living in a strange stationary yet wheeled shed, the two people charged with my care had located and purchased a sort of giant aqua wasp, brought it into our cramped living quarters still alive and now proposed to make it the focus of dinner. At this point I would have settled for a croquette potato.

But what could I do? I argued, I moaned but, deep down, I figured my parents knew best. They seemed all-powerful and all-knowing. Which shows you how stupid four-year-olds are, because now I realise that they were 31 and broke. When I was 31, I don't think I had a credit card. I was living a studenty existence in a council flat with no candles. The idea that, with only such a brief span on the planet as preparation, they felt able to make a four-year-old, take it to France and obtain a miniature monster for dinner is breathtaking. Why weren't they just hanging around London getting pissed?

And, as if to prove the very point that our four-year-old hero might go on to make 33 years later if he survives his encounter with the monster of the deep (I'm trying to build suspense), it soon transpired that my parents didn't have the first clue what to do with a live lobster other than release it back into the wild via a long, agonising and smelly death in a bin.

Actually, that's not fair. They had several clues – as I imagine you do if you're one of the many people who've never cooked a lobster but have been hanging around in a world where that's the sort of thing some other people do. You'll have vague notions about plunging it into boiling water, or maybe sticking a pin into it in a very precise way that kills it but doesn't hurt it – or, according to some, agonisingly paralyses it but stops it from wriggling around, which amounts to the same thing. You'll be simultaneously thinking about what's most humane and also what might preclude getting your finger snipped off by one of the beast's terrifying claws. What they, like you, didn't have was any facts.

But they had a secret weapon: my mother is a woman and is consequently able to ask strangers for advice and information. And my father, being a man, is able to sidle up while she does this and vaguely listen. So they formed a plan: they would ask the French couple in the caravan next door how you cook a lobster. Brilliant.

My parents don't really speak French. There is no transcript of their exchange with the French couple but, having concluded it, they returned to the caravan firmly of the opinion that the way you cook a live lobster is to put it straight in a pan of cold water, making no attempt to poke it with a pin or anything, and slowly bring it to the boil.

When I've told people about this since, reactions have varied. Some say 'Oh my God, how barbaric!' Some give a nervous 'Oh, right ...' in expectation of the horrors to come. Others say, 'Didn't they mean *boiling* water? Don't you plunge it in *boiling* water?' and still others say, 'Yes, that is how you cook a lobster.' I've noticed that responses of the last kind go up proportionally to the age and life-experience of the people I'm telling the story to. Therefore, sceptical though I have long been of the French couple's knowledge and my parents' linguistic skills, I'm forced to contemplate the possibility that that is genuinely how you cook a lobster. If so, let me tell you it's no picnic. No idiomatic picnic. It may circumstantially be a picnic but one which you will come away from humorously saying, 'That was no picnic.' If you do, may that shaft of levity help you come to terms with the horrors.

The caravan was narrow. At one end were two bedrooms, the bathroom and the door to the outside world; at the other, the main seating area. In between were the galley kitchen and dining table booth. This formed a bottle neck – you could only walk on one side, the galley kitchen side, of the table if you wanted to get out. This wasn't usually a problem. (See map.)

My mother was twitchy from the start and hovered as nervously over my father's shoulder while he put the lobster into the saucepan as she would over hers if she'd asked a stranger about local restaurants. She was, I remember clearly, on the door side of him and the hob. I wasn't – I was in the sitting room bit. At this stage the creature was docile, no doubt traumatised by having been out of water for a while. Consequently, on arriving in the pan, it relaxed. This has been a weird day, it was probably thinking, and things are still far from normal but this water, albeit under-salinated and in an unfamiliar steely environment, is definitely an improvement. I tell you what, if that really is what the lobster was thinking, I'm never eating whitebait again.

'Why can't you spare a thought for the poor creature?' you're probably screaming at the page by now. I'm sorry. You're right. Above all, this was a bad day for the lobster. I accept that intellectually. I just couldn't feel sorry for it at the time – it looked too alien and terrifying, too nasty. I was too frightened to feel mercy. Also, I ate meat. I always have and I suspect I always will. As incidents where you're brought face to face with the reality of that go, the demise of a heavily armoured, dark, eyeless, snapping creature is a lot less likely to make you reach for the nut roast than seeing a bewildered and affectionate lamb gambol past a mint sauce factory towards some rotor blades.

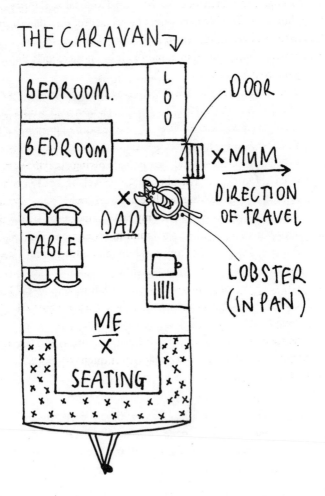

THE CARAVAN

But I'm getting ahead of myself. You don't know what happened yet. The lobster might win. So, the lobster's in the pan, my father's at the stove, my mother hovering by his side, I'm in the sitting area, moaning about this whole ill-conceived plan, and the Calor has just been ignited under the crustacean's new home. This is the calm before the storm, the phoney war.

The spell is broken by the lobster. It has begun to smell a rat. My parents had added one for flavour. Not really, I'm speaking metaphorically. The lobster is starting to suspect that the apparent improvement in its fortunes was no more than a dead cat bounce. (It's massively into animal metaphors.) It has noticed that the water has begun to get warmer.

I don't remember the details of the next few minutes. I assume my dad held on to the pan as the lobster inside moved around in an inquisitive, then concerned, then agitated and finally enraged and panicked fashion. I only remember the last stage. The pan is now full of very hot water and the lobster is throwing everything into a dramatic bid for escape. The phoney war is well and truly over. My mother breaks like the Maginot line and runs out of the caravan.

I would gladly follow her, but my father, struggling with a boiling hot pan containing an enraged mini-monster, stands in my path. I make a few hesitant steps towards him, and a furious and steaming claw flails from under the saucepan lid sending searing splashes everywhere. A droplet lands on my knee. I know, with all my heart, with a terrible, chilling certainty, that the creature wants me dead. There will be no appeasing it if it escapes.

I refuse to eat any of the lobster. I think I'm making a point, but I imagine my parents were happy enough to polish it off themselves.

Civis
Britannicus Sum

Now I come to think of it, almost half of the memories I have from family holidays come from that trip to France. I remember the children's roundabout outside the hypermarket, where, if you were lucky enough to be in one of the helicopters, there was a lever you could pull that would make it rise AS IF YOU WERE REALLY FLYING A HELICOPTER – I still feel this ride is the crowning achievement of French culture.

I remember the doctor who gave me a series of injections in my arse because, with a child's unerring instinct for inconveniencing his parents, I'd developed the first symptoms of asthma while we were on holiday (and the French will inject you in the arse on pretty much any occasion when a British doctor would go for the shoulder; the arse is apparently the better place for it and the French believe, quite wrongly, that optimising health is more important than avoiding embarrassment).

I remember the ferry trip there and back which, in my view, was more enjoyable than any other single part of the fortnight.

But one of the few things I don't remember from that holiday is arriving home again – that feeling of being glad to be back in Britain, which I remember from all my other trips abroad.

In general, you don't see Britain at its best when you re-enter it after a holiday. Places such as Heathrow airport and the docks at Portsmouth are fairly unpleasant. One worries what it looks like to foreigners and wants to make excuses for it. It's like you've just introduced an old friend to a group of people and then noticed he's got a damp patch round his crotch.

Gatwick airport is the worst. It's been there for decades and yet it never seems to be finished. It won't settle into being a mere scar on the landscape, however brutal. It remains an open sore. It also insists on putting up posters advertising how much money it's spending on all this building work, which simply make you think: 1. You should have spent that money ages ago – before you opened the airport perhaps. Or: 2. The charlatans, incompetents and security hysterics who run this hellhole somehow have lots of money – there is no justice on earth.

But in spite of Gatwick airport, or whichever unlovely point of entry to the UK I'm trying to negotiate, I always feel, and have always felt, a huge wave of pride and patriotism when I come back to Britain. I'll happily sit in traffic on the M25 contemplating how much nicer our crash barriers and motorway signs are than those in France/Spain/the USA/Italy. I'll find the drizzle atmospheric. I'll admire our number-plates, our skips, our yellow road grit containers, our keep-left signs, our pylons.

And it isn't just a fondness for the familiar. It feels like I *know* that they're better, that this is a better country, whatever its inadequacies, than anywhere else. This sounds tremendously jingoistic and doesn't, for a moment, stand to reason. But I think it's a common inclination. In its most developed forms, it leads to extremism. But I'm hoping the mild case of it that I suffer from is harmless enough and just results in my being broadly pleased with where I live.

There's an opposite and balancing prejudice from which, judging by my circle of friends, just as many people suffer. That is to be inclined, in the same knee-jerk way, to *dislike* the attributes of your own country, to find French/Mexican/Indonesian light switches/police hats/parking meters better than our own.

This is no more based on reason than my patriotic inclination, but I reckon it's more socially acceptable – or, at the very least, deemed cooler. I feel slightly bitter about that. As prejudices go, surely it's worse, more misanthropic, to be inclined unfairly *against* the country where you're brought up than it is to favour it?

Patriotism is a weird thing. I don't know whether it's at all positive or useful, but it seems pointless to suppress it. It can't be any worse than supporting a football club and probably isn't much more likely to lead to terrible violence. (I never supported my local football club, which was fifty yards from the house where I grew up – partly because I wasn't encouraged to feel rooted in my home town, partly because home games fucked up the local parking and put my parents in a bad mood, and partly because I find football intensely dull, which is why I've never supported any other football team either. But I can't deny I always hope Wales will win the rugby.)

Like following a sports team, being proud of your country allows you to take credit, or at least derive pleasure, from successes that you've actually had little or nothing to do with, like winning the Premier League or the Second World War. But unlike supporting a sports team, patriotism also involves complicity in events and activities that are downright dastardly. Britain's history provides plenty of examples: the slave trade, the potato famine, imperialism, child labour and so on. You have to find an answer to the question: 'How can you possibly support and be proud of an institution that has been responsible for these terrible acts?' (as Billy Butlin's wife used to ask as they watched the redcoats).

Different sorts of patriot have different answers to this question. I get the feeling that the French – having had so many different constitutions and regimes, as well as the discontinuity caused by German occupation – are more distanced from their country's past. They think: 'Our politicians, the country's official actions, our former empire – they've not got much to do with what France really is. We're all about café culture, baguettes, art and injecting people in the bottom.'

But this type of patriotism doesn't work for me. I love my country and am proud of its achievements, but consequently I also accept and feel shame for the bad things this state has done, even though I wasn't even born for most of them. I'd still say that, overall, Britain is a worthy object of pride because it has been guilty of terrible things less often than most civilisations that have wielded equivalent power. Humans are always being horrible to each other and I genuinely take pride in the fact that, when this country had the whip hand, it was significantly less cruel than most. A pretty slender line of reasoning to justify singing the national anthem, you might say, but it works for me.

And, oddly, that annoying bias many Britons show against their own country is something I am perversely rather proud of too. It is a matter of national pride for me that I come from a nation less than averagely inclined towards national pride. I unquestioningly admire our self-questioning inclination. I love our self-loathing. It shows cultural maturity (others would say dotage). I'm reminded of Britain's attitude by what Calgacus, the Caledonian general, said as he prepared to confront the conquering Romans:

> Here at the world's end, on its last inch of liberty, we have lived unmolested to this day, defended by our remoteness and obscurity. But there are no other tribes to come. Nothing but sea and cliffs and these more deadly Romans whose arrogance you cannot escape by obedience and self-restraint. To plunder, butcher, steal – these things they misname empire. They make a desolation and they call it peace.

It's a brilliant speech – it makes me shiver. But I expect you're wondering how that searing rejection of imperialism can possibly resonate with my pride in Britain's history. You may think it's because I associate that ancient Caledonian attitude with British steel and defiance. Well, you'd be wrong. Because it's not really a Caledonian speech at all – as Simon Schama pointed out in his BBC Two *History of Britain*, it was written by Tacitus, a Roman.

Schama skated over this detail because he was using the speech to encapsulate early Scottish feelings of defiance. But I love the fact that it's Roman – I think it's one of the greatest achievements of the Roman empire. Never mind the armies, the buildings, the roads, the central heating, the aqueducts, the statues of men with their nobs out and the popular entertainment formats gruesome enough to make Simon Cowell blush: this speech shows empathy. Within Roman civilisation, there was the sophistication to understand all that was wrong, offensive and alien about Rome to its enemies – and to express that better than those enemies ever could.

History, they say, is written by the victors. Well, here the Roman victors show the compassion, the sensitivity and also the impish cheek to make the vanquished the sympathetic characters. Two thousand years later, Robert Webb and I wrote a sketch about the SS in which they asked themselves, having noticed the skulls on their caps, 'Are we the baddies?' The Romans were asking themselves this in AD 100. I think that's amazing and I believe it's a self-analytical skill that British civilisation shares with ancient Rome (and that the Nazis, in their adolescent pomp, manifestly lacked). The Romans had it first – but then, we never fed people to lions.

- 8 -

The Mystery of the Unexplained Pole

On the Belsize Road roundabout, there's an old FRP. This stands for Flat Roofed Pub and is the coinage of my friend Jon Taylor. Pubs with flat roofs are almost always terrible – scruffy, rough estate pubs covered in tatty England flag bunting. Recently built, these are pubs that have been put there purely to supply the locals with alcohol – there's nothing historical, gastronomic or even twee about them EVER. They're just places for pit bulls to chew toddlers while their parents drunkenly watch the darts on a big screen. (In nicer pubs it's possible actually to *play* darts, but not in FRPs – the toddlers would only throw them at the pit bulls.)

I'd genuinely love to hear of any exceptions to this rule – of flat roofed pubs that have an impressive range of real ales and new world wines, or a good reputation for food (the demographic of my readership isn't all I'd hoped if I need to say that *carveries do not count*); of places where there hasn't been a fight for years and people don't bring savage-looking dogs. I suspect there'll be a few nationally that are adequate, where you probably won't get beaten up, but I'd be delighted to hear of any that are actively nice.

The Lillie Langtry, which I slagged off a couple of chapters ago, is an FRP in spirit (or rather in alcopop) but it doesn't really have a roof. It's got several storeys of flats on top of it. But I suppose flats are flat and so, if your roof is a flat, by definition your roof is flat. It's a flat roof in two senses.

This FRP on the Belsize Road roundabout – fortunately now closed – was called 'The Britannia', which name is typical of the genre in its slight overtones of nationalism. A name like that doesn't guarantee a racist clientele but it's surely more likely than in a Grapes or a Queen Charlotte – or even a Saracen's Head. 'The Albion' is another FRP favourite. If anyone knows of an FRP called The Albion where they do organic cheeses, then let me know because that's a massive outlier on the graph. It's probably in Malta.

The Britannia is now a Tesco Express, which is much more in keeping with the architecture. Very few supermarkets have pitched roofs – I've noticed a few in small Cotswold towns and it looks wrong, like a robot wearing a bobble hat – and I've never seen a thatched one. But rather oddly, Tesco has decided to preserve the tall pole in which the Britannia sign was once displayed and replace it with a sort of 'Tesco Express' pub sign. I don't really understand this. Surely that pole can't be listed? But, if not, wouldn't Tesco get rid of it?

The fact that Tesco is constantly and rapaciously expanding, choking out local businesses like bindweed smothering roses, isn't something you'd think it would want to draw attention to. Nevertheless, there the post stands, irrefutable evidence that this was once a pub – another scalp that the vicious supermarket giant has collected, drying in the wind.

Of course I know that the closure of this pub was no loss to civilisation but, in the imagination of a passer-by who doesn't, the hostelry that Tesco replaced is going to be a veritable 'Moon Under Water'. (That's the name George Orwell invented for his ideal London pub – somewhere that never actually existed. It was later adopted by Wetherspoon's, who have several pubs of that name and many other variants like 'Moon in a Shopping Centre' or 'Moon in the Face of Orwell's Memory'.) So why has Tesco drawn attention to The Britannia's ghost? It's inexplicable.

I'm not good with the low-level unexplained. I worry away at such things. I'm quite relaxed about the great mysteries of the universe; when it comes to the existence of God, for example, I figure that, as with a good episode of *Inspector Morse*, I'll find out what's going on eventually. But also like Morse I do tend to bang on about tiny details that don't quite make sense. That's used to signify a sleuth's maverick brilliance in lots of detective fiction: Columbo, Poirot, Holmes and Miss Marple are forever harping on about what happened to missing cufflinks or why there was no tea in the pot, while those around them try to bring their attention back round to the fact that there's blood and guts up the wall.

I find their impatience odd. Particularly where Captain Hastings is concerned. Do you know Captain Hastings from the early ITV Poirots? He's not in them any more, now they've got a bit mopier and more cinematic. I rather like that character – it's a very entertaining turn. And one of the funniest things about it, or most annoying things depending on my mood, is how Hastings, who shows few signs either of great intellect or an inaccurately high estimation of that intellect (basically he's an idiot and he knows it) keeps moaning on at Poirot for wasting time.

'What are we doing checking the garden shed, Poirot?'

'What possible relevance could an unexplained speck of powder have, Poirot?'

'What are we doing at Somerset House, Poirot? Who cares who's married who?'

All the time. Now, *every day* this man, this idiot, watches Poirot brilliantly solve murders on the basis of small clues. And yet the next day he has *always* forgotten and is basically saying: 'What the hell do *you* know, you Belgian twat?' Never, not once, does he say: 'Well, personally I can't see the relevance of the lipstick but, do you know what, it's your call how we investigate this because on the last two hundred or so cases I've come to the conclusion that you know what you're doing. So you decide. Let me know if there's anything I can do to help.'

Unless of course the Poirot cases in Christie's stories are supposed to be the exceptions. Maybe that's what she's implying with Hastings's moaning – that nine times out of ten Poirot *is* wasting everyone's time sweating the detail. I think that must be it, because otherwise Hastings would shut up. God knows, in real life, Poirot would be so idolised that no path of inquiry he advocated, however absurd, would be neglected. He'd be the Woody Allen of detective work: given complete creative control long after his gifts had waned.

That's how I behave about things like this inexplicable pub sign. I can't let go of them, even though there's no greater mystery – no murder – for them to be the key to. I might be guilty of the same pattern of thinking that leads people to give money, or even devote their lives, to donkey sanctuaries. People focus on saving donkeys from cruelty because the pit of human pain is too deep to contemplate. Solving donkeys' problems seems much more achievable and an appropriately humane gesture. Similarly, maybe, I worry away at small mysteries like the Tesco pub sign, and rant about tiny irritations on TV panel shows and online 'vodcasts' as a displacement activity – to avoid thinking about things that really matter.

There was an inexplicable thing about my prep school (New College School of the aforementioned non-Stalinist approach to lunches). It was a school rule which stated that: 'On no account should any boy ever enter Bath Place.' Bath Place, I should explain, isn't a weird public school name for a bathroom, or swimming pool, diving hole, or buggery nook. It's just a small cobbled courtyard off Holywell Street, just round the corner from the school.

There was a mystery surrounding this rule, which gave the picturesque Bath Place an enormous cachet. Some said that a boy from the school was murdered there, others that one of the school's former headmasters used to frequent the Turf Tavern, an ancient pub which is accessed via Bath Place, and didn't wish to be observed by his charges while drinking.

It always struck me as odd, however, because boys from the school basically weren't allowed to go anywhere at all during school hours. So why specify Bath Place? Why did the anti-Bath Place rules overlie the general anti-everywhere-that's-not-the-school ones? 'On no account should any boy ever enter Bath Place.' The implication was, even your parents weren't allowed to take you there. Bath Place must surely be the best place in the world? I don't know. I never went.

There were a few occasions when I was allowed out of school without a teacher or parent. This was when I was in a school play, which necessitated remaining at school until the evening performance. On those occasions your parents could write a note permitting you to go into town, in the company of a group of other boys, to have dinner there rather than sharing the boarders' tea. And who on earth would want anything to do with the boarders' tea if you could go to McDonald's?

McDonald's was a new arrival to Oxford and consequently had a tremendous atmosphere of transatlantic glamour. I yearned to have birthday parties there, but obviously that wasn't allowed. I had to have horrible birthday teas at home with home-made cake and sandwiches and jelly and sausages on sticks. My parents didn't seem to realise that I could have tea in the garden in the sunlit innocence of childhood any time, while opportunities to stuff down McDonald's quarter-pounders under neon lights were fleeting.

My worst birthday tea was when I was eight. It was our last summer in the Staunton Road house – we moved round the corner the following November – and, by this stage, I was too old for party games. I felt like I was practically an adult and so, instead of games, my parents agreed to take my friends and me to see *The Wrath of Khan* at the cinema.

With such a grown-up outing on the cards, I felt brave enough to invite John Wilkinson. John Wilkinson was the most popular boy in my class – the one who was best at football and cricket, who everyone wanted to be friends with. I desperately wanted to be friends with him, but was also self-aware enough to slightly despise myself for it. Nevertheless, alongside the six or seven invitations I issued to my proper friends, I sidled up to John Wilkinson and asked him nonchalantly if he fancied the birthday trip to *Wrath of Khan*.

He said yes! This was a tremendous leap forward for my social confidence, not to mention the glamour of the guest list. It's how Ricky Gervais must have felt when Ben Stiller agreed to appear on *Extras*.

Off we went to the cinema, then back to my house for tea. I asked John Wilkinson, the guest of honour, to sit next to me, pointedly distancing myself from my less popular, closer friends. Soon I wouldn't need them. It's how Ricky Gervais must feel when he sees Robin Ince.

There were sandwiches for tea, but these were just a dull routine before the main culinary event. My mum had made a special birthday cake, a sort of black forest gateau, which I considered to be extremely sophisticated. As it was set down ceremonially on the table, John Wilkinson, with the lightning-fast reactions so admired in his slip-fielding, grabbed some pepper and put it all over the cake. It was ruined.

He wasn't a nasty boy. I think he just got a bit over-excited. He was, after all, only eight. But I was enormously upset, while simultaneously knowing I had to hide that to save face. And, after all, I'd deserved it. That's what you get, I realised, for cravenly courting the favour of the popular. Know who your real friends are, I thought to myself. But don't get bitter and vengeful, like Khan.

McDonald's would have been so much better. You can't ruin anything on their menu with pepper (if there'd been a cake, I could have moved it before he got the sachet open), and it was so much more exciting than my parents' soppy old garden. But it's difficult to imagine feeling that now, as I glance at the branch I'm passing on Finchley Road in 2012. This modern McDonald's is big, unloved and usually empty. Its clientele are big, unloved and usually full. With the occasional emaciated tramp hacking into a coffee. And this is one of the posh branches which has been painted olive green and is now serving high-fat salads. It even has trendy padded sections on the walls to deaden the echo of emphysema.

I don't know whether the Oxford branch retains any sense of excitement for children – I hope so. I can never hate McDonald's completely because I remember so clearly a time when it was a massive treat to go there. It's odd, standing on this ugly section of the Finchley Road, very near the flat in Swiss Cottage where I lived when I first came to London, how McDonald's prompts memories of innocence and of home – of the happiest period of my childhood, when life revolved around school plays and bonfire nights and carol services. A period of security that I very self-consciously enjoyed, spent most of puberty trying to recapture, and still look to for comfort when I feel bewildered even now. I wonder if the tramps, huddling in McDonald's for warmth, remember going to birthday parties there.

-9-

Beatings and Crisps

I was very happy at New College School. There were only about 130 boys, of whom 16 were choristers in the New College choir, and no girls – but when I started there, this wasn't a down side. In fact, it was a plus. At the age of seven, I was extremely sexist.

It was ruled with charismatic and somehow witty strictness by the headmaster, Alan Butterworth, known by both boys and parents as 'Butch'. This was not an ironic nickname for a man who was actually incredibly camp. He was incredibly butch – terrifying yet fun, like a ride at Alton Towers – a rotund bulldog of a man with a tremendous shouting voice.

But, for all his masculinity, he wasn't unflamboyant: he drove an MG and wore immaculate pinstripe suits, brightly coloured socks and overpowering aftershave. This last could be a lifesaver, as it was often the only clue you'd get that he was lurking round the next corner with an outstretched fist. Don't misunderstand me, he didn't hit the boys. But you weren't supposed to run in the corridors, so he would provide a fist for those disobeying that rule to scamper into. At the time I considered this policy very fair – and basically I still do. What I particularly liked about it was that Butch, having allowed you to smack your face against his hand, would not then rebuke you for running. The discovery of the crime, its punishment and forgiveness were simultaneous.

And, of course, when I say he didn't hit the boys what I mean is that he occasionally hit the boys. I specifically remember his picking up Rawlinson-Winder by his hair for failing to grasp a point of Latin grammar. I hope you get a sense from that last fact not just that the man had a fiery temper but also that he was extremely comfortable with self-caricature.

He also administered the school's official corporal punishment – known as 'The Whacks' – which, I was told (I was far too much of a conformist to be sentenced to it myself), involved being hit with a gym shoe made heftier by a kitchen weight wedged in the toe. The gym shoe's name was Charlie. It is surely one of the world's great sadnesses that billions of shoes go about their benevolent business in aid of mankind, day after day, protecting feet, providing warmth and support, unselfishly getting ducked in puddles and smeared with dog shit, and yet remain unnamed. Whereas this nasty little cunt of a shoe got lavished with affection like a pet.

Butch was as entertaining as he was intimidating and had a way of making you listen to him in school assemblies which I took for granted at the time but have realised in adult life is a gift possessed by few. His most memorable assembly, however, was entertaining in a way he wasn't in control of.

He was obsessed with litter. It maddened him. He considered it, and I'm inclined to agree with him, as the thin end of some sort of anarchist wedge. He couldn't understand why there was ever litter in the school playground when it was well supplied with both bins and teachers authorised to eviscerate you if you were caught dropping so much as the 'tear here' corner of some peanuts. So why, Butch furiously pondered, was there always a small amount of litter in evidence? Who were the anarchists among us – the apparently law-abiding middle-class nine-year-olds with a hidden desire to smash and smash and smash?

It's a good question. I really don't think any of us dropped litter – it was so easy not to. And yet there were always two or three bits of crap floating around the corners of the playground, usually empty crisp packets. This led to a new Butterworth theory: the crisp packets were blowing out of the bins, in a way that a Kit Kat wrapper, for example, would not. The boys were trying to obey the rules but were being beaten, not by him on this occasion, but by physics.

His solution was simple: when you put a crisp packet into a bin, it was vital that you scrunched it up first. Otherwise you were obeying only the letter and not the spirit of the anti-littering rule. I cannot over-emphasise how often the importance of scrunching was stated to us. (Certainly more often than we were told about autumn, another subject seriously over-covered by schools in my experience and of very little use in adult life. If I had stepped into the world as an 18-year-old unaware of the distinction between deciduous and evergreen trees and the hibernation or migration habits of various vertebrates, I think it would have taken a college friend about two minutes to get me up to speed – in the unlikely event that the ignorance ever became apparent. I mean, take the word 'deciduous' – I was taught it, I think, at the age of six, taught it again at the age of seven, ditto when eight and nine – and I've only used it twice since. And that's in this paragraph, where it's actually been very useful. Thanks, Miss Boon!)

But scrunching trumped even autumn. 'Why oh why,' Alan Butterworth would scream, 'will you boys not learn the simple technique of scrunching up a crisp packet as you throw it away!? If you don't get it soon, I shall have to ban crisps from the school premises,' he threatened. He was saying this because the stray, apparently unscrunched packets were continuing to blow around in the small wind eddies in the playground's corners, alongside the dead leaves of the more littering sort of tree; he was assuming, not unreasonably, that we were all too stupid to obey this simple instruction, that the dense, untrained, anarchic schoolboys were always too light-headed from their crisp-induced mid-morning carb and salt rush to remember about the scrunching after they'd poured the last delicious potatoey shards down their young throats. In his view, it was a level of idiocy unequalled in his long career of working with unformed brains.

So, one day, he decided to do a practical demonstration. He brought a crisp packet into assembly. It was quite incongruous to see it in his signet-ringed hand, like watching the Queen brandishing a ketchup bottle. The packet was empty – he never told us who had eaten the crisps. He held the packet aloft before vigorously scrunching it between both hands and placing the neat and unaerodynamic ball on the table in front of him. We then stood to sing a hymn.

If you've eaten crisps in the last few decades, you'll know what happened next. During the hymn, the plastic packet gradually but determinedly unscrunched itself until it lay flat on the table. It stayed there for a few moments before drifting gently onto the floor. The problem with his scrunching instructions was humiliatingly laid bare – as was the towering arrogance of a man who had been banging on for years about this apparently simple solution to the littering problem without once trying it out himself. He was so sure of himself that the *first time he ever attempted to scrunch up a crisp packet was in front of the whole school.*

Now, there's confidence for you. And foolishness. It's like a metaphor for the First World War: the folly and the leadership rolled into one. He didn't mention the flattened-out packet after the hymn. The official line was that the simplicity of the plan had been brilliantly demonstrated by the headmaster. But that's not what the other teachers' faces were saying.

He ran a terrific school, though – and it was terrific largely as a result of his labours. He'd been headmaster for over 25 years when I arrived, and his techniques clearly worked – the school's academic reputation was excellent and, more importantly, it was an institution with high self-esteem.

That's quite a trick to pull off for a small provincial prep school which was neither big enough nor rich enough to win at games. Somehow the boys at New College School were made to feel clever and significant. The staff seemed to have a swagger about them too which, when I think about it, was remarkable. It's not a brilliant job, teaching in a small prep school. We do not, sadly, live in a society that values teaching very highly as a profession. We live in a society that pretends to, but gives the big money to footballers and bankers (and more to comedians and actors than they are probably worth, I'm very happy to admit, but personally I'm in it for the disproportionate praise).

But, even where teaching is valued as it should be, teachers from small independent prep schools are probably the least revered. Those little seats of learning have neither the sense of sacrifice of the state sector nor the glamour of the major public schools. But most of the staff at New College School seemed bright, interesting, fun, well-motivated and had been there years. Butch was clearly doing something right, even if it was mainly spotting clever and engaging people who weren't very ambitious.

Whenever I think about the odd alchemy – the combination of planning, tradition, flexibility, inflexibility and luck – that it takes to make a functional institution, I think of New College School. And I worry that institutions like that are less likely to exist in Britain now. We don't seem to live in a society where excellence in small but achievable aims is respected – where a man like Alan Butterworth, a very bright and charismatic Oxford graduate, would be willing to devote his entire career to making one small school as good as it could be.

Don't get me wrong, I know being a prep school headmaster isn't the same as founding an anti-malaria charity. But that's sort of the point: it wasn't saintly, neither was it glory-seeking. It was a modest, realistic goal. He didn't want to run a bigger school or to make the school that he did run bigger. He just wanted consistency, and from that he derived contentment – or at least I hope he did. He certainly did some good, albeit only to the male children of fee-paying parents.

- 10 -

The Smell of
the Crowd

I cross Finchley Road at the Swiss Cottage roundabout (there's a pub there which looks like a giant Swiss cottage, which is how the area got its name; why such a giant chalet-shaped boozer was built is a mystery to me) and wiggle left into the top of Eton Avenue. There are two theatres here now – Hampstead Theatre, which is newly rebuilt, having existed in a glorified portacabin fifty yards further south until a few years ago, and the Embassy Theatre, which belongs to the Central School of Speech and Drama.

Some students are sitting on the steps outside the theatre and I squint at them jealously. I don't want to *be* them – they're wearing loose, sensible clothing in order to facilitate the sort of balletic moves by which no production in theatrical history has ever been improved, and I'm including ballets; plus they all seem to be agreeing about something, and I've got a hunch that they're all wrong – I'm just remembering what it was like to put on plays as a student, surrounded by friends, all beer and low stakes.

But perhaps it's not like that if you're a drama school student. At university, it all just felt like fun. Maybe these students feel like they've started work already. I'm not sorry I didn't go to drama school. I've heard they make you do mime and try to 'take you apart and put you back together again' which, even if they mean it metaphorically, isn't really my cup of tea. They want to 'take you out of your comfort zone', and I think that might mean they actually confiscate your cup of tea.

My first proper theatrical performances were at New College School. I have a vague recollection of one occasion at Napier House when I was made to pretend I was a stalk of wheat, but that was just a sort of Harvest Festival show, which involved us bringing in various foods for redistribution to the bemused and needy, then some kind of activity which I'm not going to dignify with the word 'performance', on a platform which I'm not going to dignify with the word 'stage'. I remember being part of a line of children, in front of an audience of parents, and we were all pretending to grow from a seed by starting in a crouched position and slowly standing up and finally stretching out our arms. Like soldiers in a Soviet propaganda film, we were under instructions to smile. I suppose it was physical theatre really and, like a lot of physical theatre, it received a rapturous response from an unquestioning audience at pains to indulge the performers.

But my real performing career started at New College School, with an appearance as a clown. One Friday afternoon in my first year at the school, it was suddenly announced that instead of 'Field', which was what we called sport because you went to the college playing field to do it, we were going to be taught some circus skills.

It is a sign of how baffling so much of life is when you're seven that we took this news in our stride. I've often wondered since what was actually going on, and I've come to the conclusion that a bunch of out-of-work performers were making some cash on the side by doing circus skills workshops at independent schools and that one of the NCS staff either knew one of the performers or had been born yesterday.

The first piece of news about the circus skills afternoon was that, sadly, not everyone would get to have his face painted like a clown. 'Ohhhh noooo!' the class moaned – and I assume I joined in, just like I'd have joined in at Nuremberg. What I was thinking, of course, was: 'Thank God for that, I don't want my face made up like a clown's by someone I don't know. That would be awful! And what if the make-up wouldn't come off?!'

'I'm sorry but two is the absolute maximum for face painting,' lamented Miss Brown, 'and as you all obviously want to have your faces painted like clowns …'

'Oh yes, madly – please pick me, Miss Brown!' we all interjected.

'… I'm just going to have to put your names in a hat and pick out the two lucky ones who will get to spend the afternoon looking like clowns.'

I was already familiar enough with sod's law to have a sinking feeling at this news. There seemed no way of volunteering to be left out of the hat. It was just assumed that we'd all want make-up all over our faces. Where, I thought, did that idea come from? Why is there this weird consensus about this weird thing – this bizarre concept that everyone else seems to think is a lovely treat? And why am I being swept along in it?

And yet I knew any attempt I made to opt out pre-hat would be dicing with pariah status. I was facing another, and quite unexpected, challenge in my quest to be normal: I was going to have to make it seem as if I wanted to look like a clown. I really hadn't seen that coming. But still, I reasoned, it probably won't be me.

Of course it was me. First out of the hat. I forced a smile onto my soon-to-be-vandalised features. Oh God, life is awful, I thought. And I distinctly remember thinking that this was doubly unjust because, not only was I going to have to endure something terrifying, but one of the many among my classmates who, it had recently become clear, had always been obsessed with greasepaint would be denied the smearing of their dreams.

And it was fine, obviously. It didn't hurt – I walked around with everyone saying 'You look like a clown!', they cleaned it all off before I went home, and I had that buzz you get from having endured something you were dreading and found it, while not actually pleasant, less alarming than you'd feared.

Other than sitting still while a stranger daubs your face, the other 'circus skills' which the out-of-work actors were teaching turned out to be balancing a hockey stick on one finger – which takes a bit of practice but isn't that difficult, or at all impressive, or a circus skill – and lying on a bed of nails. This involves just lying on a bed of nails. If the nails aren't that sharp – they weren't – the fact that there are such a lot of them means that it's basically pain-less – your weight is comfortably distributed among the hundreds of nails. It's supposed to sound brave or impressive because you're lying on *so many* nails, so people (idiots) think it must be many times the pain of lying on the point of one nail, which is agonising. But of course it isn't. I hated Field, but there's no doubt that after-noon would have been better spent if I'd been outdoors running away from a football as usual.

You may be wondering why, as the sort of freak who wandered around inexpertly disguised as Louis XIV all weekend, I wasn't more enthusiastic about spending an afternoon disguised as a clown. I think my horror largely came from the novelty of the activ-ity and the people inflicting it on me. I'm not really attracted by novelty, as you will almost certainly already have guessed. (If not, wait until I start talking about Chinese food.)

That selection process for the clown make-up is the earliest recollection I have of my knee-jerk hatred of consensus. I just don't like it, particularly when it relates to fun or fashion. Not only did I dread the thought of having to wear make-up, I hated the feeling that I was supposed to think it would be great. I hated that pressure to join in and be like everyone else. I hated it, but I did it anyway.

Who are these morons who want stuff putting on their faces, I thought. And why does their opinion prevail? I get the same shiver of contempt when I hear inane radio DJs talk to listeners about their weekend plans to 'just chill', 'have a large one' or 'party with my mates'. These people are welcome to such pleasures, but I balk at the implication that that's what everyone's doing or what every-one should be doing; that these are the lives that the uncool are so often exhorted to get. I'd love to hear a caller to XFM or similar announce that they'll be spending all weekend at a steam fair, seeing a relative with dementia, decorating eggs, desperately looking for a vital but lost bit of paperwork or just frantically masturbating to the Eroica symphony.

This is a world where people no longer indicate their enthusiasm for a TV series, actor, celebrity, band or snack bar by saying 'Oh, I love it' but with 'I'm loving it' – you know 'I'm loving this season of *Strictly*', 'I'm loving Heston's mini fish burgers', 'We're loving Alan Carr's new glasses'. That's the fickle present continuous. There's a silent 'at the moment' after it which there isn't with 'I love'. These consumers are just passing through, waiting to get their head turned by something sparkly which, once tarnished by their gaze, they'll turn away from. They like what's cool because it's cool and for no other reason, and I hate them for it.

Another example of their hatefulness while my dander's up: in order to get themselves off the hook of sometimes liking uncool things, they refer to them as 'guilty pleasures', which is a ridiculous expression. What? So you like Abba, or Roger Moore as James Bond, but have been led to believe that this taste is somehow infra dig, so you style it a 'guilty pleasure', thus demonstrating you're sufficiently relaxed and self-deprecating to own up to it – when in fact the way you have chosen to express it lays bare your bland and inane obsession with the worthless trappings of the zeitgeist.

Doing those list-interviews which newspapers print nowadays because they lack the resources to fill their pages with proper articles – the *Guardian* Q&A, that sort of thing – I've been asked dozens of times: 'What's your guilty pleasure?' I usually reply 'A fry-up' or 'Watching *Bargain Hunt*' or 'Eating toast in bed'. On one occasion, bored, I replied: 'Well, I must say, I do like to fuck a prostitute.'

I'm proud of that (saying it, not doing it – I've never actually fucked a prostitute) but now unfortunately the pride I've confessed to will have made it less funny. Sorry.

But honestly ... 'Guilty pleasures'? It's prudish and judgemental and yet it's referring to harmless things people do in their spare time. I mean, I've watched and enjoyed *The X Factor* and I know that it's not exactly the Proms or *The Wire* or whatever worthy thing I'm supposed to be watching, but why should I feel the least bit guilty about having taken pleasure from it? Or, for that matter, from eating a Findus crispy pancake, watching a *Brittas Empire* DVD or reading *Country Life* in the bath?

It has occurred to me since, as it almost certainly occurred to you, that there was probably more than one timorous child only pretending to want his face painted. But that just makes the idea of consensus all the more terrifying.

- 11 -

Cross-Dressing, Cards and Cocaine

Having turned right after the Hampstead Theatre down Winchester Road, I am walking between two gleaming new blocks of flats, under one of which will be fragments of rubble from the first flat I rented in London – a time when I had no money and no paid work. I've been standing on stages for years, I thought in those days. If someone doesn't pay me for a public performance soon, it'll be as if they're trying to starve me into stopping.

After inexpertly miming the life cycle of a staple crop and being made to look like a clown, my next public performance (unpaid) was when I was ten years old, and it was the role of 'Dancing Girl' in a production of *A Christmas Carol*. This wasn't the lead. I was only in one scene: Mr Fezziwig's party. You know, when the Ghost of Christmas Past shows Scrooge what he used to be like when he let his hair down (or, in most productions, before he'd let it get all grey and straggly). I didn't have any lines. Basically I was an extra in drag. I was part of a group of eight boys, half of us disguised as women, who were doing a sort of line dance in order to make the atmosphere of Fezziwig's Christmas party seem appropriately festive.

It's impossible for me to infer anything flattering from being cast in this role, and God knows I've tried. Clearly the school wished to involve as many boys as possible in the production; if you auditioned, they'd try and give you something to do. Their decision to put me in a wig and a dress at the back of the stage in a single scene does not suggest that my acting showed much promise. And obviously, it was embarrassing to have to cross-dress – but then, it was an all-boys' school so I wasn't alone and some of the boys had to play actual female characters, which involved talking and (in the most nightmarish examples) pretending to be in love *as a woman* – inevitably, there being very little lesbian theatre performed at my prep school, *with a man* – which I considered much, much worse than what I had to endure. (Obviously, if there had been lesbian theatre at my prep school, both of the lesbians would have had to be played by boys, so that wouldn't have helped either.)

I've worn drag a few times on stage since then – I pretended to be Cilla Black at a college rag week version of *Blind Date*, and played the dame in a couple of pantomimes in the part of my career before anyone paid me, when I was living on the very road I'm walking down now. Later, when Robert Webb and I were doing our sketch show, I appeared on television as Mrs Danvers (Daphne Du Maurier's terrifying housekeeper), Mrs Patricia Wilberforce (our vision of a 1940s British version of Oprah) and half of a two-headed Mrs Hudson. On every occasion I enjoyed it; it's so much easier to get laughs when you're a bloke in a dress. Audiences just find it funny and seem well disposed to whatever line you deliver.

I don't really understand why that is, although I can certainly feel that hilariousness myself when I watch the *Monty Python* team pretending to be housewives – particularly, I think, the Batley Townswomen's Guild re-enactment of the Battle of Pearl Harbor (essentially they just run at each other in a muddy field wielding handbags). There is something about male impersonation of female mannerisms, however inexpert, that makes people giggly – possibly because it consists of the right combination of silliness and taboo-breaking. Fluidity of gender is not something we're culturally confident about, however much we try to be outwardly accepting.

This is one of the reasons transsexuals get such a hard time. They're doing something which, for some, offends against principles which are deeply, if only instinctively, held. A minority of the offended, the angrier, stupider minority, then lash out. But, even for those of us who aren't remotely offended by what transsexuals do with their bodies or their lives, there's the problem that, when a large man decides to live and dress as a woman – and to have what surgery in that direction they can to help the process – what most of us still see is a bloke in a dress.

And it does often seem to be quite a large man, wearing quite an old-fashioned twinset and pearls type of get-up – although they may just be the only ones we notice. And they look very much like the Batley Townswomen's Guild. So it's funny. But we're not supposed to find it funny – so it's even funnier. The person who's made that choice is deadly serious and very sensitive about it – which makes it funnier still. To the comedy-appreciating parts of the brain, it's as if someone has solemnly announced their intention, in order to be more completely themselves, to live a life of constantly slipping on banana skins. And then we see them doing it. All seriously.

Unfortunately, that immediate entertaining effect of a man in a dress didn't really happen for me when I was ten – partly because I didn't have any lines but mainly because, if you put a pre-pubescent boy in a dress and a wig, he looks exactly like a pre-pubescent girl. The very effect that large hairy blokes who feel they're women trapped in men's bodies are so desperate to achieve, I couldn't at that age avoid. The photographs of the production were humiliating, as my true gender was completely undetectable – and this was at an age when I identified quite strongly with being a boy and the thought of blurring that line was intensely threatening. I was proud to be penis-bearing and considered girls to be basically silly and unnecessary. It was disconcerting to discover that I was a few months without a haircut away from being indistinguishable from one.

On stage, I did my dancing steps as rehearsed while the action of the play continued around me. I had little or no idea what went on in any of the other scenes – it was only later that I found out the plot of *A Christmas Carol*. I was only on for two minutes and I spent the rest of the time playing cards with the other dancing boys.

That was why I fell in love with the stage: it gave me the opportunity to play pontoon in the gaps. There was a huge amount of waiting around involved in this show. School would finish, after which you'd either have boarders' tea or go to McDonald's – but then there were still hours to wait before the show, during which you'd change into your costume and get made up by one of the team of female teachers and mothers. They ran a sort of greasepaint production line to make sure that every member of the huge cast was properly painted orange with red lips (if they were pretending to be girls) or with thick black worry lines (if they were pretending to be old) and a great big scarlet dollop in the corner of their eye whoever they were pretending to be.

The older boys would earnestly explain that, without this bizarre caking, human facial features were almost totally unnoticeable under the powerful lights of the school hall's stage. Obviously this was nonsense. We would have looked completely normal under the lights without make-up; with it, we looked like we were absolutely covered in make-up. But I must say, in contrast to my experience as a clown, I found being made up for the play quite fun. It made me feel important and I liked the smell.

But during the hours of waiting for everyone to get through this process, and then the hour or so while the audience arrived, and then the hours of the show itself, which I resolutely ignored apart from my two-minute appearance, there was plenty of time for playing cards. This felt like the most fun I'd ever had in my life. I'd been taught pontoon by my grandfather (the second nicest one), but to play it with other boys of my own age – to get to teach some of them the rules – was hugely exciting. It felt very grown-up and sophisticated, particularly because it involved betting (albeit only with matchsticks) but also because it had its own little argot: not just the names of the cards but things like 'twist', 'bust' and 'five card trick'.

I was very disappointed, and slightly alienated, to discover many years later, on a stag do, that the casino version of the game not only has a different name – blackjack – but also different words and conventions for everything. You're not supposed to say things like 'twist' and you get treated like a rube if you do, so it turns out that my schoolboy sense of sophistication was illusory. And of course it struck me as illogical and unfair that 'twist' exists as a word – an obscure way of asking for a card that you have to be in the know to be aware of – but quickly becomes obsolete when you get even deeper in the know. It would be like mariners not only having the words 'port' and 'starboard' instead of left and right but also a secret rule which stated that, when you really became a seasoned seafarer, you reverted to saying left and right. For some reason, I expected better from these people who were trying to cheat me of my money.

Back at school, before I was aware that it was possible to spend an evening playing games of chance without the excuse of a theatrical production, I decided to sign up for every play going – which, unfortunately, was only two a year. In the following year's Christmas production, I was given my first line – and I've been battling cocaine ever since.

No, I've never, in fact, had cocaine. No one has ever offered me any cocaine. I work in showbusiness and no one has ever offered me any cocaine.

Can you believe that? What's wrong with me? I don't want any cocaine, by the way (in case you were offering – which, experience suggests, you weren't) but it would have been nice to be offered once or twice. It's like being a vegetarian to whom no one has ever offered any meat. They wouldn't be pleased. A vegetarian doesn't want meat but neither does he (or she – usually she, let's be honest) want the thought that, as soon as she enters a room, everyone *assumes* she's a vegetarian. No one, however merciful towards animals, wants to look so vegetarian in every way that no one has even bothered to check. That's how I am with cocaine and it makes me worry I'm not always the life and soul of the party that I feel like in my head.

Anyway, I was given my first line of dialogue in the next year's production and it was: 'Vespasian, centurion.' Two nouns, one of them proper. I think the centurion is trying to remember who the current Roman emperor is after a year of political instability and each of his soldiers, of whom I was one, makes a suggestion. On consulting Wikipedia, I learn that, after the death of Nero in AD 68, there were four Roman emperors in quick succession – Galba, Otho, Vitellius and then Vespasian. It was this fact that the author of this comic play set in Roman times, presented by and for children, who was also a Latin teacher at the school (Mr Roberts), was seeking to do a joke on. That's the sort of thing that gives dumbing down a good name.

It was very enterprising of a teacher to write the school play but I didn't feel that the line 'Vespasian, centurion' was exactly a zinger. I'm not saying I could have got full value out of 'Infamy, infamy, they've all got it in for me!' but with 'Vespasian, centurion' I didn't think I'd been given the equipment with which to amuse. I felt in need of a bed of nails or even a hockey stick. When I said 'Vespasian, centurion' at the point instructed, the audience showed no sign at all of having noticed. But the good news was that saying 'Vespasian, centurion' didn't eat seriously into my card-playing time, which kept the magic of theatre alive in my heart.

The next year's production presented a problem: I was given quite a large part. It was an adaptation of *Winnie-the-Pooh* and I was cast as Rabbit. This is the first time I can remember acting, rather than just moving and standing, and occasionally saying 'Vespasian, centurion' in exactly the way I was told. In our family car we had a tape, which I would ask to hear again and again, of Lionel Jeffries reading *Winnie-the-Pooh*. It's a brilliant reading by a terrific actor. If you think you don't know who Lionel Jeffries is,

LEFT & BELOW:
The ageing process
is terribly cruel.

The child of a thousand nervous faces

You'd have to be a sneering *Downton Abbey* sceptic to spot the anachronisms in my beloved 'eighteenth-century king' get-up. Today, His Majesty is holding the royal secateurs.

If you want to look cool, you first have to *feel* cool. You then have to do a lot of other things.

Despite the smile, I am bitterly aware that this outfit is humiliatingly baggy.

Here, I am guarding some nascent runner beans.

ABOVE:
The Kilburn High Road: 'The closer you look, the better it gets.' This is a genuine slogan used by the council.

RIGHT & BELOW:
Me and my brother Dan, in 1987 and 2012. As you can see, the age gap has widened from eight years to about twenty.

LEFT:
My parents Kathy and Ian, photographed, as usual, in front of a Christmas tree. I shou[ld] point out, however, that this tree is in my flat in Kilburn. There'[s] no way my dad would give houseroom to anything so wonky.

RIGHT:
With Grandpa, my mum's dad and my favourite person in the world at the time.

LEFT:
With Grandad, my dad's dad. I'd rather be watching *Knight Rider*.

LEFT:
A typical FRP.
Organic produce ahoy!

BELOW:
Having ordered a piano,
this young mother is
just about to embark
on the gruelling weekly
fireworks shop.

BELOW:
or many years,
was an only child.

Showbusiness!

The 1984 New College School production of *A Christmas Carol* – the Fezziwig's Party scene. I'm third from the left, in the red skirt. I've clearly got 'it'.

I am the legionary on the far right, wearing gym shoes and nervously watching the end of my neighbour's spear. I have probably already said 'Vespasian, centurion!'

If you look closely at this typical gathering of a human, a bear, a rabbit and a pig, you may notice that, in reality, they're *all* humans.

What possible explanation could there be for this sign?

I have a racist palate.

Regent's Park loos – an etiquette minefield.

The British Ambassador to the Eighth Session of the European Youth Parliament in Barcelona.

you'd probably recognise his face and bald pate. Among hundreds of roles, he played Dick Van Dyke's father in *Chitty Chitty Bang Bang* and did a rather moving turn as the patriarch of a brewing family in an episode of *Inspector Morse*.

Anyway, he read Rabbit with a sort of clipped military Field Marshal Montgomery voice, and I had the idea when auditioning for the show (and I mean 'idea' very much in the sense that advertising creatives use it) of copying him. This immediately put me head and shoulders above anyone else who read for the part – I already had a performance. When I landed the role, I remember counting my lines – I had well over a hundred! I'd hit the big time and, in that production, I had no time for playing pontoon. Fortunately for my future financial security, I found that I enjoyed the performing even more than the cards. (I say 'fortunately' but then acting is hardly the most secure financial path you can tread – and I'm reliably informed that some people make a very good living playing poker, although I don't think the same can be said for pontoon.)

And with my first stage performance of any size came my first on-stage cock-up. The approach to theatre at New College School was an old-fashioned one. Realism, wherever possible, was demanded. I have extremely fond memories of the set: no short cuts, no simplified black box staging, none of that theatrical bullshit that, in our heart of hearts, we all know is an excuse to save effort or money. No, there were trees and burrows and bushes and paths and doorways and a bridge and a river all crammed onto the stage in the school hall, all lovingly recreated in wood and paint.

For the scene in the snow – the first story from *House at Pooh Corner* in which Pooh and Piglet decide to build Eeyore a house and in the process accidentally demolish the one Eeyore has just built for himself (they mistake the structure for a pile of sticks) – the set was transformed, in a quick scene change, into a snowy land-scape, complete with cotton wool snow along the railings of the bridge. I thought that was amazing.

And the commitment to realism extended to the costumes. The animal characters weren't alluded to with, say, a pair of ears while the rest of the costume was human in a way that reflected the character's personality. Oh no. We were head to toe, fingertip to fingertip in fake fur. Only our faces showed. This led to my mistake.

There is a scene in which Rabbit has to read out a plan to drive Kanga out of the wood – it's in the form of a long list. He doesn't like immigrants basically but, like many extremists, he's attempted to rationalise his instinctive xenophobia into some sort of coherent philosophy. It's a very funny list which I had *sort of* learned. Not as well as I'd learned my other lines because this bit, I reasoned, I'd be reading out. It is not a good idea, I now know, to *sort of* learn anything – to 'become familiar' with it. It's worthless. Either learn it or don't. If you're going to read it out, just admit that and don't in any way lull yourself into a false sense that, were the piece of paper to go missing, you'd probably be okay.

The piece of paper did not go missing, by the way. I am very organised about props. People who mess with them get my full anal barrage (by this, I do not mean that I shit on them – I'm using anal in its modern slang sense). The piece of paper was where it should have been – folded up in the pocket of Rabbit's waistcoat (which I wore over the top half of the fur body suit; I did not wear anything over its bottom half, but that's okay because there is a strong convention that the anthropomorphised animals of children's stories are non-genital).

The only problem was that when I came to read out the list on stage, I couldn't unfold it because of the ridiculous furry mittens I was wearing in order to complete the illusion that I was in fact a talking rabbit. I was able, with difficulty, to fish it out of my pocket, but that was all. The words were on the inside. All I could do was stare at the blank, white, folded quarter of A4 and try to remember my lines, a process not helped by simultaneously having to surf a wave of panic.

But it could have been worse. I fluffed a bit, I approximated, I probably went slightly red but, in the context of a prep school play, the standard of professionalism probably didn't fall perceptibly below the mean. What interests me about it is that, afterwards, one of the directors of the show, Mr Sleigh, to whom I'd been recounting my mittens nightmare with a verve worthy of a classic anecdote about Gielgud getting caught cottaging, said that I should have taken the mittens off to unfold the list. He said it would have been funny.

He was right, of course. But it had never occurred to me to do that. In my mind, I was pretending to be a rabbit and the rabbit wasn't wearing gloves. I felt that to take them off, assuming people didn't scream because they thought the giant rabbit was now skinning its own hands, would have been to shatter the illusion – as surely as if I'd gone off stage and fetched the script. It would have been *cheating*. I wanted to say: 'Look, am I pretending to be a rabbit or not?' But it stayed in my head, that idea of how you could cheat in a performance – the thought that, as the audience members were suspending their disbelief anyway (I certainly didn't think that anyone believed I was a rabbit), they'll suspend it a bit further if you give them a joke.

Whether on stage, on TV or, I suppose, in a film, although I've had very little experience of that, it's a tricky thing knowing how much you can 'break the fourth wall', acknowledge the pretence. The right decision usually depends on context and, by keeping the mittens on, I was rightly erring on the cautious side even if I lost a laugh. But this early directorial note is interesting because it lodged firmly in my mind the idea that, when you're performing, what you're primarily doing is telling a story and trying to entertain, not just pretending to be something that you're not.

The other distressing event in that show was the moment towards the end when I was supposed to hug and kiss another boy. You're probably thinking: 'I don't remember that bit in *Winnie-the-Pooh*!' Don't you? That story where Rabbit professes undying love for Eeyore and starts to hump his leg? Don't worry, that's just in the fan fiction (or that's what I imagine – there's a big internet out there: get googling!).

No: this was in a story where some of the animals, Rabbit amongst them, get lost in the woods. I think it's basically Rabbit's fault – this is very much the Arnhem campaign to his getting-Pooh-unstuck-from-his-front-door El Alamein. And Tigger finds them. Tigger, to whom Rabbit, informed by the xenophobic instincts that also made him dislike Kanga, has up to this point been markedly hostile.

I can now understand why Mr Sleigh thought it would be funny if, when Tigger comes to the rescue, Rabbit throws himself at him in a massive hug and kiss of gratitude. At the time, I couldn't quite believe the suggestion. I actually thought he was joking. I wouldn't have been any more shocked if he'd suggested I should get down on my knees and take his cock in my mouth. Fortunately I didn't go to that sort of school.

I think, in the end, I managed to sort of touch Tigger's shoulders effusively. The boy in the tiger suit was no keener on the idea than I was, and was in the lucky position of only having to be hugged. He could just stay still and he chose to do this on all fours – for tigerish verisimilitude – which made hugging a tricky thing to do anyway. I completely failed to realise Mr Sleigh's comic moment of relief-driven hypocritical affection, and still that was the moment in the show that I most dreaded.

This wasn't the same awkwardness as that which attended the idea of love scenes in *A Christmas Carol* two years before. It was no longer as specific as not wanting to play another boy's love interest, or to be seen to be soppy. It had grown into a wholesale rejection of *any physical contact at all*. Even a simple hug seemed preposterous, with anyone. I was as confident in this insight as those people who can't see the point of real Christmas trees are that it's much less messy to plug in an artificial one year after year. None of their reasoning is wrong. There's just something else they're not getting.

Where did that repression come from? Not from my parents – they've always been very affectionate – and not, it seems, from the teachers at my old-fashioned prep school. But there was something in me that found even the simulation of this sort of harmless affection terrifying. Maybe all boys of that age – I think I was 12 – feel the same. Maybe it's to do with a fear of being or being perceived to be gay? Or maybe it's just that there's always something a bit disgusting about other humans that, in the absence of sexual attraction, can be gruelling to get over as an adult but, for a child, is impossible – just as an adult me could choke down disgusting gooseberry pie which I absolutely couldn't when I was little.

Whatever the reason, at the time I was happy and confident in the belief that there was really no need for one human *ever* to hug or kiss another. (You may be surprised to learn that I no longer subscribe to that view.) I would indulge my parents in such activity because they were in denial about my maturity, but basically those things were for babies and very small children – and thus they were of the past, and not in a good way like plus-fours. I'd left all that behind and this was a thought that contented me. I did not yet know the facts of life.

Presidents of the Galaxy

When are you in Regent's Park but not in Regent's Park? When you're at the Marriott Regent's Park. Or to give it its correct name which is also, in its own way, incorrect: the Marriott Regents Park.

That's the large hotel I'm passing on King Henry's Road; architecturally it looks quite holidayish. It wouldn't be out of place on the Majorcan coast. When I lived round here, we'd occasionally go for a drink in the bar, instead of going to the pub – although I think it might have been a Holiday Inn then.

You can't see the park but, to be fair, it would be a very quick taxi ride or a ten-minute walk. Globally speaking it's extremely close to Regent's Park. At the solar system level they're indistinguishable, part of the same speck. At a pan-galactic level, you'd reflect that the number of things in the universe further away from Regent's Park than the Marriott Regents Park so utterly dwarfs the number of things closer that to complain would seem churlish. But I still reckon that an inter-dimensional traveller, on being shown to his room with a view of the A41, might have to bite his tongue (or tongues) to prevent himself (or herself or itself or third-alien-gender-self) from muttering that he thought it might have been a bit closer to Regent's Park than this. And that they might have fucking kept the apostrophe.

When we drank there, I found it engagingly anonymous – a perfectly adequate hotel which could have been anywhere

– certainly its name isn't a particularly good clue. Also, the lager may have been slightly more expensive than in a pub but you got free peanuts. I think I worked out that, if you were on for a big night of peanut-eating, it might even work out cheaper. My friends were less keen to go there than I was, possibly because it was so devoid of atmosphere but possibly also because they didn't feel they belonged there. We were a bunch of scuzzy, unemployed and impecunious ex-students and this was a place full of businessmen. I don't think we were sneered at but it felt like a possibility.

I quite liked that possibility. I liked the idea of some self-important sales manager trying to assert that he had more right to buy a lager in a hotel than I did – so that I could angrily respond that my money was as good as his, while secretly thinking that it was better (even if it was far less plentiful). I suppose as a middle-class ex-public schoolboy I got a feeling of social confidence from a middle-ranking hotel (after all, my parents used to manage such places) which even the empty pockets and frayed clothes of the unsuccessful freelancer couldn't shake. In fact, it was probably those very reduced circumstances that made me seek out the reassurance of an environment of unremarkable prosperity.

And also I fancy myself a bit. I reckon I'm something (or 'summut' as they say in Yorkshire, where almost everyone reckons they're something and yet particularly resents it in others, so expressing it in fewer letters saves millions of man hours). That's not to say that I don't sometimes feel very shit about myself – I'm not always nice, organised, hard-working or sensible. But however broke, scruffy and unemployed I became, I could never quite shake my feeling that I was a man of consequence.

I really hope I don't come across as if that's what I think about myself. I'd hate to seem immodest. Not here, of course. I'm perfectly resigned to seeming immodest here – and I do so in a spirit of honesty. But I very seldom want people to realise that's what I feel. Not because I'm ashamed of feeling a bit special (I hope everyone does) but because I've been brought up to believe that behaving modestly is one of the keystones of politeness. It's something that maddens me about the direction our culture seems to be taking – led by reality TV – that this convention of modesty is being lost. In programmes such as *The X Factor* and *The Apprentice*, contestants are encouraged to voice the most megalomaniacal aspects of their self-belief and, should they be unfortunate enough actually to *be* as modest as I wish in non-autobiographical contexts to seem, to exaggerate them. We're sliding into a society where the first thing you need to do to demonstrate that you're any good at something is to say that you are. Under the old rules, boasts were assumed empty until proved otherwise. You had to impress with your actions, draw attention to yourself subtly without being seen to do so. It's a hell of a lot more fun than the pantomime of self-belief we see on reality TV today. A society where you're not allowed to blow your own trumpet is so much more nuanced, sophisticated and interesting than the grim world of literalism that's being ushered in.

One of the weird side effects of my continued adherence to this fading convention is that sometimes it makes people think I have low self-esteem. Mostly this is a misapprehension from which I profit, as people are apt to be fonder of those they think of as self-doubting. But it's annoying when people not only assume I think I'm shitter than I do, but then agree with that estimation. It reminds me of a moment in *The Hitchhiker's Guide to the Galaxy* when Arthur Dent, the hapless and very British central character, has been unusually helpful in a crisis. Zaphod Beeblebrox, the cool, preening, transatlantic-voiced President of the Galaxy, congratulates him and Dent replies: 'Oh it was nothing.' Beeblebrox says: 'Oh was it? Forget it then.'

Some might think that acting all modest and yet feeling all megalomaniacal is dishonest. I say it's a cultural thing. And of course it's not megalomania (well, if it is, I'm the worst person to judge – just don't put me in charge of soldiers), it's just general high self-esteem. And it means that when I do have moments of self-loathing, I don't feel worthless but that I've let myself down – which implies that, even when feeling low, I still sense that there's something to let down.

And to those who say to me: 'Oh I can see you're the nervous one,' or 'You seem shy,' I sometimes want to reply: 'If I'm shy, why am I standing on the shiny platform?' In showbusiness there are a lot of complete extroverts who uncomplicatedly want to be on stage being looked at. I'm a bit shyer than that; I don't always like it. But at the end of the day, people who really hate the limelight don't choose to stand in it.

I don't know where my feeling of self-confidence comes from. Being the loved child of nice intelligent people in comfortable circumstances is an excellent start – but there are plenty of doted-on kids of the middle classes who doggedly self-loathe and self-harm. If I had to pick a reason why I've avoided that, I might very well plump for Form VI, the scholarship set at New College School, for boys who might win scholarships to public school.

I was a swot – I was one of the boys who were good at exams. In fact, I don't think I'm flattering myself when I say that, in my year, I was the best at exams. I admit that this made me very proud. I loved being the best at something. I could never be best at sport – the activity that most schoolboys would probably choose to excel at – but being best at lessons was a very acceptable second-best sort of best.

I also had a sense that the disproportionate cachet which sporting prowess attracted was not something that would continue in the adult world. It's caused by evolution failing to keep up with mankind's fast-changing circumstances. Our enthusiasm for signs of physical strength and agility over the mental equivalents made a lot more sense when the economy was more reliant on catching woolly mammoth by hand than it has been for some millennia. Twenty million years from now, the boys who are good at maths will be cool and popular and get the girls – and by that time there won't be an equation on earth that isn't solved by robots.

So the swots weren't top of the boys' social tree, but they were valued, accorded grudging respect and not bullied. There were only seven of us in the scholarship set and we were, fairly ridiculously, treated like adults. The teachers enjoyed our lessons and so did we – and we didn't have to pretend otherwise. This was an environment in which Lisa Simpson would have found acceptance – if she weren't a girl.

We were constantly told that we were bright and special and that this was a brilliant academic opportunity afforded to few. It was assumed, even at that age, that we would go on to achieve things: get scholarships, go to Oxbridge, become professors (only academic success was really aspired to – no one was pushing us to become entrepreneurs). Our expectations and self-image were managed upwards. I loved it and I genuinely think that I've never quite lost the glow that being treated like that at a young age gave me. It has waxed and waned with my fortunes but never disappeared entirely.

- 13 -

Badges

While I was failing to achieve sporting prowess, I remember as I walk up onto Primrose Hill, where a group of schoolboys are playing football with the seriousness of *Guardian* readers discussing independent cinema, I was often supervised by a teacher smoking a cigar. It was Mr Roberts, the one who wrote comic plays about the politics of early imperial Rome, and he was just as averse to exercise as I was.

We were divided up for sport and I certainly wasn't in the scholarship set there. I was in 'Group B' with all the other speccy nerds and, when we were in Mr Roberts's unenthusiastic charge, we didn't have to play football – a relief all round as it's difficult to get a game going when *all* the players are running away from the ball. Mr Roberts didn't seem to own a tracksuit and so, instead of having to negotiate the muddy playing field, he just told us to run round the University Parks, where he could stand on the tarmac path in his Chelsea boots and leather jacket, puffing away.

But sometimes football was unavoidable. I didn't realise that mud had a smell before I first walked into the school's small pavilion in the corner of the sports field to change from plimsolls into football boots. The floor was littered with dried clods from the bottom of other boys' boots with holes where the studs had been – like little mud six-pack rings for cork-sized beer cans – and it gave off an odd, flat, nothingy scent. Like the olfactory equivalent of white noise. It depressed me and made me feel sorry for the boys for whom the bland smell of chalk and books was equally unsettling.

I also fiercely resisted attempts to make me try for swimming badges. These were an obsession of my parents, largely because Richard Slater kept getting them. Richard Slater was, like me (and I hope he'll forgive me for saying so), a timorous weed. We were good friends and our parents were good friends. Then, at some point, we stopped being friends – I don't really know why. From then on, it seemed, all I would hear about him was his swimming prowess. My parents wouldn't shut up about what badges he was trying for or getting, and how I should be doing the same thing. It wasn't just distance swimming but various proficiency and survival awards, named after Olympic metals, which seemed to involve a bewildering range of aqua-activities: treading water for various periods of time in various states of undress, retrieving objects from the bottom of the pool, befriending dolphins, etc. The holders of the gold awards, it seemed to me, would have been able to infiltrate Atlantis.

It was really wearing. I wanted to say: 'Look, do you want me to actually *be* Richard Slater? Is that your big idea? Because, I'd say, overall I prefer me to Richard Slater and I think you do too. You don't get to cherry-pick the good aspects of Richard Slater and add them to all my stuff. You take the Slater swimming but you'll be stuck with all the other tedious Slaterisms into the bargain!'

But I did feel a bit guilty. What was wrong with me, I wondered, that I found the prospect of going to a swimming pool for weekly lessons, building up to an unnecessary test in which you had to swim a terrifying distance and then fashion a rudimentary float out of a pair of pyjamas, so unappealing? I hated the thought of that test and its pointless survival situation. What was it supposed to prepare us for? A world where air travel has disappeared and, in this post-aeroplane future where we're all getting liners to the United States because that's where the food is, the U-boats only attack at night?

So, what did I have to fill the gap where obsessive sport-love wasn't?

Love Life: obviously not – not at that age. I'm middle-class. And don't hold your breath, by the way. If that's what you're here for, you'll have to skip forward a *long* way. But careful you don't crease the spine because you may just want to get your money back. So, no love life or crushes or trysts. By which I mean both (a) I didn't have a prepubescent sweetheart, to whom I used coyly to give daisies while wearing a straw hat and posing for a greetings card photographer and with whom I had my first fumbling sexual experiences four or five years later in a hay loft – or possibly a straw loft, full of straw waiting to be turned into hats; and (b) I wasn't abused.

At some point in 1986 I remember getting an erection watching a Madonna video, although I had absolutely no idea what to do about it and no way of getting in touch with Madonna to ask.

Hobbies: I collected badges. Non-swimming badges. But only out of duty, like a Japanese businessman glumly taking golf lessons. If we went to any tourist attraction – Warwick Castle, the Tower of London, etc. – I would always buy a badge from the gift shop and I kept all those badges in a tin. I never wore them, I never displayed them, they're probably still in the drawer in Oxford where I last added to them in about 1987.

I don't know what gift shops sell these days – I never go into them. Probably themed iPod covers, business card cases, novelty condoms, cheese knives and melon ballers. Maybe porn? Maybe you can get tourist-attraction-themed jazz mags where the Madame Tussauds waxworks are all doing each other in a big gangbang. I wouldn't be surprised. Honestly, what is the world coming to? I'm really surprised.

Speaking of gangbangs, or gangs at the very least, I didn't join the Cub Scouts. That's what you had to do if you wanted to become a proper human – or so my parents heavily implied. It would be a great way of meeting other children and broadening my range of interests, so that I didn't just spend all my time watching *Knight Rider* – that was their view. I did not share it. I had an aversion to fresh air and didn't want to go camping. That seemed to be the jewel in the cubs' crown of activities – or the turd in their cesspit, as I saw it. The concept of the cubs was bad enough: on top of having had to develop friendships and a survival strategy for school, this was a new group where you had to find allies and evade enemies.

Also, it would wipe out an evening a week. I jealously guarded my TV-watching time. It was always being encroached upon by homework (or 'prep' as we called it – that's one of Britain's hidden class signifiers). I saw no reason to commit to anything else. And also, all the cubs' activities that didn't involve going away from home and sleeping outdoors (something my parents were so keen to encourage and, yet, if I'd mooted it in my late teens under the influence of heroin, you can bet they'd have raised objections – honestly, you can't win with some people) were almost as bad: lighting fires, cooking, sewing, chopping, climbing. All the wholesome shit that I hated and, when brought into contact with, hated myself for hating.

The only hobby I really enjoyed was writing. I developed the habit, whenever we were watching TV as a family and I wasn't particularly gripped by the programme, of writing a sort of endless fantasy epic. It involved kings and emperors and wizards and dragons and wars. It was sort of cod-Tolkien, I suppose, but even less likely to come to a satisfying conclusion before you lost the will to live.

I wasn't a Tolkien fan. I spent the best part of a year trying to get through *The Lord of the Rings*, finally grinding to a halt halfway through *The Two Towers*. I don't know why there are adults who treat its tedious daftness with such awed solemnity. That just makes it less fun. And it's zero fun to start with. Even something that is a tiny bit fun, like pressing the button to make an electric garage door go up, is infinitely more fun than the endless moaning of a jewellery-obsessed, hairy-footed midget.

Anyway, I would write and write and write this epic. It wasn't supposed to be entertaining – I just did it for the pleasure of filling the pages. I wrote it in play form, enjoying the escapism of seeing drab mundanities being exchanged between people supposedly living in fantastical circumstances. It probably read like an *EastEnders* script except all the characters were wearing armour or capes or crowns or wizards' hats. Like an *EastEnders* Hallowe'en special.

I also loved the look of the playscript format: writing the character's name in capital letters with the dialogue next to it and how they might say it ('angrily', 'quietly', 'waving his wand', 'dropping his axe in horror') and putting all other business in stage directions. I sat there, night after night, filling page after page, gaining satisfaction merely from there being more of it, with no thought of it ever being staged or even read. No wonder my parents encouraged me to join the cubs.

Family: Yes, I had a family, who loved me and whom I took completely for granted. My brother Daniel was born when I was seven and a half, which was an event I was more or less against to be perfectly honest. His arrival was an unsettling experience. I was too old to display a toddler's resentment that my place at the centre of the universe had been supplanted, but I still experienced those feelings.

Years later, when I was best man at his wedding, this is what I said about it in my speech:

Unlike most best men, I can take the story of the groom right back to the beginning. Well, almost. I'm not going to start discussing my parents' love life of the early '80s. That never goes well on occasions such as these. But I do remember when I was told, at the age of seven, that I was soon going to have a little brother or sister. I think my parents were concerned about what my reaction would be because they presented the news as if it was an event entirely designed to please me.

'You know how you like having friends round to play? And you get annoyed that that can't happen more often?' they said. 'Well, soon there'll be someone for you to play with all the time!'

I was good at maths. I did a quick calculation. This sibling, I reasoned, was still some months away and I was getting older all the time. So, when this new person was nought, I would be seven and a half. When I was nine, he would be one and a half.

'Someone for me to play with?!' I exclaimed to my parents. 'I don't play with people who are six! People who are eight don't play with me! How long will it be before he can talk?'

'A year and a half,' ventured my mother.

A year and a half?! That was more time than I could imagine. And presumably, even then, my one-and-a-half-year-old brother wouldn't exactly be a sophisticated conversationalist. It appeared that my parents' well-meaning 'get David a friend to play with' scheme was hopelessly ill thought-through.

'Is there any way it can be stopped?' I asked. I must be one of the few best men ever to have toasted the marriage of a man he initially advocated aborting.

That's not to say I didn't love him as soon as he arrived. I did. I worried about him. I wanted to protect him. It would have been awful if anything had happened to him. That all came naturally to me. But I'm afraid I had the imagination to realise that, had Dan never existed, I logically wouldn't be able to miss him – and neither would I have had to deal with all the changes to our circumstances: the noise, the nappies, the tiredness of my parents, the necessity of moving house. I resented all this even if I didn't resent him for it.

And I had a strong sense that the standards my parents expected of their offspring were dropping. He seemed to get away with stuff that I didn't (even when making allowances for infancy – I wasn't envious of his right to shit on the go). For example, I was pretty convinced that I was *never* allowed to draw on the walls. When going round the supermarket with Dan and my mum, he would be given a packet of crisps to eat *for which we had not yet paid*. And we had to leave *Santa Claus: the Movie* halfway through because he was screaming blue murder. I *still* don't know how that ends.

But I hope you've inferred from the fact that I was later to be best man at his wedding that our relationship improved after that. By the time he was five, I was properly pleased he was there. I realised I'd be lonely without him. By the time he was 11, I was leaving home and sorry to be abandoning him. Not that he needed my help with our parents, of course. They let him draw on the bloody walls.

Dan still lives in Oxford, where he works for a hedge fund as their 'official historian'. I don't know what he tells them other than that, in the long run, you're fucked whatever you invest in. I don't see him as often as I'd like, but when I do we generally go to the pub to drink and talk about real ale. We both enjoy that. Deal with it.

The other major change our family underwent while I was at New College School was Grandpa dying. I was ten. In some ways, this is the worst thing that has ever happened to me. It's definitely the worst thing that ever happened to him.

He was relatively old – 73, I think – which is about par for a death in the mid 1980s, I believe. Not strictly a tragedy, anyway. And I think he'd had a happy life. His marriage was incredibly happy and he loved his daughter and grandchildren very much. He was also properly and unselfconsciously religious which, as a muddle-headed agnostic, I rather envy.

We were very close and I officially considered him the best person in the world. I remember he was a bit fat and he wore black-framed glasses. I remember that he smoked Silk Cut and would send me upstairs to fetch a new packet from a cupboard in which he had also secreted Lindt chocolate animals. I remember that he made very good chips and swam in the sea with a slow, confident crawl. I remember that he was a big fan of *Minder*. But mainly I remember a feeling of being loved by someone kind and special, who knew that the important things in life were fish and chips, ice cream and the seaside. Had he lived another ten years or so, I would have undoubtedly seen him differently, he wouldn't have remained perfect in my eyes – no human could. But I would like to have known him with an older brain.

I cried for hours when I heard the news. I went over the awfulness of it hundreds of times and instinctively wrung grief out of myself. It was the most emotionally healthy thing I've ever done in my life and, as a result, saddened and oddly aged though I remained as a result, I genuinely came to terms with his death. What worries me about this is that I never cry these days. I lost the ability at some point in my late teens which makes me fear that I'm now emotionally unfused. Or perhaps it's just because nothing as bad as that has happened to me since?

How ridiculous is it – how absurdly blessed am I – that the death of my grandfather in the middle of my childhood is the worst single event in my life? I've had a tremendous run of luck for which I am enormously grateful, but I'm also enormously fearful of it running out.

Friends: I was all right for friends – it wasn't just aqua-Slater. In fact, I made some very good ones. I'm still in touch with some of the other boys from Form VI, and a few of them are proper friends – people you have things in common with other than your past.

Obviously I didn't get together and play football with Leo, Ed and Harry. Neither did we dress up and pretend to be The Professionals. Although I'd quite like to do that now, which I must remember the next time I see them. I'd reached the stage where we mostly just sat around and played board games, which wasn't as exciting as watching *Knight Rider* – but unfortunately *Knight Rider* was only on for an hour a week. That's partly why I was so resentful when my parents complained that I spent 'all my time' watching it.

Home: We had dry rot. If you've ever had anything to do with dry rot, I know that will have got your attention. 'Bloody hell, dry rot!' you'll be saying like someone with a bad back hearing about a bad back. (If, like me, you've had a life blighted by both dry rot and a bad back, my God you must be enjoying this book.) If not, let me tell you, dry rot is a nightmare. It is literally the worst sort of rot.

We had moved house to a place round the corner which was definitely better but in a much worse state of repair. My brother was changing from an incredibly unruly baby, who seemed never to sleep, into a fearless toddler. As a result of having to eradicate the dry rot, my parents were short of money, which worried me. It felt like the writing was on the wall – but that was Dan's fault. I didn't want us to become like Lacey's family from *Cagney and Lacey*. I wanted us to be like the Bellamys from *Upstairs, Downstairs*.

But, other than the dry rot and the felt-tip on the skirting-boards, I liked being at home. It was where the television was.

- 14 -

Play It Nice
and Cool, Son

I'm at the top of Primrose Hill. You get an excellent view of London from here. Everyone likes views. They're an extremely mainstream form of entertainment, yet one which nobody considers beneath them – other than literally. They have universal fun appeal, like food, drink, fireworks and mammalian cuteness – and unlike comedy, where the things that are widely appealing and enjoyed by the majority are perversely off-putting to fans of the niche comedy that only a minority get.

This is frustrating for comedians. You want to be popular, you want people to like you. But if too many do, those who liked you most intensely at the outset start to turn away – they think you've sold out. They don't realise that, in one sense, you were always trying to sell out but now you've got more buyers. It's bad stage-craft for a comedian to seem eager to please, but that doesn't mean we're not. The primary aim of even the most edgy stand-up is to get laughs from whoever will listen.

Early fans' sense of betrayal is no more justifiable than that of a man who sees another man walking off with a hooker he once enjoyed paying to fuck. Except the whole situation should be much less charged with the potential to feel betrayed, because this isn't an intimate physical act we're talking about, but just the telling and hearing of jokes. Dark or light, satirical or wacky, message-bearing or surreal, comedians are just fools capering for a king's pleasure.

We shouldn't get above ourselves, but neither does the king have cause to complain if we also raise a smile from an emperor.

I was slightly disappointed by something the comedian Stewart Lee once said on this subject. I think Stewart Lee is very funny. But a routine he did on his BBC Two show cut right to the heart of something I feel very deeply about comedy – and about life in general. It's about being cool.

This was a long rant in which Lee hyperbolically expressed his frustration that the bit in *Only Fools and Horses* when Del Boy falls through the bar was voted the funniest clip ever on British TV. He found it incredibly depressing that such a mindless moment of slapstick should have so caught the public's imagination – that in a world of such comic sophistication, this should be the moment they consider most brilliant.

But what I feel is: the audience don't find the clip funny just because it's a good piece of slapstick – they find it funny because it's happening to a character they feel they know. Del Boy, by being in a popular and long-running sitcom, has achieved the status in millions of households of a friend – that friend who's funny down the pub, the friend who gets into scrapes. The person you say should be a comedian.

Slapstick on its own is never more than fleetingly amusing. To really get the belly laughs, it has to be surrounded by character. This is why Peter Sellers is a genius and Norman Wisdom is not. Wisdom falls beautifully, with acrobatic comic skill, but his characters always look like they're going to fall. They are ready and willing to slip, tumble and crack their skulls to get laughs. Sellers, particularly as Clouseau, has dignity. He comes across as someone who would be mortified to be involved in even the most low-key of pratfalls. Despite his long history of accidents and clumsiness, his expectation is still, inexplicably, that he will meet every new situation with unruffled savoir-faire. It is making that unlikely attitude so plausible and likeable that is the mark of a brilliant comic actor. So when Clouseau falls face first into his hostess's tits, or puts his hand into a wedding cake to steady himself or has his trousers blown off by a bomb, we believe that he is mortified. It's not the physical but the emotional pain that really makes us laugh. It's not about how Sellers falls, it's about how he gets up.

Del Boy's pratfall is far from a cheap laugh. It has years of the writer's narrative skill and the actor's characterisation invested in it. It is a culmination – a sign of mainstream comedy's power to move people, to be welcomed into the homes it initially invaded. This is something all comedians (whether they're at the dark/cult/ niche end of the spectrum like Jerry Sadowitz, or mainstream stars like Graham Norton, or somewhere in between like me) should celebrate. It shows the power of comedy. It's why television commissioners persevere with it when it's much more expensive than, for example, cookery programmes. They know how great the potential rewards in audience numbers and appreciation can be.

Those cool comedy fans, who turn their noses up at *Only Fools and Horses*, never sneer at Basil Fawlty thrashing his car with a sapling. That scene also usually comes high in the favourite clip polls and, in isolation, is equally unsophisticated. But *Fawlty Towers* isn't such a slow-moving target. For all its popularity, it also has comic credibility. When the aficionados of edgy comedy see that clip, they don't just see slapstick – they see the greatest sitcom character ever created giving vent to his frustration. Yet they don't give *Only Fools and Horses* fans credit for appreciating Del Boy in the same way.

Fawlty Towers is in fact a rare exception to the sell-out argument: the certainty of some fans that cultish comedy gets worse when it gets successful. This argument makes me uncomfortable. While wide appeal is no guarantee of artistic merit, neither is obscurity. The cachet of non-mainstream or obscure comedy is all tied in, to my mind, with notions of what's cool. And that gets my hackles up. Comedy shouldn't be swayed by what's cool. Some people say it's cool to be funny – if so, that has to remain completely incidental. Let's not allow the comedy world to become any more infected with empty-headed notions of trendiness, fashion and zeitgeist or we'll be reduced to the absurdities of the music industry.

It may be cool to be funny, but people who try too hard to be cool, who make that their primary aim, are laughable. It's no coincidence that Del Boy's exact words, before falling through the bar, are: 'Play it nice and cool, son, nice and cool.'

People who aspire to be cool are one of the main groups that comedians prey on. But it's difficult for us to do that if we've been reduced to having the same hollow aim ourselves. Far better to aspire to be a mainstream family comedian. The very greatest comedies – *Fawlty Towers* is a shining example, as are *The Morecambe and Wise Show* and *The Simpsons* – are as funny for niche comedy fans as they are for the mainstream family audience. Like panoramic views, they can be enjoyed by all.

As I stare down Primrose Hill, taking in the London skyline, I feel somehow important and victorious. I'm sure the appeal of high ground is an evolutionary thing. When you've got a good vantage point, you know you're relatively safe.

By the end of prep school, I had this feeling a lot of the time. Nervous though I was about it, the whole growing up thing was basically going okay. It felt like I was occupying high ground with a good view of a promising future. I wasn't just a tedious, bookish nerd – I had the beginnings of a personality. I'd also had a tiny but instructive experience of injustice and adversity, and been given a few ideas about how to cope with it.

I'm a bit worried about telling this story because I'm not sure it reflects very well on me. I might come across as a little shit who bears grudges, and that is the last thing that even little shits who bear grudges want to come across as. Well, I say last – it's preferable to 'paedophile'. But it's not ideal. Still, I'm going to take the plunge because one of the things you've presumably bought this book for is to find out what I might actually be like. So even if I reveal truths that make you think less of me, you'll also think more of me for revealing those truths honestly, right? I might end up about evens, in terms of what you think, and a quid up for what you paid for the book in Poundland. Unless you've borrowed it from a library – but fortunately, libraries are all being closed down while Poundlands are opening everywhere. I think it's to do with the Big Society.

Okay, here we go then. There was an annual academic prize called the 'Form Prize'. In my second year, I won it. In my third year, Butch called me into his study to explain that, while I deserved to win it again, they'd decided to give it to another boy because I'd won it the previous year and they wanted to spread around the encouraging book tokens. Magnanimously, I thanked him and said that I understood.

The following year, I once again did best in the exams and was not awarded the prize – but neither, on this occasion, was I granted an explanatory interview with Butch. My mother went spare. She had a bit of a chip on her shoulder about the school's attitude, you see. She thought that it was biased in favour of boys whose parents were dons at the university and slightly scornful of the likes of us – former hotel managers, now lowly polytechnic lecturers. The father of the boy who won was an English fellow of an ancient college. Furthermore, a boy in another form whose family also had university connections had won a prize *every year*. There was no talk of giving it to someone else to spread the love where he was concerned.

Mum felt, and told me, that the school didn't quite like the idea of a bright boy not coming from academic stock but from trade. She also, in rather more respectful language, made her feelings known to the headmaster. It's interesting to note that this is a woman who, only four or five years earlier, seemed perfectly happy for another school to send me home covered in sick. But this suspicion of bias was enough to make her speak out. I don't know if this was a sign of her growing confidence, her prioritising of the academic over the alimentary, or just inconsistency. I've never asked her. I suspect I will get an answer soon after publication.

Anyway, she extorted an apology from Butch, delivered personally to me in a moment of acute embarrassment for both of us, and got him to concede that the prize was rightfully mine (although I didn't actually receive it – nobody suggested that the winner should be stripped of it like an Olympic medallist after a drugs test). The following year I won it again – and the year after that. She'd made her point. Or perhaps she'd just terrified him.

I don't know if my mum was right about this bias. At the time, I accepted unquestioningly that she was. After all, I was being told it by the same person who had introduced me to the notion that it might not always be a good idea to shit in my trousers; looking to corroborate all facts when dealing with your parents can be a barrier to development in early childhood. Bias or not, it was unfair I hadn't won, but was she right to speak out? Or should she have told me to accept the injustice as the way of the world, or reminded me that one boy's academic attainment in a prep school didn't amount to a hill of beans in this crazy world? (My mother talks exactly like Humphrey Bogart.) Whose sense of perspective was at fault – hers (and mine) at the time, or mine remembering years later and wishing she hadn't said anything because the teachers must have thought I was a horrible, snotty little swot? And an unconnected one at that.

I think I'm now glad she spoke out and explained her reasons to me. It gave me a small insight into how authority can be flawed and unjust – that the people in charge aren't always right. I don't want this to sound like a clip from *The X Factor* but, in order to succeed, you have to endure periods where the only support your ambitions receive is from your own self-belief. And your mum.

But what the hell, it's an unfortunate world. The majority of the vast population of Bangladesh live on a flood plain. It was good for me that, when I turned thirteen and strode out from New College School with as much confidence as I ever have about any new experience (i.e. not much), I was armed not only with a reasonable level of belief in my own intelligence and personality but also with the unsettling knowledge that life isn't fair.

- 15 -

Teenage Thrills: First Love, and the Rotary Club Public Speaking Competition

Down from Primrose Hill, parked on Regent's Canal near London Zoo, teetering on the edge of the water, is a Chinese restaurant. On a boat. It's one of the most inviting-looking restaurants I've ever seen: two storeys high and delicate, like an elaborate, claret-coloured imperial barge. It actually looks delicious. I've passed it many times, so the fact that I've never gone in must show how much I dislike Chinese food.

Whenever a plan to eat out is in the offing, my priority is always to push fellow diners towards a venue where one of the many things I already know I like will be available – which means that my comparative unfamiliarity with Chinese, and for that matter Japanese, cuisine becomes self-perpetuating.

I realise it's not logical. If I'd never tried new things I'd still be eating rusks and goo. Somehow my food tastes have become accept-ably broad and I'm grateful for that, even as I call a halt to further broadening. I'm glad I'm not one of those people who are genuinely intimidated by menus and are always trying to order something plain. They get silently sneered at for their fussiness – it's considered unsophisticated.

These people, I'm afraid, include those who suffer from 'wheat intolerance'. I know there is such a thing, which can afflict even the sturdiest, most no-nonsense of souls and causes the consumption of foods containing wheat to bring on unpleasant symptoms that, while not at the same level as an allergic reaction, the sufferer would still want to do something about, such as stopping eating wheat, and that wouldn't necessarily make them a tedious, attention-seeking wuss.

However, I think the vast majority of people who cite the condition *are* tedious, attention-seeking wusses who mistake the normal symptoms of daily life – feeling sluggish after meals, tired in the morning, hungry before breakfast and generally not as though they want to leap around like someone in an advert – for there being something wrong with them. It's not just wheat they're intolerant of, it's everything. They're so dissatisfied with the sensation of being human, with the world's constant assaults on the temples that are their bodies, that they're now unwilling even to coexist with a grain.

I sometimes think about this when I'm sitting on my special back-pain-reducing giant yoga ball. Basically, I've become chair intolerant. For me, the furniture equivalent of a wheat rejector, the long-established human way of sitting, handed down through the millennia, has been dispensed with in under a generation. Now we suddenly know better. Unlike all those stupid twats from the past who were wrong about everything. Those sexist, racist, homophobic idiots like Henry VIII, Vlad the Impaler, Hitler, Beethoven, Aristotle, Florence Nightingale and Julius Caesar. They didn't understand human rights and the solar system, so why should we have any faith in their recipes or furniture designs? We're so much wiser now, so let's throw the eating bread and milk, using normal soap and sitting on proper chairs baby out with the stopping women from voting bathwater.

That's my problem with new-age stuff. In common with many irrational views it harks back to a sense of something ancient while rejecting anything provably historical. It's like the miserable concept of Original Sin. There seems to be an obsession with the idea that there were ancient humans, uncorrupted by their capricious intellects, who lived in the 'right way'.

They didn't eat too much dairy or any wheat. They didn't sit down too long for their spines or walk around in posture-ruining shoes. They didn't consume too many sugars or fats for their unblemished guts to digest, or pop painkilling and antibiotic tablets to deal with the short-term symptoms of long-term problems that should be dealt with by wholesale lifestyle change. They didn't drink or smoke. They were perfect and we should sling out all our stuff and emulate them. Except they had an average life expectancy of about 18 and the planet could only support a few hundred thousand of them. Apart from that, good plan.

But I am capable of sitting on a normal chair to have a meal. So nobody could call me fussy. I don't insist on a ball. I won't even mention it. To see me out dining, you'd never suspect I was anything other than a conventional, non-intolerant fellow. And the last thing I'd want to do is cock up this excellent semblance of normality by being fussy about my food. So, I avoid going to Chinese restaurants. I never know what everything is, what to order, how many of these things constitute a proper meal. I can just about cope with chopsticks but I'm not comfortable with them and I feel self-conscious. Yet I lack the social confidence to ask for a knife and fork.

I know I should get a grip (metaphorically – a lighter grasp seems better with chopsticks) but the trouble is that I don't tire readily enough of the dishes I already like to incentivise a search for new flavours. I would get bored if I had steak and chips for every meal. But I'm pretty sure that if I had it for one in four meals, I'd be fine. If it were one in ten, I'd be thrilled every time. Which means I only really need ten things I like in order not to be bored – and I've long since overshot that. So why would I go to restaurants with weird cutlery where they don't serve any of them?

The culinarily adventurous often deploy the phrase 'You don't know what you're missing' to try and persuade me – but I just think: 'Well that's all right then.' Imagine if I'd never tried alcohol and didn't know what I was missing there – well, that would be brilliant! I'd find other ways of avoiding boredom – read more, work harder, go to the theatre and cinema more often, and I wouldn't have this expensive, health-jeopardising habit. I'm very glad I don't know what I'm missing where cocaine's concerned.

I'm not saying Chinese food is a global scourge similar to alcohol and cocaine. But there was a terrible Chinese takeaway in Abingdon which once made me iller than either of them ever has. (To be fair, cocaine hasn't really had a fair crack of the whip.) It left me with images of beansprouts and gloop, saccharine-tasting, psychedelic-coloured sauces clinging to gristly lumps of meat, of which Chinese restaurant food today, although better, still puts me in mind.

The takeaway was near my new school. My awful new school. An avoidable takeaway was the least of my problems. Abingdon School was big – there were over a hundred boys in each year. It took me an hour to get there every day from Oxford, on two buses. And there was school on Saturday mornings.

It had a paramilitary wing. And as well as the 'Combined Cadet Force', it pushed pupils towards the 'Ten Tors Challenge', an annual attempt by thousands of schoolchildren to die of exposure on Dartmoor; and, most unprepossessingly, the 'Duke of Edinburgh's Award', which seemed to involve pretty much any kind of plucky unpleasantness you'd want to put yourself in for, but somehow with overtones of a posh man shouting at you – very much like the Spartan, self-improving education the Duke subjected his sons to at Gordonstoun.

I wasn't the cleverest any more. This was despite the fact that the boys from state primary schools (who arrived two years before those from private prep schools) had been warned by their teachers that we newcomers would be academically ahead of them.

This was a public relations disaster as far as I was concerned. We were pre-stamped as snooty swots. There's no doubt that, if people have told you that I'm a snooty swot and then you meet me, you're going to think that it's plausible. I don't think I really was a snooty swot but there was something about my attempts to deny it that seemed snooty, swottish even, to my detractors.

Underlying all this was the extremely unsettling hormonal change of puberty. Thirteen is a very stupid age to make boys change schools.

Abingdon School in the 1980s was trapped between its fears and aspirations, between jeopardy and hope. That's the classic sitcom trait – it makes shows seem dynamic without the basic situation ever changing. Basil Fawlty is terrified of his hotel being closed down or going out of business and spends half his energy averting crises related to that. The other half is spent on scheming to escape his mediocre circumstances – to make the hotel posher, to be able to hobnob with the great and the good, to get rid of the riff-raff.

Abingdon was in a similar bind. It was caught between its fears of being indistinguishable from the state sector and its aspiration to be as much like Eton, Harrow, Westminster and, most particularly, Radley, a nearby and much more expensive school, as possible.

It was a genuinely old school. It had existed since at least 1563, at which point a man called John Roysse was known to have given it some money. That would make it an Elizabethan grammar school – like the one Shakespeare went to. Since the sixteenth century, it had moved sites and expanded in size and become a 'direct grant' school. The direct grant schools were independent schools which got a fair bit of state funding in exchange for charging lower fees and providing a wide range of bursaries. When the direct grant scheme was wound up in the mid 1970s, Abingdon decided to go fully private.

Basically, the school was an honest place where a decent but unremarkable education had been provided for respectable townspeople for centuries. Abingdon's headmaster wasn't content with that. He's the central comic character here except, if it really were a sitcom, you'd think they'd overdone it with the hair and make-up. He was a tall man with a large hooked nose, thick glasses and the most extreme comb-over I have ever seen anywhere, including Hamlet cigar adverts. He looked kind of magnificent but enormously daft. His name was Michael St John Parker, known to boys (in honour of his nose and authority) as 'Beak'.

Beak's predecessor in the job, Eric Anderson, had gone on to be head of Shrewsbury and then Eton – so Abingdon seemed like a perfect springboard for high flying. Unfortunately, the next head-mastership for Beak, of a richer swankier school, didn't seem to come five years after he'd arrived, as it had for Anderson. Or ten years. By twelve years in, when I turned up, I think he'd begun to suspect he was there for the long haul. The boys' theory was that, in the absence of the headship of a posh school, he was trying to make the one he was already head of as posh as possible.

He often spoke of evidence of a school in Abingdon long before 1563, with links to Edmund of Abingdon, who was a thirteenth-century Archbishop of Canterbury and then a saint. Beak desper-ately wanted St Edmund to have gone to or founded the school, and he may have done. And he may not have done. But it really seemed to matter to Beak: in the absence of any Prime Ministers among the Old Abingdonians, someone who may be hobnobbing with the apostles in the next life is a pretty good substitute.

The official foundation date of the school has since been adjusted by 300 years. I joined a 424-year-old institution, but now get letters from one that's over 700. Boy, does that make me feel old.

The boys, sons of the provincial middle class, had a normal old-fashioned snobbery about the local state schools. On the other hand, there was an even stronger inverse snobbery that led us to despise Radley. We played them at sport and desperately wanted to win but seldom did. Their money, it seemed, had made them physi-cally better than us. Why do we play them, I always wondered, if it causes us such pain? These are *their* games – we'll never win.

The boys' insecurity at losing was only intensified by the suspi-cion that Beak would rather have been headmaster of Radley. We felt like the dowdy wife of an ambitious man who nags us that we let him down and, when he takes us to parties, spends the whole time flirting with someone thinner.

But maybe we were wrong. After all, he did co-write a history of the school, published in 1997, four years before he retired. So perhaps he came to love the place in the end. And perhaps he with-stood an avalanche of offers from other schools. But I prefer to think of him as like Windsor Davies in *Never the Twain*, bitterly shaking his fist at supercilious Radley's Donald Sinden.

Of course, the social gap between Radley and Abingdon is far narrower than it used to be; the gulf now is between independent schools and any other sort. Over the last two decades, they've become, as a sector, vastly more expensive; fees have gone up way ahead of inflation. There is no way that two polytechnic lecturers like my parents could afford to send their sons to Abingdon nowadays. That's always in my mind when I get newsletters from the school and am asked to lend my support – always very nicely and by charming, well-meaning people. But I can't escape the thought that this place isn't for the likes of me any more. Independent schools have never served the majority of society, but, in a generation, they've gone from being within the financial reach of perhaps 20 per cent of the population to well under 10.

I started to enjoy Abingdon more when I was about fifteen. It had a debating society. I loved the way the motions were expressed as 'This House' would do such and such – withdraw from the EEC, become vegetarian, institute communism, ban immigration, make Morrissey king, abolish the monarchy, etc. It sounded so parliamentary. The boys who were good at debating seemed popular while also being a bit swotty – I was heartened that such a combination was allowed.

So, nervously, falteringly, I started to get involved. At first, I was intimidated. Then the society went through a really bad patch of pointless, childish, ill-attended debates: I was in my element. My debating technique was entirely based on raising as many laughs as I could in the hope that this would then make people vote for whichever side of the motion I was advocating. It completely worked – and it was immediately obvious to me that I didn't really care about winning the argument. It was the laughter that made me feel good.

By the Fifth Form, I was enough of a debating regular to be chosen to represent the school in the Rotary Club Public Speaking Competition alongside Daniel Seward, one of the state primary boys who was already at Abingdon when I arrived but whom I managed to befriend across this great cultural divide, and Leo Carey, a friend from Form VI at NCS. I'm pleased to be able to say that I'm still good friends with both of them. Daniel is now a Catholic priest and Leo is an editor at the *New Yorker*. With hindsight, we were quite an interesting team. Without it, we were three spotty nerds.

Most of the teams in the Rotary Club Public Speaking Competition were dire: three girls from a convent school primly reading out something worthy about the environment, or three chippy lads from a local comprehensive explaining their interest in the guitar, while the Rotarians fatly glazed over. In contrast, we were *very slightly* amusing. Not so as to be entertaining in any other context but, like a donkey's fart in a vacuum, we were the nearest thing the judges got to a breath of fresh air. We took part three times and we always won. This gave me something to feel good about and focus on other than academic work, now that I was no longer the cleverest. It was a setting that gave me the confidence to be the centre of attention.

Unlike the school play. I was cast in *Much Ado about Nothing*. Leo played Benedick, the romantic lead. I wasn't so fortunate and was cast in the tiny role of Verges, Dogberry's sidekick. Not even Dogberry. Still, my friend Harry was even worse off than me, playing Third Watchman. At least my character has a name, I thought.

Creatively there wasn't much about this production to get my teeth into. I decided to play Verges as very, very old. Humorously old, was the idea. It also occurred to me that, if I was to be noticed by the audience, I would have to make something special out of the few bits I had to do. This, with great solemnity and energy, is what I did. I dread to think how over-the-top, scene-stealing and yet unwatchable I was. I imagine that I drew the eye like a pile-up.

At one point in rehearsal, Harry did an impression of my exaggeratedly doddering gait and the weird intense expression, with jaw thrust forward, that I'd decided to assemble on my face. Thankfully Harry wasn't a very popular boy, so this moment of mockery wasn't picked up on by the group. The fact that I remember it, however, suggests it touched a nerve and that he was making a fair point. So the evidence points to my performance being awful. No one, apart from my parents who were, as always, effusive in their praise, commented at all, either positively or negatively.

The sad truth is that you can't triumph with a part like Verges. People tell you that you can – that a small, perfectly formed jewel of a performance will draw the eye and mean you land the lead next time. But that's only possible if you get at least one moment when you're supposed to be the centre of attention: one scene, one speech, one pratfall. When you're just there to say a handful of lines and populate the stage, you won't be noticed unless you do something incongruous to get attention – and that very incongruity will, almost invariably, be a bad acting choice.

This is what is so sad for extras (or 'supporting artists' as they're now known) on TV. Most of them want to be actors and for that to happen they think, quite reasonably, that they need to get noticed. But in 99 per cent of situations where extras are used, they're not supposed to be noticeable – not individually anyway. They're there to fill the back of the screen, to make it look like there are people at this party/pub/shop/public execution. But if any one of them does something to make you look at them, he or she has already made a mistake. As an extra, if you do your job well, no one will notice.

The main reason I wanted to be noticed and praised for my performance as Verges was that I had fallen in love. That's probably a rather grandiose term for a schoolboy crush, but I use it because that's exactly how I felt about it at the time. It was unlike anything else I'd previously experienced. This was very exciting. The object of my affections was the girl playing Beatrice, the female lead. (She was from one of the two private girls' schools in Abingdon – they were allowed to come and be in plays with us, which meant that the dancing girl roles such as the one I'd so memorably filled, aged ten, at Mr Fezziwig's party were no longer open to me.)

As soon as I spotted her, I was obsessed. I couldn't stop looking at her, watching her move and listening to her speak. I desperately wanted to get near her and spend time with her. Obviously I knew about sex at this stage, though I was far too innocent to have any organised thoughts in that direction – but I had lots of disorganised ones.

I quite wrongly thought that these powerful new feelings were a good thing. I was going to be happy forever with a wonderful new girlfriend who I'd probably have sex with quite soon and then marry at some point and just generally everything would now be fine. It never really occurred to me that she wouldn't fall in love with me. Such was the strength of my sudden feelings that I assumed she would have reciprocal ones about me. I wasn't hoping for that – I just took it for granted that it would be the case. That's how I thought the universe was constituted.

One of the advantages of that assumption was it meant I didn't have to make any sort of move, or so I thought. This girl, I should explain, was in the year above me and had a reputation for being a bit of a goer. Who knows what that meant she actually got up to – maybe nothing, maybe she was an embodiment of the Kama Sutra – but she certainly usually had a boyfriend. So it was for her, I reasoned, to broach the subject of our colossal mutual attraction and thus officially inaugurate Happily Ever After.

Consequently, I barely spoke to her. I smiled, I was pleasant but I in no way even courted her company. In fact, I had no idea what she was like, only what she looked like which, from memory, was absolutely fucking terrific. As the weeks of rehearsal wore on, I very gradually became concerned that her attitude, of not really know-ing who I was, might not just be a front. I had absolutely no idea what to do about this. I decided that if I went a bit quiet, she might ask me what was wrong. You won't be surprised to hear that this approach was not blessed with success.

The school play, it seems to me now, had a different status with boys than it did with girls. The girls who had roles in the boys' school play were the cool ones – the alpha girls. The boys involved in the play were not their male equivalents. We were much nerdier, much less cool. Some boys in the play had a slightly musical, aesthetey or gothy sort of aura about them and were a bit cool. Leo, for example, played several musical instruments and had an absent-minded aloofness that brought him a measure of cachet. But not like being the captain of the rugby team. That was the sort of boy with whom this sort of girl expected to go out.

I'm amused by how that problem didn't occur to me at the time – by how sure I was that this very pretty cool girl, who might even have actually had sex, was going to fall into the arms of a spindly, bespectacled, shy nerd with a sideline in massive over-acting. I wasn't seeing the bigger picture. Or maybe, to be fair, I was seeing the even bigger picture that we might actually have had a lot in common and found each other fun and got on well and then … who knows? She may have been out of my league at the time, but a few years later she would have been exactly the sort of woman I was much more realistically aspiring to get off with. And failing.

After that play, I was left with the terrible dark realisation that love, what really felt like genuine love, albeit for someone with whom I'd barely exchanged a dozen sentences, is not guaranteed to be requited. My only consolation was that at least I hadn't humiliated myself by making my feelings known. And of course I was wrong about that too. For all that it felt impossible at the time, I really wish I'd said something to her. However ridiculous and sad it would have made me feel, I would have learned much earlier that amorous feelings can be addressed and talked about without shame and with only a finite amount of embarrassment. And you never know! I think it extremely unlikely, almost unthinkable, that that girl would have fancied me at all. But my behaviour was such that, even if she had, nothing would have happened. Don't ask, don't get.

16

Where Did You Get That Hat?

The central London parks are the closest thing you get to a civic idyll. They're splendidly laid out, well maintained and still being used to realise the Victorian vision of good, wholesome, egalitarian recreation (although it's difficult to read that sentence without imagining a girl in a white lace frock being eagerly beaten by Gladstone).

Regent's Park, across which I'm following a broad path through an avenue of trees, is not a deft modern conversion – like a failed pub that's been turned into flats or a trendy restaurant/bar. It's not a former coal barge that's now an adorable second home in Maida Vale, or an old Unitarian chapel that's now a party venue or a community centre. This has not been creatively reimagined. It's something that's as fit now for the purpose for which it was designed as it ever was – and needed just as much.

There are even a couple of friendly-looking police officers wandering through it to complete the image that all is well with the world. If I were a policeman on the beat, I'd make doubly sure – in fact, I'd triple check – that no crimes were being perpetrated in the Royal Parks before I moved on to urine-smelling back alleys and started searching skips for clues. But actually, I now realise they're not both policemen; one of them is a Community Support Officer.

Robert Webb and I once wrote a slightly unkind series of sketches about a policeman and a Community Support Officer. The two of them are walking along together apparently happily – as you often see, much like this pair in the park – but the policeman is whispering bullying remarks throughout. Here's a sample:

POLICEMAN: Is that the theme tune to *The Bill* you're humming?

CSO: Er … yeah. Cos this is a bit like –

POLICEMAN: How dare you! The old opening credits to *The Bill* featured the feet of two *police* officers. Two sets of police officer shoes. Not one set of police shoes and some flippers. Or one set of police shoes and some espadrilles, or wellies or the rear legs of a cat. It was a policeman and a policewoman. And you're not even a policewoman.

CSO: I think that's a bit sexist.

POLICEMAN: At least it's institutional sexism. If *you* said it, it would just be sexism – you haven't got an institution, or not one that anyone cares about. Did you see Britain's most senior Community Support Officer on the news last night?

CSO: No?

POLICEMAN: Neither did I.

I have no idea whether this is an accurate depiction of how policemen view CSOs. Actually, I have some idea. A year or so ago, I was standing in the street outside a party (it was a party to which I'd been invited, I hasten to add, and I was with a group of guests smoking outside; some people are surprised to hear that I cadge and smoke the odd cigarette when drunk; of those people a minority are disappointed; people like that need to invest their hopes with more care) when a couple of policemen came up and told me how much they'd enjoyed the sketch and said it was fair comment – so it obviously rang true for them. But I'm sure lots of police have a huge amount of respect for their CSO colleagues. Well, it's possible.

The reason I have a problem believing that it's a harmonious relationship of mutual respect is that I think that both jobs attract the same sort of people. People who are usually well-meaning and want to do good but also want to be in charge of things – they want the overt trappings of authority. In short, both policemen and CSOs are people who want to be policemen. And yet the CSOs aren't. Why?

I'm convinced that almost all CSOs would prefer to be proper policemen – I expect there are about two weird contrarians who wouldn't, like that heterosexual couple who campaigned to be allowed to have a civil partnership instead of a marriage in order to prove a point. But I think basically CSOs want to be in the proper police and aren't allowed. If I have a certain amount of involuntary disdain for someone who tries to be a policeman and fails, how much more will be felt by an actual policeman? And I'm afraid to say, while I'm sure there are many noble and brilliant officers, one can't read the newspapers and conclude that police recruitment procedures have excluded all incompetence and dishonesty from their ranks. And the CSOs *still* couldn't get in?

But I know what it's like to grasp at a tiny and despised amount of authority in order to try and feel better about yourself because, in the Sixth Form at Abingdon, I strove desperately to become a prefect. Looking back, I wish I hadn't.

You know how some teenagers, often the arty creative ones, seem to have an attitude of immunity to the outside world – of poise and calm? I'm sure that's not how they feel, or behave to their families, but it's how they can come across. I have a sense that they're often in bands – or maybe they paint or sculpt or something. They seem unselfconsciously artistic and above the usual teenage concerns of friendship and acceptance and dealing with authority.

Well that wasn't me. But neither was I conventionally success-ful, cool or popular. I had no idea that parties were a thing that happened to people my age. I'd been to parties when I was six which involved jelly and Pass the Parcel; I later went to parties as a student which involved £3 bottles of wine and Stella cans full of cigarette ends; and I go to parties now which involve canapés and commissioning editors – but in my teens I was almost completely off the party grid. I went to two, I think. Both were cast parties for plays, at which I awkwardly hung around sipping cider, bored out of my mind and baffled, absolutely baffled, that this could be an environment that anyone would enjoy. And vaguely wondering how long I had to wait before an attractive girl would throw herself at me.

No, in my teens I fell squarely between the stools of conventional acceptance by my peers and arty indifference to such notions. I knew I couldn't be a star of the former group but neither did I have a sufficient sense of self-worth to reject a value system that was rejecting me. I was into acting and debating and watching TV comedy – I could have styled myself as left-wing and creative and anti-establishmentarian. I wish I had. But I didn't have it in me. I wanted to gain official acceptance – I wanted to be a prefect.

The school authorities, particularly Beak, made a big deal out of the prefects. They were the favoured few. So it really is regrettable that I wasn't sufficiently contrarian to think, 'Look, this doesn't matter. What an absurd way to judge people. Why take a tiny minority of a group of teenagers, put them in charge of supervising the lunch queue and then talk about them as if they're the next generation of world leaders?' Some boys did have that insight and, to them, I must have looked like a twat.

I *was* made a prefect, by the way – which is marginally less tragic than having wanted it as much as I did and not been. So I was able to swagger around the school as if I was a winner. But I didn't really feel like it. I didn't have enough respect for the system that had given me this tiny amount of authority to fully enjoy it. I was probably put off by the institution's own insecurities – its self-loathing, its wanting to be posher or less posh, the persistent middle-English aura of something mediocre bitterly trying to shake off its own mediocrity. I mean, mediocrity's fine – if you accept it. Abingdon didn't and yet seldom seemed to do anything sufficiently distinguished to leave it behind.

As I approach the drinking fountain in the middle of the park – a small white spike like the top of a buried cathedral – I pass a man wearing a wide-brimmed black trilby. I immediately assume he's an idiot, which I suppose is unfair. I like hats – I slightly regret that I don't live in an era when all men still wear them. I'd enjoy wearing one, having different hats for different occasions, taking them off to go indoors, worrying about losing them, putting important slips of paper in the brim, maybe even sporting them at a rakish angle and tipping them to ladies in the park (if I'd completely changed personality). But that's not the age we live in and I'm wary of those whose hat-wearing seems to be a denial of that. I can't help thinking they're exactly the sort of contrarian who would have refused to wear a hat when it was the convention to do so. They wear them now as a sign of disdain for consensus. 'Why aren't *you* wearing a hat, square?' their hat-wearing proclaims. I'm suspicious of consensus and I wish I'd been a more contrarian teenager, but that doesn't stop me looking at him with immense annoyance. Or perhaps that's why I do.

Also I have a hat exactly like that and it has not brought me happiness. I last wore it five or six years ago when Robert Thorogood, a friend of mine who's a big fan of John le Carré, was being surprised on his birthday by a sort of espionage day. His wife Katie had organised various spy-themed encounters for him in central London. Friends would sidle up to him in various filmic locations and disguises and give him clues leading to other encounters and it all finished up with a jolly night in the pub. That's love for you – she actually *made him a spy for a day*, which is probably the optimum length of time to be a spy, any longer leading to boredom, suicide or a desperate desire to shout 'Hey, everyone, I'm a spy!'

Another friend, Tom Hilton, who lives near me in Kilburn, was also involved and we were both supposed to rendezvous with Robert in the National Gallery, in front of a certain painting. We decided to get the Tube together, both wearing trilbies which I had provided to make us look, if not like spies, at least as if we'd made an effort to look like spies.

It was about noon on a Saturday. As we walked up Kilburn High Road towards the station, the traffic was, as usual, terrible – almost stationary. We were feeling slightly self-conscious in our hats, particularly Tom who works in IT and isn't used to dressing up. 'Don't worry,' I told him. 'Some people wear hats all the time. It may feel slightly eccentric but it's basically a conventional, if somewhat outmoded, form of clothing.' I'd be amazed if I uttered those exact words, but then again I am quite pompous. Anyway, that was my gist.

All went well for 45 seconds until we walked past a builders' van, stuck in the traffic, its side door open to reveal four or five men, covered in paint and plaster dust, drinking cans of lager and in general exuding the exhausted high spirits of people who have just knocked off work. They spotted us in our hats. They sensed our self-consciousness. There is piss to be taken here, they intuited.

They thought we looked like cowboys. That's what I inferred from their cries of 'Yee-hah!' I think they may have mimed shooting guns in the air. Even in the humiliation of the moment, I was irritated that they'd mistaken trilbies for cowboy hats. And we were also wearing long overcoats. Their instinct for mockery may have been bang on but they were pretty ignorant when it came to costume.

Maybe it was this thought that prevented me from acknowledging them with a friendly, self-mocking smile or wave and defusing the moment. Or maybe I just thought we'd have walked past them in a couple of seconds so we might as well ignore them. Tom's instinct, it appears, was the same as mine. We did get a short distance ahead of the van and out of mockery range, but then the traffic shunted slightly forwards and they drove past us by a few yards. This was a disaster, as it meant we'd have to walk through their raking broadside of disdain once again. And it was definitely too late for the good-humoured acknowledgement this time. All we could do was pull the brims of our hats down further over our eyes.

When we got past them for the second time, the traffic moved again. It's not a long walk from the end of my road to Kilburn Tube station – it takes perhaps four minutes. But I can tell you, if you're ever in a situation of only having minutes to live, get a gang of cockney builders to enthusiastically rip the piss out of you and it'll feel like aeons. When we finally reached the Tube station, old men by then, we took off our hats and kept them off until we were in the National Gallery waiting to pass on some fake microfilm. We didn't stand out there; there are loads of twats in the National Gallery.

But this wasn't my worst experience with that black trilby. Aged seventeen, on the brink of leaving Abingdon School, I gazed into that hat in a moment of utter defeat. Just stared into its silky lining, reading the words 'Dunn and Co' again and again – feeling the contrast of a pleasing sight made ridiculous by failure. It was the Christmas holidays and I'd just come home from a shopping trip to be greeted by a letter from Merton College, Oxford saying they were not going to offer me a place to read Modern History.

I'd bought the hat a few months earlier. I thought it was quite stylish. I knew I could never be properly trendy but I'd begun to affect a slightly more flamboyant, if young-fogeyish, taste. I'd started to wear brown brogues instead of trainers and was one of the boys at school who'd taken to waistcoats. Awful, I know – but no worse than most teenagers' fashion crimes, just slightly more Wodehousean.

How absurd it suddenly was, this hat, in the light of my Merton failure. This affectation of adulthood by a boy. It had cost me quite a lot of pocket money – not that that mattered, I had precious little else to spend it on – but what had been the point? To look quirky, mature, artistic, intelligent? Well, I wasn't intelligent – I just used to be. All those years of being a swot, all those exam triumphs at prep school, had just been a waste of time because, on the first occasion that such aptitudes might have achieved something concrete, something which would have materially affected my life, they'd let me down. It had all slipped away at the eleventh hour. I'd been reduced to a fogeyish, hat-buying teenager who was okay at debating and liked amateur dramatics. So what.

I hope you'll excuse the lapse in my sense of proportion that occurred at that moment. Going to Oxford University isn't the be-all and end-all of life but it felt like it at the time. The pill of failure was further embittered by the fact that Leo, Ed and Daniel had all got into Oxford. Harry hadn't applied. I felt like the failure of our group. It had always felt to me – and I'm sure growing up in Oxford has something, but not everything, to do with this – that Oxbridge was where you went if you wanted a chance at real success in almost any field except skiing. And glutton for glory though I've always been, I've never yearned for mastery of the slopes.

As I remember it now, that was an epiphanic moment. It wasn't, of course. In fact, my parents said, 'We're so sorry but, don't worry, let's just try and have a nice Christmas,' and I did my best to suppress the sense of failure by shoving mince pies into my mouth. (This did not, in case you're worried, result in weight gain. As a teenager I had, in common with most of my friends, a ferociously inefficient metabolism. I was stick-thin and perpetually starving. An hour of solid ingestion would stop me feeling hungry for perhaps twenty minutes. Then the peckishness would start to set in and gradually intensify as I prepared for another massive feed. It was like I had a tapeworm. It was brilliant.)

But the more gradual epiphany which I associate with that moment was realising that I'd had it with academe. From now on, I decided, school work was a means to an end and that end wasn't 'coming top in exams'. I would get to Oxbridge somehow – I would exchange all the prep school exam results and thousands of hours of pre-pubescent swotting for that at least – but then I was done with it. I genuinely remember thinking about it like that – as if, after the Oxford failure, I was coming out of academic retirement for one last job: to get three A's at A-level so that I could reapply with a realistic hope of success. (Not to be rude about 'all our hard-working youngsters', as politicians put it, but three A's at A-level was still quite difficult to get in 1992.)

By all means now imagine a training montage of my buckling down to work. I made my revision plan as if I was studying flaws in the ventilation system of a Swiss bank. The blueprints: A-level past papers. The weapons: a fountain pen, a glasses-cleaning cloth, a ream of A4 and a copy of *Aristocracy and People: Britain, 1815–65* by Norman Gash. The mission: to break into Oxbridge.

17

I Am Not a
Cider Drinker

Two thirds of the way through the park, I pass the public lavatories. Do I need a piss? Yes. Do I need a piss enough to go to the park loos? No. They're weird and cold. The surfaces are all damp and, while it's probably condensation, it could be urine. Sometimes it's definitely going to be urine. And also, aren't park loos basically for closet gay men to have sex? Or the sort of gay man who isn't in the closet but is still turned on by the trappings of an illicit act? It would be rather rude of me to be getting in the way of assignations, using my penis for the less glamorous of its two purposes.

And what if I were propositioned? Unlikely, I know, but that would be a moment of such acute embarrassment that it's worth considerable bladder discomfort to avoid. How do you deal with that, socially? If someone says hello in the loos, you can't assume they want to have sex – that would be incredibly presumptuous even if it's what you'd immediately suspect. In order not to be either the kind of person who thinks they're so desirable that any unsolicited greeting must be a seduction attempt, or the kind who reckons anyone showing civility in a public toilet is on a cottaging expedition, you'd have to behave like you thought it was all innocent friendliness – until the last minute, the awful moment of having to say, 'I'm terribly sorry, I think you've got the wrong idea,' while removing their tongue from your face or trousers.

A female friend once told me that this often happened to her with meals out that weren't definitely dates but probably were. Some male friend or other would suggest dinner in a way that was *probably* romantically intended but (because it wasn't specifically expressed as such) there was no opportunity to say, 'Thank you but I don't think of you that way,' without sounding rude. She had to say yes. Then, throughout the meal, the suspected ulterior motive would gradually and agonisingly manifest itself in coy smiles and lingering eye contact and she'd realise that there was no polite way out of this before the inevitable awkward lunge. (As she was explaining this, I nodded and asked for the bill.) I wouldn't want to go through a quicker version of her experience in a cold room with my cock out.

In my year off after leaving school, I had a job as a cottager. Or so the others in the office must have thought, because I was always in the loos. Officially, I was a general office assistant at Oxford University Press. Unfortunately I worked in the department that published dictionaries for learners of English (i.e. dictionaries without the interesting words) and one of my duties was proofreading. I took every plausible opportunity to get away from this job for a few minutes: lots of trips to the loo, or the water cooler, which itself necessitated lots of trips to the loo.

The loo was quiet and clean and calm and I didn't have to stare at words on a screen. I would sit there wondering how much longer I could plausibly be in there before I had to return to my desk. I don't think I was so bored that, had an urgent member appeared through a glory hole beside me, I'd have given it a rub – but who knows? It would have used up valuable seconds before going back to double-checking the pronunciation guides in the International Phonetic Alphabet. Maybe it's that sort of boredom that has always led to sexual experimentation? God knows what must go on at the Inland Revenue.

It had always been my plan to take a 'gap' year between school and university – and by 'my plan' I of course mean 'my mother's plan'. She felt very strongly that I needed that time to become a more rounded person. Basically I think she was worried that I was boring – not really, properly, actually boring, just that people would think that I was boring. That I would seem boring to everyone else. That they would become bored when I was there. Which I suppose is the definition of boring.

At my mother's urging, I spent some of my OUP money on an interrailing trip round Europe. It wasn't a success. I'd secretly known it wouldn't be. I'd suspected it was going to be Barcelona all over again.

Eighteen months before, in the Upper Sixth at Abingdon, I'd been appointed 'British Ambassador to the European Youth Parliament', which simply meant going to Barcelona for a lot of dry political discussion with other nerds and a two-day 'team-building' event in the Pyrenees.

I was even more nervous than most of the other swots. But in fact the European Youth Parliament wasn't nearly as dominated by nerds as I'd expected or considered appropriate. It turned out there were plenty of cooler kids there who weren't really into debating but had got wind of a foreign trip and all the opportunities for drinking and dry humping that that afforded and so scrambled onto the band-wagon, undoubtedly pushing aside some of the less articulate of my fellow dorks as they did so.

We had to do a bit of rock climbing and abseiling. As you can imagine, I was delighted. There was a certain amount of trying to rig up a net between trees for some reason, as well as some capering about in a mountain stream with some logs. We were given point-less tasks to complete with kids from other countries. Just picture me, miserable, damp and cold – consumed by concern about whether I'd ever be relaxed enough in the weird youth hostel where we were staying to be able to do a shit, surrounded by some like-minded compatriots and dozens of other teenagers from all over the continent who were perfectly happy to scramble over treacherous rocks as a means of flirting with members of the opposite sex rendered even sexier by virtue of being foreign – and ask yourself why you ever thought the Euro might work.

Later in the week, a few of the cooler kids organised an evening in a nightclub which I bewilderedly went along to, before discovering that all it involved was drinking, which I was too law-abiding to do illicitly (even if I had an ignorant suspicion that it might be legal, or somehow closer to legal, in Spain), and dancing, which was an unthinkably embarrassing act in my view then. And now. (But not always in between. I was able to disco dance drunk on a regular basis from about 1994 to 2000. That particular ray of unselfconsciousness has now once again been obscured by cloud.)

I did have a bit of alcohol in Barcelona, though. There was a reception to welcome all the teenage delegates, with glasses of fizzy wine going round. (At the time, I assumed it was champagne. I now assume it was Cava, both because we were in Spain and because it was a party for teenagers.) I liked the warm fuzzy feeling and it was beginning to give the taste positive associations for me. Drinking alcohol was ceasing to be a chore. For a few years, my dad had been giving me a bit of wine and beer now and again, if we were eating in a restaurant – just for me to try, before wincing and ordering a Coke. His well-meant booze-pushing was beginning to take hold.

I remember thinking, around the time of this trip, that there was something wrong with me because I couldn't get drunk. I tried at the cast parties I was invited to, and occasionally at the houses of friends, to little or no effect. I now know the reason for this: I'd somehow got it into my head – as many teenagers do – that I liked cider. I did not, but I assumed, cider seeming to be an entry-level drink, that the alternatives tasted even worse. It was sweeter and fizzier than other boozes and therefore surely less unpleasant. At first sip, it seemed nicer than beer or wine.

But, when you don't really like it, cider is quite difficult to get down in any quantity. Its acrid, acidic sugariness precludes quaffing for all but the most alcohol-calloused tramp's throat. It's very easy to accidentally nurse it. So, on several occasions, I'd been 'on the cider' for some hours while hardly consuming any of it. At the time, I worried that my apparent inability to get drunk was due to some terrible lurking physical failing. I worried that the normal human metabolic reaction to alcohol was beyond me. That might give you some sense of the scale of my teenage doubts: I was one step away from fretting that gravity might cease to have an effect on me and I'd start to float helplessly out into space. Because I was such a loser.

Of course that kind of doubt is common to most teenagers. It is, in fact, the norm. The real freaks are the tiny and influential minority of teenagers who actually enjoy life at that age; who embrace the dating, partying, music, dancing, drinking, socialising, sport-playing of the pubescent years with gusto. In general, they are to be pitied. Few of us leave this vale of tears on a high: medical science and decades of relative peace mean that most Britons expire decrepit, with our happiest, most exciting years behind us. That's always sad. But it's sadder still when those high points came so early on in life – when the nostalgia kicks in at twenty. That's a high price to pay for avoiding acne and mood swings.

My Barcelonan inkling that drunkenness might not, after all, be beyond me, was proved right the following summer at Leo's house. It was a strange occasion on which to get drunk for the first time. Not a proper party, an afternoon gathering in a field, a pub where they'll serve you underage, or a covert late-night raid of a parental drinks cabinet. It was a very self-consciously 'civilised' evening. Leo, Ed, Daniel, Harry and I were behaving like adults, taking a break from our A-level revision to unwind, relax, chat, recharge – there was a thick veneer of bullshit maturity laid over the whole occasion. Leo's parents were out. Their house was tastefully deco-rated and full of musical instruments. There was no television in the sitting room – how posh is that? We chatted, we watched a film, we ate pizza, we drank wine.

I drank a lot of wine. For the first time in my life, it was really going down a treat. That horrid sour drink had become delicious.

I wanted to guzzle it – now a sensation I'm all too familiar with. I suppose we must all have got a bit tipsy but I'm pretty sure I was further gone than the others. I only became aware of the situation on the way to the loo: I noticed that the corridor had become slightly difficult to negotiate. I was swaying, like someone drunk in a film. It was weird, unsettling, basically unpleasant – but, at the same time, I was thrilled that it had finally happened to me. I was experiencing in real life something I'd previously only known from fiction – it was like seeing a white Christmas or someone ripping off the end of a cigar with their teeth.

I also felt embarrassed. I hadn't behaved as responsibly or maturely as people might have expected. In a tiny way, I'd been stereotypically teenage and, in a stereotypically teenage way, I was ashamed of myself. So after an awkward swaying piss and a careful journey back to the living room, I tried to act as sober as possible. Yet somehow, while doing a gesture to illustrate some remark, I managed to break a plate. I was unmasked. I sat with a guilty expression, quietly burping. My friends observed the state to which I'd reduced myself with sage, judgemental looks that ill concealed their glee.

The next day, I had my first sensation of wondering how much of a fool I'd made of myself. That's so often the strongest feeling after you've got pissed – worse than the hangover. You're seldom convinced that you were a tit, you're just not convinced you weren't. You feel the urge to make phone calls to test the water. You hope that you can determine whether you should be embarrassed and apologetic by the tone of voice with which your call is answered. You think they're unlikely to sound offended – but it's a warning sign if they sound amused.

Of course I also had my first hangover, which I didn't realise was a hangover as my expectations of what one would be like were solely informed by Alka Seltzer adverts. What I know now but didn't then is that you often don't get the bad headache they illustrated, just an overall feeling of unease, clumsiness and delicacy.

The stomach is usually more upset than the head, which Alka Seltzer failed to mention – largely because, if your stomach's feeling peaky, the last thing you want is Alka Seltzer, a horrible salty fizzy drink. Its pain-killing powers are dwarfed by the massive downside of taking on a gallon of stomach-troubling slosh. So, at the time, I was relieved to escape the dreaded hangover but puzzled to coincidentally have no appetite and crave water. It's not much to be proud of, managing to get drunk for the first time. But, like mumps, I was glad to get it out of the way.

I'm just leaving Regent's Park now. On a bench near the gate, there's a tramp swigging from a can of Special Brew. Now there's someone whose first experience of alcohol probably wasn't swiftly followed by the offer of work at Oxford University Press. I wonder if he got into booze under pressure from his parents to stop watching *Blackadder* and develop a social life? I wonder if they were half glad, the first couple of times he threw up in public, that he was beginning to live a little?

I wonder if they nagged him into taking an interrailing trip round Europe so that his gap year wouldn't be entirely frittered away doing clerical work for £4.50 an hour? I wonder if he sat nervously in beautiful squares in Florence, eating supermarket sandwiches and worrying about wasps, utterly oblivious to all the opportunities of high- and low-brow fun that lay around him? I wonder if he dutifully got up from youth hostel beds at eight in the morning to trudge round museums and galleries, bored out of his mind but feeling ashamed of that boredom? I wonder if his terror of running out of money while away from home prevented him from buying more than tiny amounts of horrible cheap food, while salivating as he passed restaurants? I wonder if he worried about how much more life frightened him than excited him, about how he longed to take refuge in things he knew? Did he feel inadequate at the thought of contemporaries who'd travelled to the Third World to build schools and get off with one another, thus rubbing his nose in his own encumbrance with shyness and fear? Did he return home from this holiday in Paris, Rome, Florence, Venice, Vienna and Prague just hugely relieved that it was over and looking forward to eating beans on toast and watching *Telly Addicts*?

Probably not, that would be a bit too much of a coincidence. I walk out of the park and continue heading south.

-18-

Enthusiasm in Basements

I hope I don't bump into Michael Palin. I don't know why I would, but it's always possible. He might be standing at a bus stop. Or browsing in a shop window. I hope he isn't.

I feel bad about saying that. And thinking it. I was once having a conversation about who was the worst person to bump into on holiday, to find staying at your hotel, and I concluded that, for me, it would be Michael Palin. Not Hitler. Not my worst enemy. Lovely Michael Palin.

This was my reasoning: first of all, on holiday, you don't really want to bump into anyone unexpected at all. You want to spend time with the person or people you're holidaying with – so bumping into anyone is bad news. I appreciate that this is a misanthropic attitude and I'm sorry about that but it's how I feel. I actually like people, in lots of cases, and want to spend time with them. In a *planned* way – I'm not up for chance encounters.

There are various sorts of chance encounter I dismissed before deciding Palin would be worst. For example, there's that category of acquaintance you're tempted to ignore when you pass them in the street. Not because you don't like them or hardly know them but because you know them to just the wrong and annoying extent. You're not really friends, but you know them well enough for acknowledging them to necessitate a 'catch-up'. You have to go through the whole 'My God, how are *you*!?' pantomime, as if the fact that you're not often in touch has been a tremendous and regrettable lapse rather than a tacit agreement.

Don't get me wrong: I know the world is basically a better place for these pleasantries and I wouldn't want to live without such lubricating hypocrisy, but it's just sometimes easier, when you spot someone whose level of acquaintanceship with you is in this category, to pretend not to see them. They may well be doing the same and I don't think that makes either person evil – just not particularly warm. And there are genuinely warm people – my mother, for example – who like to have such passing catch-ups with people they would never otherwise think about. They enjoy those little purposeless chats, the moment of human interaction and contact. Such people, I freely admit, are better than I am. But I won't become one by pretending.

Now, on holiday, almost anyone unexpected falls into this category. If you met a real bosom buddy, which is unlikely because you'd probably know the holiday plans of anyone that close, it might be okay. You could have a meal together one evening and otherwise continue with your plans. But everyone else is trouble. The oddness of the circumstances would be so unavoidably worthy of remark that you'd have to chat fully with people you'd barely speak to in the context that you know them from: 'Oh my God, you work in that shop round the corner from me, I see you there a lot, we've never exchanged more than a nod and now you're in exactly the same Portuguese hotel and it's so weird we have to say hi and chat for a bit – and because we're beside a swimming pool we've now seen much more of each other's naked flesh than either of us is comfortable with. Hooray!' The 'My God, how are *you*!?' hypocrisy levels are sky high.

So it would be worse to bump into someone you're neutral about than someone you hate. In the latter case, you'd have to assume the hatred went both ways and you'd naturally avoid each other on the beach, in the restaurant and going round the interesting local church. If you hate them and they *don't* hate you, just behave like an arsehole when they say hello and you've killed two birds with one stone.

Back to Michael Palin. For me, he's the nightmare scenario: someone I massively admire and would feel incredibly self-conscious in front of. It would ruin the holiday. A different sort of person would love it: they'd think, 'What a great opportunity to become friends with my hero Michael Palin!' and merrily set about ruining Palin's trip. I'm no such optimist. Why should Michael Palin want to be friends with me? I'm sure he has enough friends. And so do I, actually. How would Palin–Mitchell socialising work? He's much older than me. He's a big star. What would we do? Would I go round to his house and play board games? Would we go to the cinema? Would I hold dinner parties for all my university friends and Michael Palin as well, sitting in the corner being exactly, uncannily, off-puttingly like Michael Palin and making everyone worried about their table manners?

As things stand, I get to enjoy Michael Palin's work while satisfying my friendship needs with people who aren't part of the Monty Python team. Knowing him won't make *The Life of Brian* any funnier – in fact, if familiarity breeds contempt, it might make it less so. What a disaster that would be! I'd lose the pleasure I derive from some of the most brilliant comedy ever made, and get saddled with a friend my parents' age who makes me feel self-conscious. Perhaps you begin to understand why the Michael Palin encounter would be my holiday hell – and I'd get no help from the British consul.

Or you might be wondering why I can't just ignore Michael Palin on this theoretical Portuguese beach. Not an option.

Perhaps I should explain that I have met Michael Palin before. I was in the pub in Kilburn with my friend Toby, on an ordinary Saturday night about four years ago. I was unshaven and greasy-haired – I was getting pissed at my local, which felt like an extension of my living room. I didn't feel like I was 'out in public' – I was probably comfortable enough to scratch my balls without thinking about it – when suddenly Michael Palin walked into the pub, came up to me and introduced himself.

Can you imagine how weird that was? There was no seeing him across the room and hoarsely whispering:

'Is that Michael Palin or just someone who looks like him?'

'I think it's him – maybe you should say hello? You're on TV.'

'No! That would be really annoying of me – he won't want to be pestered by fans. Besides I'm not presentable and I keep scratching my balls!'

Toby and I had no such opportunity. Instead we got an instant 'Hello, I'm Michael Palin – I've seen you in *Jam and Jerusalem*, which I really enjoyed.' Or something like that – something nice. He definitely said 'Michael Palin'. I heard Michael Palin say 'Michael Palin', live in the Black Lion in Kilburn.

And of course being a weird, shy and socially maladroit fan, I don't think I was very nice to Michael Palin. I wasn't rude – I was just quiet. I said hello, I introduced Toby, and Michael Palin went away to sit with his friends while I interrogated the part of my brain that seemed to think Michael Palin would have minded if I'd said, 'I'm a huge admirer of your work.' Exactly how had I come to the conclusion that this remark could wait for the next time Michael Palin came up to me in the pub? Obviously I was thrilled and amazed – one of my biggest comedy heroes had recognised me and said hello. Yet the thrill and amazement was dwarfed by shame at having dealt with the situation so poorly. So I was left with the strong net feeling that I'd rather the whole thing hadn't happened. But at least I wasn't wearing trunks and trying to drink out of a coconut.

I've met Michael Palin again since, in the building I'm just passing now: BBC Broadcasting House, at the bottom of Portland Place. That's probably why I'm jumpy about bumping into him again. We were both on an episode of *Loose Ends*. This encounter went much better, I'm relieved to say. But then I was ready for him. Broadcasting House is the sort of place where you expect to meet people, where you don't go without having your shit together. So, having managed to give a reasonable account of myself with Michael Palin at last, why on earth would I want to bump into him under a palm tree and cock it up again?

In a tweedy way, there's something momentous and sacred about BBC Radio Comedy. It's a world in which new performers and writers, aspirant and broke, desperate to turn promising Edinburgh Fringes into ways to pay the rent, are thrust together with some of the grand old men of comedy. Never is this more apparent than at the BBC Radio Comedy Christmas party. The tatty clothes of the skint and keen are punctuated by the occasional gleaming blazer of the likes of Nicholas Parsons or Barry Cryer.

There's a sense of amazing continuity – that an unbroken tradition from the days of *It's That Man Again*, through *The Goon Show* and *Round the Horne*, into the era of the three great and surviving radio panel shows, *Just a Minute*, *I'm Sorry I Haven't a Clue* and *The News Quiz* and taking in brilliant shows like *The Hitchhiker's Guide to the Galaxy* and *On the Hour*, is still alive here. There's a bookishness alongside a sense of possibility. This is a place where pipe-smoking and ale-drinking sit alongside surrealism and satire – a perfect environment for a conservative who thinks the world needs to change. I love working in radio: it's quick, you don't have to learn your lines, they always give you sandwiches and you're encouraged to go to the pub afterwards. I feel I belong there, and I'm proud of that feeling.

But that's not how I felt when I first entered Broadcasting House as a keen undergraduate on a day trip to London. James Bachman, who had already graduated, took Matthew Holness and me to a *Week Ending* non-commissioned writers' meeting. This was in a basement 'Writers' Room' which, in 1996, was still equipped with typewriters. The three of us sat quietly in a corner as a harassed and tubby script editor or producer, wearing round glasses and a bright waistcoat, went through the news stories they were looking for sketches about, while a handful of braying smart alecks chipped in and announced their writing intentions.

It was not a happy atmosphere, probably because we all knew that we were the bottom of the heap – most of the material would come from the commissioned writers who had already been briefed and had taken the juiciest stories. They were on the princely retainer of £50 a week and were gods to us. In the non-commissioned writers' room, it was intimidating to be a newbie, shouted down by older hands, conscious of how hard it was to get noticed even by one tiny satirical radio show. But it was worse to be an old hand, because there was really no excuse for not having become a commissioned writer by now. Anyone who'd been going to those meetings for more than a couple of years was officially deemed to have failed. And I have to say, from what I heard of the ideas they loudly chipped in with, rightly so.

But it's no good getting lost in reveries about Broadcasting House. I have to plan what I'll say if I bump into Michael Palin. Be prepared, as I didn't learn in the cubs. I managed to say that I admired his work when I saw him at *Loose Ends*, but I probably shouldn't just say that every time I see him. I need something else, possibly urgently. As I turn down Regent Street, I'm amazed by the number of people who, from a distance, could be Michael Palin. It's crowded; he could come at me from nowhere. By the time he was close enough for me to be sure, it would be too late to plan. That's one of the many ways in which Michael Palin differs from Mr Blobby.

Maybe I'd tell Michael Palin about having to play a dancing girl at Mr Fezziwig's party. He, of all people, might be sympathetic. Michael Palin's first stage role was Martha Cratchit, daughter of Scrooge's hapless clerk. He played her at primary school in Sheffield, I've read.

But he was only five and I was ten. Maybe at five it wouldn't have been so embarrassing to cross-dress and look exactly like a girl? Or maybe Palin's masculinity shone through? I'd hate to try and swap stories about our shared misery only to find that he loved it, and thus my attempt to bond over common ground with Michael

Palin would actually result in the exact opposite. He'd walk away thinking I was weird and incomprehensible.

Also, I reckon Martha Cratchit's a better part than Dancing Girl. I bet he had lines. At five! He was a prodigy – he was six years younger than I was when I was finally trusted with 'Vespasian, centurion', which I reckon Palin would have made more of and was also, when I think about it, slightly embarrassingly *Life of Brian*-ey. Thanks, Mr Roberts! Way to make me look like a dick in front of Michael Palin! Yes, it would definitely be better not to bump into him.

Michael Palin's first comedy experience at university was, I've also read, performing sketches at a Christmas party. That means he waited weeks, months before trying to break into the performing scene at college. Not me; I went to fifteen auditions in my first weekend.

Yes: following some successful A-level results and an interview, I discovered halfway through my gap year that I'd got into Cambridge. I'd decided to apply there instead of Oxford because, having left school, it struck me as a good idea to spread my wings a little and get away from the place where I grew up – albeit only to somewhere unbelievably similar.

Getting in felt like more of a relief than a triumph. By then, I'd managed to persuade myself that, after all the years of obsessing about exams, not to get to Oxbridge would be a disastrous failure. Ridiculous though this view is, I felt it sufficiently strongly that, psychologically, I'd probably made it true and, had I not got to Cambridge, I would have slunk to whatever other perfectly good university had admitted me with an irreversible sense of defeat. Or perhaps I would have been stung by the rejection into intense hard work and made billions out of a dotcom. Nevertheless, my over-whelming emotion was of having averted a disaster – which, if anything, feels better than a triumph.

When I arrived at Peterhouse, Cambridge, in October 1993 it was time for Phase 2 of my plan: reject academe and get stuck into drama immediately. (If my admissions tutor is reading this, I'm sorry. It's Oxford I was angry with. But I couldn't take it out on them, because they hadn't let me in.)

The two largest drama societies in Cambridge, the Amateur Dramatic Club and Footlights, both held Freshers' week 'squashes' – the Cambridge name for drinks dos aimed at attracting new members. (Cambridge University has lots of its own words for things that there are perfectly good words for in wider circulation. This is one of the ways in which Cambridge University is like sailors.) The Footlights squash was held in its clubroom – a dark, damp, spider-infested room in the Union Society cellars, which had been expensively decorated to the height of fashion in 1978.

As soon as I arrived, I was offered a drink: 'There's red or white wine – I'm afraid the lager's just run out.' The significance of that remark was lost on me at the time – more of that later. I joined Footlights; it seemed you didn't have to audition to be a member, just pay a fiver. However, you did have to audition to be in any of the shows or 'smokers' (late-night cabaret evenings). The next show was the Christmas pantomime – I made a note of when and where to audition and then attempted, in a shy 18-year-old way, to 'work the room'. This involved walking round the room without talking to anyone in it. Finally I managed to introduce myself to Dan Mazer, later producer of *Ali G Indahouse*, at that point Footlights vice-president and in his third year at Peterhouse, the same college as me. We had an awkward chat and then I left.

At the Amateur Dramatic Club squash, people were more helpful and welcoming, in a way that immediately made me think less of the institution. I'm not proud of that but there's no doubt Footlights' shabby standoffishness, coupled with its fame, projected greater cachet than the ADC's inclusive efficiency. The ADC welcomed those keen on any and every element of theatre production: not just acting and writing but all the boring ones as well. In fact, those seemed to be the priority, possibly because the ADC had its own theatre and so was very focused on everything you could do with and in it: lighting, set-building, publicity, front of house, costume, make-up, etc. I was slightly put off by all that. But what I was much more put off by was the fact that, scandalisingly, one of the committee members, a student only two years older than me, had a baby – her own baby – which she was sort of wielding like it was the most natural thing in the world. I reckoned that meant she'd definitely had sex.

Keeping on the opposite side of the room from the girl with the baby, I finally managed to ask someone wearing an authoritative T-shirt about acting and how to get involved.

'The standard,' I was told, 'is incredibly high.' (This was a lie.) 'You probably won't get a part in anything in your first year – certainly not in your first term – but you should audition for everything to give yourself a chance.'

Everything. Right.

'Alternatively, if you'd like to learn lighting design, we've got people who can teach you.'

I did not want to learn lighting design. Undaunted by this evidence of widespread electricity, drill, hammer and penis use in Cambridge drama, I decided to audition for everything.

Play auditions at Cambridge, in my day at least, were all advertised in *Varsity*, the student newspaper, and always happened at the weekend so that even students who had lectures all day every day of the week (scientists, basically) could still audition. (Obviously, they'd hardly be able to make any of the rehearsals but that issue was glossed over. Throughout my time at Cambridge, the acting and writing scene was dominated by people reading for arts and humanities degrees because our workload was so much lighter than the scientists'. Those who read Natural Sciences or Medicine practically had full-time jobs, while all I had to attend was one weekly supervision for which, strictly speaking, I had to write one weekly essay although I usually didn't. All lectures were voluntary and I didn't go to a single one after week four of my first term. So there was lots of time for messing around in plays.)

The first weekend of the Michaelmas (autumn) term was the busiest of the year for auditions. In any given week, there are several student shows on at Cambridge University, not just at the ADC Theatre but in many of the colleges: Trinity, Queens', Robinson, Peterhouse, Christ's, Corpus Christi and St John's all had service-able performance spaces. In the first weekend, when they cast many of the plays for the whole term, there were more auditions than one person could physically go to. I managed to get to 15 and learned a fair bit about Cambridge geography in the process.

Walking around that beautiful city on a sunny autumn week-end, I was properly excited. I loved where I was, I was relieved to be allowed to be there and, for the first time, I seemed to be in possession of some of the energy and enthusiasm I'd previously associated with people who went bungee jumping in Thailand. The mist of puberty was lifting and things were beginning to seem possible.

The auditions were held in a wide range of venues – some were in newer college buildings and felt municipal and drab. But many were in old college rooms with dusty medieval staircases, up which you would queue for your chance to be in some pseud's production of *The Changeling* while looking at shabby old posters for previous productions.

These were first-round auditions. Outside the room would be photocopied sheets of speeches to prepare (not necessarily anything from the play you were auditioning for – this stage was a general trawl for acting talent). You'd practise the speech in the queue outside – there seemed to be loads of people auditioning for all of these productions, although I noticed some recurring faces, from which I inferred that I wasn't the only one doing the rounds. When your time came, you'd go in, give your name and college, read the piece out, get told to do it differently, read it out again with that in mind and leave. It was all done with the seriousness and self-conscious professionalism that only enthusiastic amateurs ever possess. A couple of days later, a list would be posted on the noticeboard of the ADC Clubroom of those invited to a 'recall' audition. Of those, less than half would be cast.

Everyone involved in this process was a student. There were no grown-ups. You can't read drama at Cambridge, so it's only ever something people do alongside their degrees, as a hobby. This is a brilliant system as it prevents anyone in a teaching capacity from interfering – from saying there's a right way and a wrong way of putting on a play. You get to learn by experience, from your mistakes, from each other and from each other's mistakes. And the main thing you learn from this whole process is how much entertaining people, telling them a story, moving them, making them laugh, is about instinct and luck. Those who succeed are, in general, those who don't let the failures or the successes turn their heads too much, and who keep at it.

The audition I was most excited about, and felt I had the least chance of succeeding in, was for the Footlights pantomime, *Cinderella*. As a comedy-obsessed teenager, I'd obviously heard of Footlights. It was the club of which so many of the comedians I admired seemed to have been members: Peter Cook, John Cleese, Douglas Adams, Stephen Fry – these were the brightest stars in the firmament but, like a night sky in the countryside, the more you looked, the more stars you saw: writers like Michael Frayn and Clive James; producers like David Hatch, John Lloyd and Jonathan James Moore; directors like Jonathan Miller and Trevor Nunn; actors like Eleanor Bron, Miriam Margolyes and Simon Jones; Cecil Beaton, Germaine Greer, Bill Oddie, Julian Slade. The more you found out, the more Footlights seemed to be behind about half of the stuff worth paying attention to.

And there was something intriguing about that clubroom. I mean, it was horrible. It stank of stale beer. It was unpleasantly dark, but it would have been worse if you could see into the corners. Getting in involved a long walk through the union cellars, down a corridor so narrow it felt like it had been hewn out of the earth by Morlocks and as weirdly, frighteningly and garishly painted as a punk's squat. But I'd noticed there were posters on the wall of shows that looked old and significant, and photographs of famous people sporting haircuts from the era preceding that of their breakthrough.

The director of the pantomime wasn't present at the first-round audition – it was left to Footlights committee members to separate the wheat from the chaff. I auditioned in front of the two vice-presidents, Dan Mazer and James Bachman. I read out an Alan Bennett monologue in which a man is speaking on the phone, trying to arrange for a saucy telegram to be sent to his girlfriend. What James told me later is that, just before I came in, Dan had groaned, 'Oh no, here comes that keen one.'

That interests me. First because it gives an insight into my own uncool naïvety – that in one conversation with Dan at the squash, in which I was just attempting to be appropriately enthusiastic and upbeat as minor public schoolboys are trained to do, I'd transmitted a desperate and unattractive keenness. They were looking for people who were keen, presumably. But I had obviously seemed keen in a way that, in Dan's view, almost precluded my also being funny.

And it also interests me that such a category of people exists at all – that we go beyond the insight that enthusiasm is no guarantee of talent to the conclusion that it actually makes talent less likely, and indeed that a snooty take-it-or-leave-it standoffishness suggests you're likely to be hot stuff. It's a sort of Groucho Marx perversity: like the club who'll accept him as a member, my enthusiasm was somehow repellent. If Dan had felt he had to court my enthusiasm for Footlights, he'd probably have found it easier to believe I might show promise.

I don't mean to criticise the 21-year-old Mazer here. I'm just using him as an example of how pervasive is our culture's attraction to cool and sangfroid. I was guilty of it myself when I found the unfriendly Footlights squash more attractive than the more open ADC one – I was almost *directly* conforming to the Groucho quote there. But, for all that I'm susceptible to it, it's a phenomenon I hate. I hate cool. I'm impatient with disingenuous affectations of having better things to do, being untroubled, being an unflappable presence disdainfully moving through the world. What's particularly daft is that people who affect such an attitude are often incredibly fashionably dressed, giving the lie to their claims of immunity to a desire to be included. I prefer less hypocritical expressions of human frailty, where saying things like 'Yes I'd be really keen to get involved in your comedy club' doesn't immediately get you marked down as a cunt.

I'm really not as bitter as this makes me sound, or at least not in the case of the *Cinderella* audition. They thought I was funny and gave me a recall for the show, which I was hugely excited about, a feeling I didn't yet know I was supposed to conceal. Like a goth looking at a winkle-picker, all my desire was flaming in contemplation of Cambridge, acting, the theatre and, most of all, Footlights.

- 19 -

God Is Love

I'm passing a round church: All Souls', at the top of Regent Street, next to Broadcasting House. It's only really the entrance that's round – the porch bit under the spire. In Cambridge, next to the Footlights clubroom, there's a properly round church. A lot of students from my college seemed to attend services there – people I was chatty with for the first few weeks and seldom spoke to afterwards. With that guilty thought, I'm glad to turn down Cavendish Place and leave it behind.

For the first couple of weeks at Cambridge, I thought maybe everyone was Christian. When I arrived at Peterhouse, there was a nice note in my pigeon-hole from a group of second-years asking me round for a cup of tea. I jumped at this opportunity, as I'm sure most people jump at any sign of friendliness when they first arrive somewhere strange. Certainly, when I went round for tea, a lot of other freshers seemed to be there. It was all very friendly – a bit boring, a bit safe, as conversations between strangers often are, particularly when most of them are nervous and homesick – but a reassuring induction into a new place and a good way of meeting the other recent arrivals.

And that's how the first few days were. We freshers would meet up for cups of tea and biscuits with one or other of this friendly group of half a dozen second years who had taken it upon themselves to be so welcoming. And, as you will have suspected, they kept mentioning church – in a very natural, low-key way. 'We'll be going to church on Sunday' ... 'We go to the Round Church' ... 'Do come to the college Christian society lunch' ... and all we freshers nodded along.

I don't think there was anything sinister about this. They were never nasty about my not going and, as people who thought it was good to go to church, it's natural that they should advocate it. They thought it would be a good use of my time, to say the least. And I'm not even sure they really advocated it, they just mentioned they were going.

What amuses me in retrospect is that I was so baffled by the experience of being somewhere new on my own, so weirdly deracinated, that I genuinely thought: of course! This is a Christian country. I've massively over-estimated the pace of historical change and my background must be much less normal than I've always assumed. It turns out, basically, *everyone* is still C of E. That's what's still going on: everyone's still going to church every week apart from my mother, who's a Christian Scientist and goes somewhere different (Why does our family always have to do something weird, I used to grumble. It was the same when they bought me that odd brand of disc drive for my BBC Micro which my dad said was better, but I just wanted the one everyone else was getting), and my dad, whose religion is 'Ask your mother'. So fine, everyone in Britain is still Christian.

I'm not being sarcastic when I say 'fine'. I really would have been fine with that, if that was the system. I can spare an hour a week and I like a bit of ritual, a bit of a routine. If I'd grown up, as most humans have throughout history, in an unquestioning religious community I would happily have gone along with that – probably not got too involved but certainly not been the first to quibble with it. In fact, I would have been grateful not to be encouraged to address the eternal questions on my own. I would have been soothed by the solace it provided and avoided over-analysing it for fear that it might collapse in my head if I did. And I wouldn't have been stuck, as I am now, an agnostic who vaguely feels there might be a God and likes carol services, hemmed in by enthusiastic worshippers pushing various morally discredited organisations on the one hand, and the Dawkins brigade gleefully telling children that Father Christmas doesn't exist on the other. For the week when I was duped into thinking that we were still a Christian country, I was happily looking forward to some hymn-singing and certainty.

A lot of people assume I'm an atheist. I can see why. I don't seem to be practising any religion and I slag off homeopathy and astrology a lot. I think there is a perception that I have a rational and analytical approach to the world. I certainly try to, as far as is consistent with an aversion to the cracks between paving stones and to page numbers in books containing recurrent digits. But, yes, I try to analyse things rigorously – partly because that's a good approach to life in general and partly because it's easier to find comic angles that way than by trying to nudge myself into flights of surreal invention.

What I don't understand is why so many people, the religious and the irreligious alike, have swallowed the idea that atheism is the most rational conclusion to draw about humanity's position and state of grace. Even those who oppose atheism do so in terms of its being too rational: lacking imagination or faith. 'Just because there's no actual reason to believe in something doesn't mean it can't be there,' they say.

But atheism isn't the most rational approach – agnosticism is. You can't know, so it's irrational to say that you do. An atheist or religious observant might counter that agnosticism – saying you don't know if there's a God or gods – isn't a conclusion at all. They'd have a point – but in that case, I say it's irrational to draw a conclusion. We don't know and we can't know.

Atheism also requires a leap of faith, albeit a nihilistic one. It might as well be a religion – many of its adherents evangelise about their philosophy and beliefs as much as the religious do. They claim their opinions to be certainties. They viciously criticise those who believe otherwise. They are, in some cases, emotionally attached to the idea that there's no God and dislike being gainsaid as much as a Pope or an Ayatollah does. They then wrap up this annoyance as anger at the terrible suffering religion has brought to the world – as if they truly think it's the religious beliefs themselves, rather than humanity's in-built urges to kill, persecute and suppress, that led to the Crusades or the Troubles or the failure to address the AIDS Pandemic.

Don't they get it? Humans will always find an excuse. The avowedly atheist communist states of the twentieth century killed greater numbers than any regimes before or since and needed no religious justification. A politically ideological one served just as well. Humans don't kill, or boss each other around, or say sex is evil and should be controlled or that certain people are wicked and should be oppressed, or that certain clothes are inappropriate or compulsory, because of their religious beliefs – we do it because some of us want to and religion is a convenient excuse. Atheists are being incredibly naïve if they think that, in the absence of religion, other reasons won't be found for disguising violence as virtue – or indeed that atheist belief systems aren't just as potentially susceptible to murderous extremism as any of the religions they oppose.

Sorry, I don't mean this to be a diatribe against atheism. Believe me, I get just as cross with aggressive god-botherers. Just as cross, though. No crosser. I'm always struck by how similar the two groups seem, and how we poor agnostics, who aren't trying to convince anyone of anything, are laid siege to by these irreconcilable yet uncannily similar groups.

I'm striding along the north side of Cavendish Square now, heading west. I pass a man with lots of piercings, including one of those massive ones where the lobe-hole is widened by the earring so that you could almost get an egg through it. You can see air and sky the other side, as if you're peering into another dimension. I try not to stare – but at the same time, surely, on some level, he wants me to stare? I mean, it's there to be noticeable, right? Maybe even to look nice? Is it okay to stare as long as, if questioned, I say: 'I like the huge hole you've fashioned in your ear'?

But have I stooped to the reasoning of the tit-starers? 'If she didn't want me to gawp, she shouldn't wear a low-cut dress!' That's certainly not a line of argument with which I want to associate myself even if, to be honest, I can't immediately see the flaw in it. But it's definitely a very stupid thing to say, as I assume it's likely to annoy women showing a lot of cleavage – and that's not something that it's in the interests of anyone apt to tit-stare to do.

Or is the ear hole supposed to look challenging? A big 'fuck you' to all the tweedy hypocrisy that I stand for, striding through Cavendish Square in my jacket and cords, too complacent to self-mutilate in the face of a horrible world. Or maybe, among his group of friends, everyone's got massive holes in their ears so it just seems normal. Perhaps, if I asked him, he'd say: 'Ooh, I don't really think about it – I'm just used to it being there' – like I am with a pocket handkerchief.

The second thing I noticed about Robert Webb was his earring. The first was that he was holding a gun. That's a lie. I was just trying to take a leaf out of Raymond Chandler's book but I haven't lived an exciting enough life. No, the first thing was his long hair – by which I mean the fact that it was long. I don't want to accidentally sound romantic: 'As soon as he walked in I was dazzled by the sheen of his golden locks.' No, I noticed he had long hair which, I'm sure he'll mind me saying, at that point in his life was a touch mullety.

He looked like a bit of a rebel, a bit cool, left-wing, metrosexual. 'Even if almost everyone's Christian, I bet he isn't,' I thought. He certainly didn't seem very Footlights, which was surprising because he was one of only two second-years on the Footlights committee and, consequently, automatically got through to the recall audition stage for *Cinderella*. The recalls were held in groups, which was the occasion of our meeting.

I know it's a bit of an obvious thing to say about someone with whom I was soon to form a twenty-year double act but, as soon as the audition started, I thought he was funny. We were reading out little sections of script as a group and he made every character he played properly, physically funny. One of the reasons I was struck by it is that he didn't look like he was going to be funny. He looked like he was going to be serious and talk about politics and betrayal – he came across a bit mopey, a bit damaged. But then suddenly he was putting on a silly voice and pretending to be an old-school musical entertainer, a pampered effete prince, an unhinged and impish king or a comedically tedious palace servant. Those were the parts we were auditioning for. I expect you can guess which ones he and I were cast in. Unfortunately I can't hear if your guesses are correct because this medium is so damned uninteractive. Well, he was the prince and I was the palace servant. Did you get it right? Why aren't you answering me?

That Footlights show, *Cinderella*, was by far the most exciting thing that I'd had anything to do with in my life so far. I don't know that it was a particularly brilliant show – although I think it had its moments, and it was well received by packed houses of drunken students – but being involved in it felt amazing. Comedy and acting had been obsessions of mine throughout my teens but I'd hardly ever got the chance, or been enterprising enough to make the chance, to actually do much of it. It had all been watching videos, listening to cassettes and writing a few sketches that were never performed. Saying you wanted to be a comedian didn't feel any more worth the breath at Abingdon School or Oxford University Press than saying you wanted to fly. But suddenly I was in an environment where loads of people were openly sharing their ambitions to act, write, sing, improvise comic characters or do stand-up.

And we were getting to put on this huge show, with a large cast and a band and an original comic script and songs and a big colourful set and even a couple of pyros for the finale. I suppose I'd doubted that Footlights, and Cambridge drama in general, would turn out to be all it was cracked up to be. In that term of rehearsals and performances, I found it to be so much more than I'd hoped. Not necessarily in terms of the quality of the shows we put on (they were seldom 'professional standard' although that was always the boast) but in the vibrancy of the creative atmosphere. This was a place to play, full of people of like mind. My hopes and ambitions crystallised very quickly in the autumn of 1993. I realised I wanted to be a comedian and an actor – to entertain, to write jokes, to be on TV like the people I'd admired through my teens. And I was in an environment where that all felt eminently achievable. It didn't feel like the ridiculous long-shot that in fact it was.

Robert Webb – Rob to me – wasn't the only friend and future collaborator I met on *Cinderella*. I got to know a whole new circle of exciting people, many of whom went into entertainment or broadcasting in one way or another: there were the writers of the show, Dan Mazer (who I met at the squash) and James Bachman, a comic actor and writer who I think I find more naturally, effortlessly amusing than anyone else I've met. There was Robert Thorogood, then president of Footlights, who played one of the ugly sisters and now writes the BBC One drama *Death in Paradise*, and his girlfriend Katie Breathwick, now a radio presenter. They got married after leaving Cambridge; it was at Katie's behest that I wore a spy's trilby to the National Gallery in order to pass Robert T a special birthday microfilm.

And of course Olivia Colman – Sarah Colman then, but always known as Collie – a brilliant actress with whom I've been lucky enough to work almost as often as I have with Rob. She's tremendously nice and kind, without being the sort of tremendously nice person who doesn't like it when you make horrible jokes about other people. On *Peep Show*, I married her. I think I made a good choice. Shame we got divorced.

I think it was Collie more than anyone else who made me realise that Footlights was a totally different environment from a school play. She was a first-year (at Homerton, the teacher training college

– in fact, she never finished her degree but subsequently went to drama school) so I had her pegged as a beginner in the acting world, like me. She certainly seemed a bit ditzy – fun, funny, good company, but not what you'd call focused. She seemed talented in rehearsals, but slightly 'all over the place' and easily distracted.

Then came the first night, when everything feels different. You're not marking through your lines in a strip-lit room any more, you're under theatre lights, alternately dazzled or in the dark. And lurking beyond these pools of light are people, an audience, strangers. It can easily put you off. I staggered through competently but certainly wasn't as assured as I'd hoped. But Collie was transformed. Suddenly she was shining with talent – working the audience, timing her lines, drawing out new laughs but without ever seeming hammy. I was amazed. I was also flattered to be on the same stage as her and terribly worried that I was being visibly outclassed. This didn't feel like amateur dramatics any more.

'If this is what other first-years are like,' I thought, 'I'm going to have to run pretty quickly to keep up.' Fortunately for me, while there were many talented actors at Cambridge when I was there, very few were as good as Collie – certainly no one better. Performing with Collie and Rob gave me an exaggerated impression of what I was up against in general.

The other thing that was exciting me in my first term at Cambridge was that I had fallen in love again – with a lovely girl who was very happily going out with someone else. (I won't tell you her name because I never said I was in love with her then so it would seem like a perverse thing to mention years later, now that I'm not.) I hadn't felt this sensation since the wordless understanding of eternal passion that it turned out I wasn't sharing with Beatrice from *Much Ado about Nothing* four years earlier. I mean, I'd fancied girls since then, but I hadn't had that feeling of overwhelming significance.

I had that feeling constantly at Cambridge, for several different women, none of whom I ever either got off with or – and here's the remarkable part – in any way propositioned. No lunges, no suggested trips to the cinema, no roses, no chocolates, no Valentine's cards, no broaching of the subject in any way whatsoever with any of them. I did occasionally get off with someone, usually when I was too drunk to spoil my chances by thinking, but never with any of the ones I thought I was in love with.

I know this seems like a terribly illogical approach, particularly coming from a heartless automaton like me. The hopeless crushes, the fallings in love – I don't know which to call them because they definitely *were* the former but sincerely *felt* like the latter – didn't make me happy. In general, I was very happy as a student, but the crushes got me down. And yet I did nothing about them apart from endless dissection with male friends over late-night drinks who told me, in thousands of different ways: 'Look, you should just say something, tell her – probably nothing will come of it but you never know, and then at least you can move on.'

But I was incapable of taking that advice. There are various possible reasons for that. Perhaps I just liked the sensation of unrequited love, even though I thought I didn't, and felt it would be spoiled by doing anything about it – probably by rejection, but maybe too, at some unconscious level, I felt I would be put off the object of my desire if she became attainable. Maybe I liked the thrill of the not-bothering-to-chase.

I would have denied that at the time. My explanation then would probably have been that rejection was more than I could bear the thought of living with. Also, as I stacked up a series of these crushes, even though I always claimed that the current one had eclipsed all previous ones, on some level I was aware that the same thing was happening over and over again – which means I knew they eventually wore off, without my having to go through the blow and embarrassment of rejection.

Still, it was the wrong approach. I went through a lot of unnecessary heartache as a result of never addressing the problem, never ripping the plaster off and enduring one excruciating moment of kindly refusal. I'm sure my recoveries from these infatuations would have been much swifter if I'd found the nerve to do that. My course of non-action also eliminated the chance that I might have got somewhere with any of these women. Had I got lucky, I doubt I would have turned out to be as in love as I thought I was – but, still, to have had a bit of a relationship with someone you've got a massive crush on is something I would have enjoyed. To say the fucking least.

I think the key reason for my perverse approach is that being practical about how I felt – trying to address the situation sensibly to optimise my happiness – would have seemed like a denial of the strength of my feelings. It would have been admitting that I was only in the grip of a crush, not a grand passion. It would have meant that the feelings of significance, importance, magic that unrequited love gives you were illusory, and those feelings were probably as much what drew me to the crush as the charms of its object.

Ambition can feel like that. Dreams of your future career can be exciting just like a crush, and I suspect faith can. In a way, asking the object of a crush-that-feels-like-love on a date is like trying to prove the existence of God. It's not a rational approach if you know that what you need to get up in the morning is hope.

The Cause of and Answer to All of Life's Problems

'Basically, I'm a three bottles of wine bisexual,' said Ellis, taking a slurp from his pint of Kronenbourg. I secretly hoped he wouldn't have another. He drew heavily on his cigarette and then did an elaborate French inhale which involved an almost musical popping sound followed by smoke pouring upwards like a liquid across his top lip and into his nose. I began to worry that I'd chosen the wrong person to teach me to smoke. I wanted it to look natural.

We were rehearsing a production of *Death of a Salesman*. Ellis, who was only nineteen (like me) despite being a second-year, had been cast in the role of Willy Loman. It's the sort of part that great actors wait a lifetime to play – they bring to it decades of experience, not just of acting, but of life. The weariness and defeat that only the triumph, disaster, boredom, excitement, worry and disappointment of years lived to the full can etch on your face and lend to your bearing is deployed, as they attempt to personify the American dream laid low. Ellis had a bash in his teens by putting on a gravelly voice and walking stiffly. It was basically fine.

I needed the smoking lesson so that I could appear more cool and mature. That was what the director told me. I was playing Bernard, the snotty kid next door who grows up to be a lawyer – barely at university and already typecast. Will (the director) wanted something for the scene in later life where I'm a big shot professional, to differentiate me from the kid in shorts with the whining voice. The shorts could be replaced but obviously we were stuck with the voice. Maybe if I was smoking, Will thought, I'd seem older, cooler and in control.

I was incensed. As a fervent anti-smoker – someone who at this point genuinely couldn't understand why anyone smoked (and what an admission of a lack of imagination that statement always is) – I didn't want to have anything to do with portraying nicotine in a good light (in this case a Zippo), let alone an environment where that was the unthinking assumption. Also, I'd never smoked in my life and I was scared.

After a lot of persuasion that it would really help the scene and that virtually everyone smoked in the 1940s (when the play was written and is set), I agreed to have a go. Will wasn't much of a smoker but Ellis very much was and he gave me my first lesson with one of his Marlboro Reds. The only instruction I got, when handed the small papery burning object, was to 'inhale'.

'Go on, inhale!'

'Why aren't you inhaling!'

'Are you scared of cancer – is that why you won't inhale?'

He thought I was an idiot, and I was perplexed because I was inhaling with all my might – I was positively hyper-ventilating, filling my lungs with oxygen but somehow unable to ingest any more than trace quantities of smoke.

The verb that hadn't been used – and this isn't something I can say about every aspect of my theatrical career – was 'suck'. To smoke a cigarette, you may or may not know, you have first to suck. *Then* inhale. I didn't realise you sucked, just like on a straw. I thought you put it in your mouth and then sort of breathed through it. If you do that, it will not look as if you are smoking – in my case, it merely intensified the incongruity that having a cigarette in my mouth at the age of nineteen already projected. I was very young-looking. But for the fact that I'd already attained my full height, I could probably have passed for thirteen. With a cigarette in my mouth, oddly breathing round it, I didn't project the image of sophisticated American maturity, more of slightly humorous, slightly sinister innocence inexpertly attempting to lose itself – like Iggle-Piggle trying to shoot up.

I got the hang of it eventually and moved on to stage two of smoking technique: how to light a cigarette. The look of lawyerish savoir-faire wasn't going to be improved by my holding the light a foot away from my face and tentatively moving it closer. Worse still, Will insisted I use a Zippo – much more appropriate to New York in the 1940s than the bright plastic lighters you get at the newsagents', but much trickier to ignite and much more like a small, smelly can of petrol that you're trying to set fire to in your hand. Drinking lager, I couldn't help thinking, was much easier than this.

Ellis was on both stimulants in the Pickerel pub on Magdalene Street, when he brought up the subject of how drunk he'd have to be to fuck me. A dangerous place to be when he's in that frame of mind, you might think. Or a good place to be. I haven't made it clear whether or not I wanted to fuck him, have I?

I did not. He is a very good friend of mine but that is not something there is enough wine in the world to make me do. And to be fair on Ellis, he was talking in general terms about an alcohol-induced sexuality flip. It wouldn't necessarily have been enough to make him stoop to me. Maybe three bottles of wine was for Brad Pitt.

Ellis Wolfe Sareen is an unusual man with an unusual name, although the two things aren't directly connected. The name's a family thing – someone once every two generations gets called that, apparently, which I suppose saves on decision-making time. Now you'll assume he's American when, in fact, he's from Manchester. He was a slightly controversial figure in the Cambridge drama scene when I arrived. He had a lot of friends but had also managed to annoy quite a few other thesps, possibly because of his enthusiasm for getting drunk and making passes at people (almost exclusively women, even when he'd drunk three bottles of wine, which was often); but more likely because of his disarming refusal to take himself or other people seriously.

Ellis's ruthless jollity was coupled with a deep, and largely justified, confidence in his own skills. He is blessed with great intellectual and practical abilities and there are few things that he absolutely can't do – hit a tennis ball without weirdly opening his mouth as if he's trying to swallow it is one. But that's not to say his confidence doesn't sometimes go too far, as you'll know if you were unlucky enough to see his production of *The Recruiting Officer* in November 1994.

I'm now walking west along Wigmore Street, passing the Cock and Lion pub on my right, which reminds me of the Pickerel in Cambridge. Both have low and dark ground floors where, like punters in a casino, the drinkers won't be disturbed by natural light.

The Pickerel enjoys the twin blessings of an authentic wooden-beamed building – medieval in places – and a riverside location. Unfortunately, they rather cancel each other out. Medieval builders are notoriously complacent about natural beauty – think of all those castles in lovely countryside where you can only see the view through an arrow slit. I suppose, in a world where there are hardly any buildings, and all of them olde-worlde, the sheer availability of rustic views inevitably suppresses people's sense of their value. There's no doubt that, had the architect of the older parts of the Pickerel been around today, he'd laugh at people's obsession with the river but be transfixed by the fruit machine. So, you can't see the river when you're in the Pickerel, a picture window being beyond the builders' ken, but it has the pleasing atmosphere of a place where people have been getting unglamorously pissed for centuries.

That was an activity that Ellis encouraged and, in me, he found a keen student. Of drinking, that is. Less so of smoking. And I was very much not a keen student in the conventional sense because I was very enthusiastic about going to the pub all the time. I mean, we didn't drink at breakfast, or particularly long into the night, Cambridge being a place where you couldn't buy a drink after 11 o'clock except at the ADC Theatre bar; and having alcohol in our rooms took a level of organisation that was usually beyond us. But by the end of my first term, I'd slipped very easily into a lifestyle of getting up late, pottering along to the ADC via a sandwich shop for an afternoon rehearsal or a meeting about a show, going to another rehearsal in the evening and then settling into the Maypole pub or the ADC bar until it closed. On Saturday nights there was usually a party and I'd get properly pissed. It would not be fair to say that I was consequently sick more often than not on such occasions, but it wasn't as less often than not as I'd have liked.

When the ADC Theatre bar was shut, the Maypole was our regular haunt. The Maypole is not picturesque: in a city of beautiful buildings and views, it looks out on a multi-storey car park. It's an unremarkable if inoffensive building with an insensitive 1970s flat-roofed extension at the front. It's possibly my favourite pub in the world and, I've just realised, it's virtually an FRP. But what it lacked in architectural merit, it made up for in the attitude of its management. It was, and still is, owned and run by an Italian family who brought to this unremarkable British pub the unfamiliar, alien notion that it should be a pleasant and hospitable place to spend time. They did all the normal pub things but also served food they'd be happy to eat themselves and had a menu of fancy cocktails. More than anything else, they were friendly and welcoming. They learned your name and made shy, spotty students feel like they were beloved old regulars with a tankard behind the bar. This strikes me as both canny and kind, and I'm very grateful to the Castigliones for making me feel so welcome and so grown-up. Their attitude made the Maypole the pub of choice for actors from the ADC, sportspeople from the nearby Hawks Club, and anyone in the university who fancied a pina colada.

Getting quite drunk very often, and very drunk quite often, was a revelation to me. From being something that I'd only realised a couple of years earlier I had the ability to do, it quickly grew at Cambridge into a major hobby – not as major as acting or writing sketches, but one that seemed to complement those activities perfectly. This was expensive and unhealthy but, as I had very few other costs, I was able to clear a substantial budget for it and I didn't give my health a second thought. I was occasionally hungover, although not in the way I get hangovers now, but seldom ill. And the upsides were massive: it made you feel great, it made endless conversations endlessly interesting, it brought together nervous, shy, repressed, swotty teenagers by making them feel comfortable with each other. Boozing was an imprudence that I felt safe with – a recklessness that didn't make me stressed.

This isn't heading towards a confession of alcoholism, by the way – not of the whisky on cornflakes type anyway. These days I drink more than doctors would recommend, but not that much more. I still get drunk occasionally, but not very often. I wouldn't deny a certain sort of social dependence on it, but I think it's a dependence I share with most of our culture. This society doesn't work without booze – our parties aren't good enough, our conversations aren't sufficiently interesting, nor is our self-confidence high enough to sustain our interactions without alcohol. It's everywhere, lubricating everything. My mother has never drunk alcohol and consequently finds most parties or meetings of friends in pubs to be inexplicable and tedious encounters. 'How can people stand for hours in rooms just chatting?' she asks. 'I can take it for half an hour but then my feet hurt, I'm bored of making chit-chat and I'm desperate to leave.' The answer is that if you drink a bit, it becomes fun. Just as people say some dance music is only worth listening to if you take Ecstasy, so the vast majority of our socialising is only viable if you take the edge off your nerves/perceptions/inhibitions/foot-ache with booze.

I find this an unsettling thought. I don't like to think of myself as dependent on a chemical – I can potter around working, watching TV, going to the cinema, etc., perfectly happily without either drinking or getting the shakes – but there's no way I'm ever getting through a wedding without several glasses of wine. Only that will sustain me through chit-chat with someone's humourless Canadian cousin, or them through chit-chat with me. The link between drinking and being able to confidently socialise, feeling ready and in the mood for chatting, is hard-wired in me and I think those particular cerebral electrics were installed at Cambridge with friends like Ellis when I learned to love the pub.

And it gave me great joy. At Cambridge, I became a happier, more relaxed, more jolly person. I didn't manage to stay like that forever, but neither have I quite returned to the levels of angst I felt before university. When I think of my first year there, I am tremendously warmed by remembering my sense of relief – things felt like they were going to be all right. It was okay, suddenly, to be slapdash, to screw things up, to get up late, to fail to write essays, to be imperfect and fun-loving.

Love of theatre, comedy and acting was part of what lightened my mood, but the fun of talking shit and drinking too much was a big part of it as well. Booze is a complicated issue in our society and in lots of people's lives. There are many occasions on which I've drunk more than I should and I wish I could live some of them again and behave differently. But I don't regret being a boozy student: it didn't stop me doing other things, it was fun, and I befriended people I still love going to the pub with today.

Besides, when I got to Cambridge, I'd had a stressful few years. I needed a drink.

- 21 -

Attention

I need pants. I've needed pants for some time but now it's getting critical. A lot of them are 'rogue' pairs now – basically just waistbands with some cloth hanging down, not really doing whatever pants are supposed to do that justifies not washing trousers nearly as often, and also increasing the likelihood of a penis or bollock becoming noticeable in a trousers-down scenario.

When I say 'trousers-down scenario', I'm less worried about a sexual one (where the visibility of penis or testicles is probably on the agenda anyway – though it's embarrassing to be clothed in rags) than about costume fittings or changes while filming. When you're making a sketch show, you're forever being helped from one awkward outfit into the next, and the good people who are there to deal with hooks, zips and buttons shouldn't have to avert their eyes to avoid a genital glimpse. In so many areas of my work, all my clothes are provided apart from pants, and yet it seems that even maintaining a supply of those is beyond me.

My collection of pants is now about fifty per cent rogue, and almost all of the 'good' pants, ones for special occasions or stressful days when you want to feel that everything is in order, are deteriorating into 'okay' pairs, while most of those are wearing down towards 'rogue'. There's sort of a tipping point: when you've only got three or four pairs you're properly happy with left, they get worn and washed so much that the rate of their decline is vastly increased.

There's an obvious solution to this problem, so I turn left off Wigmore Street, down Orchard Street, towards it: Marks and Spencer. One of the two big ones on Oxford Street. I know it's a cliché that everyone gets their pants from Marks and Spencer but, as far as I'm concerned, it's also a fact. I don't know if they do good or bad pants, as I have never compared them to those available anywhere else and think that it would be a vanity to do so – although I do have one pair from John Lewis which I was given by a costume lady after a sketch involving my getting doused in fake cream had put my own pair beyond use.

I hadn't known John Lewis did pants and I'm confused by the fact that they do. Where's the market? I would have thought that the kind of middle English conventional attitude, expecting quality but shunning showiness, that is the hallmark of a John Lewis customer would lead inexorably to buying pants at Marks. Marks and Spencer's is the John Lewis equivalent for pants. But those who shun the Marks-pants-buying societal rule are surely unlikely to seek their alternative at the High Street's other citadel of conventionality? That would be like a rebellious son of a Baptist minister running away to join the Methodists. Anyway, I find the waistband on my John Lewis pants slightly annoying and frankly consider that to be the least inconvenience I deserve for owning them.

Am I really going to be able to buy pants? Marks looks quite busy. Maybe that's good – I'll blend in with the crowd. But what if I get recognised, while I'm holding pants? I'd be terribly self-conscious. I'd look all embarrassed, which would make things worse. People might laugh, because I'm a comedian – I'd be a comedian holding pants, which must be hard-wired into the British psyche as a scenario in which laughter is expected. But that would be being laughed *at*, having accidentally elicited a laugh, one I wasn't in control of. What if someone asks for a photo? I couldn't say no – but there I'd be, holding my pants. It would be up on Twitter in seconds – me all embarrassed, my choice of underwear being analysed by well-meaning thousands. 'Pants' would instantly be the first word that came up after my name when you typed it into Google.

I should have bought them on the internet, but that relies on being able to hear my doorbell, which I can't. That's because door-bells all need batteries these days rather than being wired into the mains. And, unlike smoke alarms, the new doorbells don't start making warning beeps when they're running out of power. To be fair, that would be confusing because you'd keep thinking someone was at the door. As it is, my flatmate and I just assumed nobody ever came to see us any more, until we realised the batteries had run out and, so far, we've failed to replace them. So buying pants on the internet would mean in effect sending money to some strangers for some pants to be moved from their warehouse to the Post Office one, while my scrotum continues to abrade its way through to the inner corduroy.

I think most people hope, when buying pants, or condoms, pile cream or even loo roll, that they don't bump into someone they know – some professional acquaintance in front of whom they want to come across well. If you're on TV, the chances of a slightly mortifying encounter are massively increased, as anyone who recognises you is effectively just such an acquaintance, and the moment of your meeting will be all the more memorable if you're doing something embarrassing (I imagine that's why so many celebs get into scrapes with brothels – it's so awkward trying to sign auto-graphs when your cock's in someone's mouth). And in the camera-phone and internet age, everyone is equipped to record and broadcast the awkward moment in seconds, leaving an indelible, searchable record of the frail humanity of any poor sod with a DVD out. In self-pitying moods, I feel like the iPhone, Twitter, Facebook and the battery-operated doorbell are all conspiring to make this the worst time in history to become famous.

I don't want to turn into someone who has ceased to live a normal life – who won't take the Tube in a normal way, shop normally for pants, go and get a normal haircut, quite normally pay a hooker to fellate me – but I'm so self-conscious about it, maybe the battle is lost? It doesn't count if I'm bloody-mindedly still getting the Tube as a sort of performance – I've only properly kept my feet on the ground if I find it a useful means of transport which I get on without thinking about it. 'Without thinking about it' is the key phrase. I hardly do anything without thinking about it.

I know I asked for this, though. At Cambridge, I almost literally asked for it. One of the things I wanted was to be famous. And I wasn't ashamed to say it, which I am now ashamed to say. I must have sounded like a contestant on *Britain's Got Talent*. I wanted to be a famous comedian and actor on TV, I said. And first I wanted to be famous within Cambridge, in that odd way a student can be. I was aware that the president of the Union Society, the Marlowe Society or the Amateur Dramatic Club, the editor of *Varsity* and the various student union officials all had status within the university – were talked about, envied and tipped for success. I wanted that, both because it appealed to my vanity and because such status seemed like the closest you could get to securing future employment – particularly if you'd utterly given up on getting a 2:1.

And the position I wanted more than any of those, the one that seemed to bring status, artistic acclaim and glorious if unnerving historical associations, was president of Footlights. My time at Cambridge, however academically disappointing, surely couldn't be deemed a failure if I got myself onto the list of people who'd held that office.

It sounds like a feeble ambition to me now – largely because I've long since both realised it and realised that it didn't matter. Anyway, there were only really two people who were considered for the job in my year: me and Matthew Holness. I think we were both deemed funny, but I was thought to be better at admin. I probably was better at admin, to be honest. So he was made vice-president.

When I say it didn't matter, I don't mean that Footlights didn't matter. Doing shows, learning how to write sketches by trial and error, making friends of like mind – these things were all massively fun and hugely important to my future career. But it didn't matter who was nominally in charge of the club. I think I had an inkling at the time that it wasn't really as crucial as I felt it to be – but then I thought, and this reasoning still holds good: 'Well, maybe it doesn't make much difference, but it can't *hurt*.' And a certain amount of university-wide status definitely came with the job title and I'm afraid I liked that.

Here's a moment that gives an insight into the darker parts of my soul. At the ADC Theatre, if you signed up on a list to tear audience tickets at the door, you could see the show for free. On one occasion in my third year, when I was a reasonably big cheese on the small cheeseboard of Cambridge drama, I was doing this job with Jon Taylor, an actor, writer and future coiner of the term 'FRP', who'd graduated the previous summer but had popped back for the weekend. It was the interval and we were standing in the bar in our theatre T-shirts drinking a couple of pints which, strictly speaking, we weren't supposed to do on duty. But, you know, everyone did. We weren't flying a fucking airliner.

Anyway, a stranger came up to me and said: 'You're not supposed to drink if you're doing front of house, but maybe those rules don't apply to *you*,' and walked off. Jon was furious on my behalf.

'It's so unfair,' he said. 'I can't stand the injustice of it. Why does he assume it's favouritism? Everyone has a drink at the interval. *I'm* having one – but he didn't know who I am so he didn't criticise!'

My reaction was different. I was delighted.

'But can't you see how *envious* he was?' I said. I was basking in the back-handed compliment that the insult ill concealed. This guy seemed to think everything was different for me – that I was privileged, a VIP, sailing unchallenged through the world. If enough people bitterly assumed that to be the case, it might become true. I liked the feeling of being lucky in a stranger's eyes – my revenge for his unpleasantness was the resentment I suspected he felt.

What a little shit I was! I don't feel like that any more. I've come to recognise that other people's envy, and related anger, is a nasty thing – for them, but also for me. I don't think it's politic to come across as too much of a jammy sod. But I try to recapture that attitude occasionally, when I read hurtful internet comments, for example. In the aggression, the insults, the nastiness, there is envy for the job I've got and the life they assume I lead. Well, anyone who calls me a cunt without even having met me can wallow in that envy, as far as I'm concerned.

But a stranger's envy wasn't my only ill-gotten gain from meaningless office. I had my first experience of a groupie. It was after a Footlights performance; we were having a few drinks and a very attractive girl in a little black dress introduced herself, struck up a conversation and basically threw herself at me. I was quite drunk, she was very sexy and had kindly obviated the need for me to make any kind of approach to her (which, you'll know by now, was not my style), and soon we were snogging outside, with my hand discovering the enormously exciting fact that she was actually wearing stockings and had no objection to my investigating that. I'm not sure which of my series of doomed infatuations was obsessing me at that point, but this was an extremely effective distraction.

I don't remember much about that night – because I was drunk, not because it blurs in with the myriad of other, similar encounters. I remember going back to her room. I remember having to go off and perform a sketch in a late-night revue at the ADC. I stumbled onto the stage, just about spat my lines out, got the giggles, finished the sketch and then hurried back to her. And I remember, quite clearly, forming the impression early on in the evening that the main reason she'd been attracted to me was that I was president of Footlights. I was one of the 'famous' people in the university and, because of that, she liked the idea of having got off with me. And, do you know what? I didn't mind that at all. I was turned on by it. That status was something I valued and was proud of, so it seemed reasonable, complimentary even, that someone else should value it in me. This office, this job title, was, to my mind, the closest I could get to a proof of achievement – to having something to show for a string of successful but fleeting attempts to amuse students. So, if she found that attractive, it was fine by me.

It all felt terribly exciting. The next day it all felt terribly terrible. I was consumed by embarrassment and guilt and I didn't really know why. I somehow felt as though I'd taken advantage of her. I didn't *think* that – I knew it had all been her idea, even if I hadn't taken much persuading – but that's how I felt. I also didn't want to see her ever again and felt guilty about that. Half of my brain felt that she must now think I was loathsome or ridiculous; the other half was scared that she might now want to be my girlfriend, the thought of which utterly appalled me. Not because she wasn't perfectly nice but, I suppose, because she wasn't perfect – unlike whoever it was I was hung up on at that point. The thought of having been intimate with someone I didn't really know and, in the cold light of day, wasn't particularly keen on, was excruciating. And I knew I couldn't explain that to her. Of course I was wrong in thinking I'd have to. But I couldn't shake the horrible sensation of having been dishonest and unfair.

I've had a few one-night stands since – not many but a few – and I've always felt the same. I've always deeply regretted it but never been quite sure why. I don't think I've ever been nasty or unfair – I think that in every case the encounter was embraced in a mutually casual spirit by both parties. And in every case I've thought in advance: 'Why not? You're single. This is what people do.' And I've thought, while it was happening: 'This is great.' And then afterwards I've *hated* myself. Hated the thought that I'd behaved differently because I was drunk, hated the fake shared intimacy of sex with a stranger.

Still, I'll never forget sliding my hand above her stocking – that was a good bit.

Back in my first year at Cambridge, I wasn't yet president of Footlights; if women were going to let me touch their arses, it was down to my rugged good looks and smooth chat-up lines alone. So I had plenty of spare time for comedy. Unfortunately Footlights seemed to have had enough of me for the moment. After the pantomime, the next big Footlights show of the academic year is the Spring Revue in the middle of the Lent (spring) term. This is a sketch show made up of new material written by the cast, director and other prominent Footlighters. It usually has a cast of about eight, of whom five or six will go on to be in the May Week Revue, Footlights' main show of the year which goes on national tour and to the Edinburgh Fringe.

Having been in *Cinderella*, I fell at the second hurdle – I wasn't cast in the Spring Revue. This was the decision, and by 'decision' I mean fault, of Tristram Hunt, the director of the show and now MP for Stoke-on-Trent Central. I was incredibly disappointed and slightly bitter about this at the time, but it was a perfectly fair call. There were lots of funny people around, and it was unusual for a first-year to be in a Footlights revue (although of course Collie was, talented cow). So I have long since dropped any grievance I had against Tristram – and I'm a slow grievance dropper. He was a tremendously enthusiastic, energetic and irreverent influence on Footlights, certainly never pegged by me as a future TV historian, serious opinion former and democratic representative of the Midlands. But I will say that he passed up the opportunity to have my undying gratitude.

I had to make do with appearing in normal plays: in the Lent term, I played Dr Rance in *What the Butler Saw* and the Reverend Parris in *The Crucible* and even helped out as assistant stage manager for *Into the Woods*, which mainly involved pushing a wooden cow on and off stage (I am not referring to an inexpressive and truculent actress). Boring though that was, the excuse to hang around the theatre even more was irresistible.

But I was obsessed with Footlights and desperately wanted to break back in – and I knew the key to that was writing and performing my own material. I'd written some sketches at school

– Leo, Harry, Daniel, Ed and I spent several months pretending we were going to do a sketch show, amassed reams of material, and then very sensibly decided to put on a production of *Ten Times Table* by Alan Ayckbourn instead. On closer inspection, the reams of material, certainly the ones I'd written, were unusable shit. My approach had been to take a potentially comic situation – say the boardroom of an old company – populate it with comic stereotypes and then make them converse for page after page. I must have been watching *You Rang, M'Lud* at the time. It was uncomfortably close to the technique I'd used to write that playscript fantasy epic in front of the TV as a child. The sketches were very long and had no point to them, no premise. Clearly I needed a completely different approach.

Though not a cast member, I was invited to help write for the Spring Revue. The Footlights writing system was straightforward and ruthlessly effective. The writing team would meet at eleven in the morning for a general chat about the sort of material that was needed. Then we would divide up into pairs who would go off for an hour or so, write a sketch or maybe even two, and return at an appointed time to read them out. This process would be repeated in the afternoon. If you do that for a couple of weeks, you'll generate quite a large pile of material from which to construct a show.

This system may sound plodding and uncreative, but I am a big admirer of it (or should that be 'so I'm a big admirer of it'?). In my experience, if you want to write comedy, you just have to get on with it. You have to crash through the invisible barrier caused by the combination of the vast sense of possibility – a sketch could be about anything, could be the wackiest, most surreal, yet most satirical, wide-ranging, specific, general, flippant, profound piece of material ever written – and the terrifying, narrowing, diminishing feeling caused by scratching the first inadequate words of it onto a sheet of A4. As soon as you start to write, you also start to close doors (metaphorical ones as well as the one to the shop where the sketch is inevitably set). The new sketch emerges and obviously isn't the next 'Parrot Sketch' or 'One Leg Too Few' but just today's effort, something that'll do.

There's no point in resisting that or being ashamed of it. Brilliance will strike you, if it ever does, as a complete surprise sailing out of the clear blue sky of competence. The key is to get stuff written down, and this Footlights system forces you to. It gives you a simple, achievable task – writing a sketch in an hour – and a friend to do it with. It doesn't have to be funny, it just has to be written. You can write a funny one in the afternoon or the next day, you tell yourself – your task in any given moment is not to go back empty-handed. Great sketches come out of that approach, as well as unusable ones. But, most precious of all, it produces sketches that aren't good enough but have the kernel of a good idea which someone else, later in the process, can often turn into something better. When that happens, you're genuinely mobilising the creative power of a team.

The best stuff generated by this system went into the show, but anything you wrote that was left over, you were free to use yourself – which meant you could audition it for a 'smoker'. That's the name Footlights gives its informal late-night performances. A contraction of 'smoking concerts', in the old days smokers were cabaret nights watched exclusively by cigar-smoking men in dinner jackets. By the early '90s, they were under-rehearsed one-night-only comedy shows made up of songs, sketches, character monologues and stand-up, where smoking was no longer allowed but women were. They played to packed houses of drunken and easily-amused students.

The first big roar for a joke you've written yourself is the best laugh you'll ever get in your life, the rest of which you spend trying to recapture it. It's a transformative moment. You are redeemed from your own personal hell and launched into the firmament. There you are, a foolhardy unoriginal idiot who's engineered a situation where hundreds of people are sitting looking at you, expecting you to say something so good that it will make them spontaneously and simultaneously emit noises of amusement. It felt doable before you wrote the sketch; it felt possible afterwards; in rehearsal there were moments when it felt likely. But in the two hours preceding the performance, it has gradually dawned on you that, of course, it's impossible – particularly with the irredeemably unfunny piece of material you've perversely saddled yourself with. You've watched all the other acts, many of which have gone well, and thought of each of them: 'Of course! That's the sort of thing to do! A sketch using the word fuck, some stand-up about wanking, that mad thing about a man with a dog called Fisticuffs who keeps getting into scrapes.' But not *your* thing – not your stupid, risky, obscure, uninventive piece of nothing.

And then it works! The joke works! They get it, they laugh loudly, you can feel their warmth, their appreciation. They like you – it's like a Vitamin B shot of confidence to your whole system.

My first smoker sketch was about the Samaritans, I'm not particularly proud to say. There've been lots of sketches about the Samaritans so I wasn't at any great risk of originality. Then again, in my defence, putting an organisation with associations of people in despair, who are possibly suicidal, into an overtly comic scenario is a pretty solid approach. You get the credit for being daring and edgy, in a context where you're not in much danger of causing offence.

The sketch, which I'd written with a friend from college, Robin Koerner, opened in a risky way laugh-wise. A man (me) is on the phone (probably because the Alan Bennett sketch I'd read out to audition for the panto was on the phone and it had gone well, so I was trying to recapture that success) saying something like this:

MAN: *(on phone, in a dry unconcerned way)* Oh. Oh. Yes. Oh dear. Yes, I see. Oh dear. Well, yes, I should go ahead then. Yes, absolutely. I can see why you would. Yes, I completely understand your position. I'd do that, if I were you. Yes. All right then. Bye then. Bye bye.

He puts the phone down. It rings.

By this point, as comedy connoisseurs will realise, nothing funny has been said. To be honest, I think the man talking into the phone went on even longer than that but I can't remember it. Anyway, there hasn't been a joke. Maybe I've got a couple of warm titters of expectation, maybe not. The joke is coming up. Having told you the subject of the sketch, you've probably anticipated it. So I hope you can imagine my stress levels, my intense concern at this instant, as I sat under a bright light in front of a couple of hundred people, twenty seconds into my first ever performance of something I'd written. Suddenly there's nowhere to hide – they either laugh at the next line or the sketch has been a disaster. There'll be no redeeming it, no winning them round. It's all or nothing. Not all sketches are all or nothing, you know. You can have material that slowly wins people round and doesn't stand or fall on one surprising moment. And I knew it at the time. So why had I decided to debut with one that does? Because I am a stupid cunt, I thought in my whirring, self-loathing, idiot's brain as I tried to time the next bit of the sketch:

He answers the phone.
MAN:　　　　　Hello, Samaritans.

Massive laugh.

I know it's not the best joke in the world, but it worked – I promise you it really worked. The satisfaction of having made an audience think backwards and laugh at the fact that the character had been casually advocating suicide was immense – of having taken a punt, reasoned that people might find something funny and been proved right. I can't remember any of the jokes from the rest of the sketch but I'll never forget that moment.

It was my laugh – I'd thought of the joke, I'd written it down, I'd learned it and I'd delivered it. This is just the best thing in the world, I thought. I want to do this again.

Mitchell and Webb

'Bread for the ducks, nice to get ooooouuuuuttttt!' Rob and I sang, to the tune of the 'Eton Boating Song' – desperately but also with a tinge of relief because that was one of the few lyrics we were confident on. Somehow the crowd sensed that and laughed. But was that why they were laughing? No, we were somehow out of sync with the music – it was ahead of us, or behind us. Only now was it doing the 'Nice to get oooouuuttttt!' bit, so we sang that again. And the audience laughed, screamed, howled.

Now we couldn't hear the backing track at all. I was supposed to sing the next verse. I think it was something else about a duck – I'd known it earlier this afternoon, but my brain couldn't multi-task to this extent. I was simultaneously trying to listen through the screams of audience mockery for the moment to come in, remember the hastily learned lyrics, compose my features into a look other than that of absolute bafflement and defeat, and work out whether the fact that we were getting laughs was basically good news, or whether our having completely lost control of why we were getting them undermined the achievement entirely and disqualified us from taking any credit.

This was the first night of *Innocent Millions Dead or Dying – A Wry Look at the Post-Apocalyptic Age (With Songs)*, the first two-man show I performed with Robert Webb. It was a late show at the ADC and, by mid-afternoon of the day we were to open, panic was setting in. We'd just remembered that we needed props. Usually, in shows, someone sorts out all the props. What we'd just discovered was that, for that to happen, someone else has to ask them. A low point had been during the technical rehearsal when Ellis had popped in to see how we were getting on and said:

'Yeah, you've got a bit of work to do, chaps.'

Ellis had said that. The personification of the 'it'll all be fine – let's just kick back and get pissed' approach. He had a look in his eye of concern, but also of respect. 'These guys,' he was thinking, 'have managed to fuck themselves even more royally than I could have done in their place.'

All was not lost, though. We were thanking our lucky stars that we'd been too disorganised to put any posters up, because we reckoned that would cancel out our having been too disorganised to learn our lines or rehearse the show. A handful of mates might turn up and we could do a sort of open rehearsal in front of them – it was all going to feel very casual and relaxed, a work in progress. That's what we hoped.

But, no, the theatre was almost full. This was unheard-of for a late show other than a Footlights smoker. There was nowhere to hide. Except the wings. Which would leave the stage bare. Which would mean they'd ask for their money back – and we were both secretly totting up the amount of money we stood to make and what that bought in Kronenbourg. Backstage beforehand, we listened to the auditorium filling up excitedly and were conscious of a huge opportunity that we were about to screw up.

'But what's going on?' you may be asking if you're in the habit of talking to books. 'A minute ago you were doing a short and derivative sketch taking the piss out of people so unhappy they want to kill themselves. Now you're fucking up a show with Robert Webb. What happened in between?'

I'll tell you. The genesis of this flawed theatrical creation, or conception of this sickly comic child or the botched laser surgery behind this fuzzy humorous vision, had occurred six months earlier.

When we were both in Edinburgh for the 1994 Fringe, Rob asked me if I wanted to do a show with him. Rob was one of the stars of that year's Footlights tour show, *The Barracuda Jazz Option*, and I was there in a play called *Colin*, written by Charlie Hartill, the new Footlights president and starring Robert Thorogood, the old one. I was just a lowly first-year but I found the whole presidential vibe very exciting and hoped it augured well for me.

As a play, *Colin* was fine but nothing special. It was about a man called Colin, but the main reason it was called *Colin* was because the writer-performers of the previous year's Footlights tour had been prevented from calling their show *Colin* by ... well, the story goes that it was the tour manager and the techies, but I don't really believe that as, in my experience of Footlights, the tour manager and techies were never consulted over the name of the show. I suspect it was the director and then the tour manager and techies agreed. The view was that you 'can't' call a show *Colin* – the joke that Colin is more usually a name for a human or pet than a comedy revue would not come across. So the show had been called *Some Wood and a Pie* instead. How bizarre that *Some Wood and a Pie* is deemed a sensible, apposite, appropriately wacky name for a sketch show but *Colin* is seen to be taking the piss – but not taking the piss in a good way. Taking too much, or the wrong sort, of piss.

I'm not sure that the joke of calling a sketch show *Colin* would have worked – but jokes in show titles seldom do. They're hilarious when you think of them and then they get printed on everything and read constantly and have the mickey taken out of them by hostile reviewers, and the joke slowly and painfully dies while you helplessly listen to its screams – like a fridge-magnet joke, impaled there by physics, miserably catching your eye every time you go for the milk, losing its humour at a hundred times the rate that the natural light can bleach the writing.

But *Some Wood and a Pie* is a *terrible* name for a comedy show. It reeks of unthinking, artless, unjustifiably self-confident wackiness – the very thing that Footlights is always accused of and should be doing everything it can to distance itself from. It's an off-the-shelf kind of revue title; the people who insisted on it must have thought that (even if it wasn't amusing) it was safe, a usual sort of comedy name. But audience members or reviewers will assume that the writer-performers think it's funny – not just appropriate but actually comical. They'll imagine those young people pissing themselves at the hilarious randomness of 'Some Wood' and 'a Pie', these two unconnected things, ho ho ho, how simply *mad* – and consequently hate them. That's not the end of the world – some people will hate you whatever you do, particularly if you're an enthusiastic Oxbridge student, but they might as well hate you for something you actually find funny, not something that you think is a bit of a lame compromise.

Calling the show *Colin* at least would have had an idea behind it. People might not get it but there's something to get. I think it would work better if they'd given it a surname – called it *Colin Jenkins* or even *Mr Jenkins*. But it would definitely have been preferable to *Some Wood and a Pie*.

You may wonder why I've got so much to say about the controversy over the naming of a Footlights show I was never in and didn't see. It's because I think it's illustrative of an interesting and maddening phenomenon in creative circles: fundamentally unentertaining people trying to make things like other things that have gone before. They believe that properly creative people, who actually have ideas, will try and drag a project off track. So, a student sketch show should have a wacky name, a TV programme should begin with the host saying: 'This is the show in which ...' and then summarising the format, a pop song should be three minutes long, people will be more entertained by daytime TV if the presenters constantly use puns, a TV detective should always have an assistant who relentlessly questions his judgement and books should be described on their covers as 'rollercoasters'.

Conventions like these are clung to and defended by people who have no real ideas of their own, and lack the self-knowledge to forge careers using other skills such as their efficiency, diplomacy or application. They want to make things that are like other things – to 'play shop', which means you've got to have a till and a brown coat and a counter with a shelf of tins behind it like in real shops. When they hear something that diverges from that – say a series of aisles with all the produce and then a bank of checkouts where people pay – they instinctively oppose it because they can seldom tell the difference between a properly original piece of thinking and a mad divergence from sensible practice. As in this case. There is no earthly reason to consider *Some Wood and a Pie* more appropriate than *Colin* as a name for a random collection of sketches – but one title has an unsettling air of originality which this type of person shrinks from, apparently without realising that such originality is where comedy comes from and therefore exactly what they should be attracted to.

Charlie Hartill was a man very much of my mind in this regard, and called his own play *Colin* as a sort of revenge on the dullards who overruled the comedians the previous year. (Of course, it was a completely hollow revenge. The play was about a man called Colin. The title wasn't off-kilter at all. The *Some Wood and a Pie* advocates would have been fine with it. If he'd really wanted to rattle their cages, he'd have called it *Some Wood and a Pie*.)

Unfortunately it was a pretty patchy play. It had some good bits, some good lines, some nice characterisation, but the story didn't really cut the mustard. My main memory of it is a scene where, while the hero is talking or doing some work or somehow otherwise engaged, my character, an argumentative, tweedy man, reaches into his inside pocket and removes a large battered sausage which he then proceeds to eat. We'd hoped people would laugh at this more than they did.

But Charlie was a talented man, albeit one who combined moments of frightening drive and intensity with long periods where he lost focus. He could be very funny in an angry, analytical way, which influenced me enormously. I remember his doing a long analysis, as part of a stand-up routine, of the rhyme 'See a penny, pick it up and all the day you'll have good luck' which ended with him emphatically saying: 'And a penny isn't worth making yourself blind for, is it?' I can't recall how he got there but it involved dog shit.

As president of Footlights, he could be withering in the face of incompetence. Rob told me of an occasion at a production meeting for the 1994 Footlights pantomime *Dick Whittington*, to which Charlie arrived late to find an argument going on. He interrupted everyone, saying, 'What is the problem? I shall solve it instantly' – and then did.

Charlie adopted a lot of his managerial technique from his mentor Christopher Richardson, who founded and ran The Pleasance, an all-conquering Edinburgh Fringe venue where Charlie had a summer job. My favourite quotation attributed to Christopher Richardson, said in the context of a technical rehearsal in a theatre, is: 'I find these inexplicable delays intensely depressing.' If I were the sort of person who got phrases printed on T-shirts, that's what I'd go for. It so perfectly encapsulates my feelings for about 60 per cent of the time I spend working in theatres, television studios or on location, where getting up early and then waiting around for hours is the order of the day. It's also a fairly appropriate general response to life.

Charlie Hartill wrote plays and sketches, performed stand-up, acted, was a brilliant designer of posters and programmes, organised the Pleasance computer system and was a director of the Edinburgh Fringe for eight years. He was often an inspiring leader for Footlights and he was an intensely loyal friend. Sadly, that was only one side of him. The other was dominated by an unfathomable anger and unhappiness that were the root of his less impressive and dependable periods of behaviour, his heavy drinking and ultimately his suicide in 2004.

Charlie and I were both fans of John Buchan novels, both for the exciting plots and the slightly laughable boys-own adventure style. After a mixed run at Edinburgh for *Colin*, in which Charlie had been by turns fun, funny, supportive, irritable, busy, absent and drunk, he wasn't my favourite person in the world. Then, soon after the end of the Fringe, he gave me a beautifully preserved copy of John Buchan's autobiography in which he'd written, rather formally: 'To David Mitchell, With gratitude and fond memory for Colin! Charlie Hartill' – and I forgave him all. I treasure it and yet it's probably the saddest object I own, reminding me not just of Charlie's death but of the times when his behaviour led me to resent or avoid him, not realising the time limit on our friendship. The book's title is *Memory Hold the Door*.

The Edinburgh run of *Colin* was a slightly muted end to my first year as a theatre-obsessed student. While the Festival itself was a dazzling event, the reality of trying to sell a mediocre show starring nobody anyone had heard of was even more of an uphill struggle than the sweaty walk across Edinburgh from the flat to the Pleasance. We sold a respectable number of tickets but, having spent the year playing to full ADC houses of enthusiastic students in *Noises Off* and *What the Butler Saw*, doing some patchy new writing in front of fifteen indifferent punters was an anticlimax.

But when Rob asked me to do a show with him, it more than made up for that. I was incredibly excited. He popped the question in the Pleasance bar on a very drunken night which ended with my having a long row with Richard Herring about Eric Morecambe. Richard Herring had come over to say that he'd enjoyed Rob's performance in the Footlights show and we'd got talking and I was hammered. I'm not sure how the subject of Eric Morecambe came up, though I fear that I probably introduced it. My feelings of insecurity about the Edinburgh comedy world, on which I was dismayed not to have immediately made an impact, led me to be dismissive of it. These transient stars of the Fringe are nothing compared to the great treasures of the golden age of television, I thought bitterly. 'You can't beat Eric Morecambe' was basically my argument.

Richard Herring didn't refute this, but contended that other sorts of comedy were also valid. I'm afraid that line of reasoning was slightly too sophisticated for me after so many lagers and I became incensed and basically accused Richard of saying he was funnier than Eric Morecambe. Eventually Richard managed to extricate himself. I should have apologised when I saw him at the Pleasance the next day, but to do so would have been too much of a tacit admission about my own behaviour. It was many years before I was comfortable admitting even to myself what a dick I must have seemed to him. Having worked with Richard on several occasions since, and always found him a very nice and funny guy, I hope he's never made the connection between me now and some spotty kid who had a drunken go at him in Edinburgh 1994. If he has, he's a very forgiving man.

Despite my embarrassing him in front of someone off the telly only minutes after our double act was formed, Rob remained willing to stick with the plan of doing a show with me. And I was hyper-keen. Rob was a Footlights committee member, star of the tour show and the next year's vice-president. Doing a show with him meant I'd arrived.

My own credentials, for a first-year, weren't bad. I'd been in the panto, taken part in smokers and written material for both the Spring Revue and the tour show – including the worst sketch they performed. This was an item entitled 'Most Feet Competition', the details of which you can probably make a reasonably accurate guess at. I felt that I was unlucky to have written the worst sketch in the show. The material was chosen from a huge pile, so to be the worst that made the cut it had to be well above the average standard of what was written. Yet, because it wasn't great but had to be performed dozens of times, the cast *hated* it, while they fondly remembered worse items that failed to make the cut at all, and consequently didn't die a death every night at the Wimborne Theatre.

I had also organised my own sketch show, *Go to Work on an Egg*, with Robert Hudson (now a novelist and my flatmate) and a few others. It had gone down very well. I, if not gorged, at least heavily snacked on that joyous sensation of getting a laugh from my own material which I'd felt at my first smoker.

One of the sketches in that show was the first thing I ever wrote with Rob, entitled 'War Farce'. We'd written it for the tour show but the director, Mark Evans, had refused to include it on the basis that it was terrible. Nevertheless I foisted it on the *Go to Work on an Egg* team because of its glamorous associations with a member of the Footlights committee. Rob had come to see the show and ('War Farce' apart) pronounced it very amusing and congratulated me in a meaningful way which, what with Rob's whole metrosexual earring-wearing schtick, a man more sexually and less comedically confident than I might have taken as a come-on. But I knew it meant he thought I was funny, in a way that he hadn't particularly in *Cinderella*. Aglow with the triumphs of such sketches as 'Date Date', 'Librarian' and 'Use Them as Trestles', I knew that he was right.

And now he was suggesting we write a whole show together! We didn't start work for a few months after that, during which time I was able to narrow the gap a bit between me and my glamorous comedy senior. Most of the old Footlights committee had graduated; only Rob, Charlie and Tristram were still around, so Matthew Holness and I were quickly co-opted to organise smokers, reel in freshers and hold panto auditions. I realised how green Rob must have been feeling when I'd met him at the *Cinderella* recall audition a year before, and had an important epiphany: 'knowing what you're doing' largely involves pretending to know what you're doing. Or, at least, it does in showbusiness. I choose to believe that it isn't like that with surgery or nuclear power.

Alongside these exciting new responsibilities, I played Mr Worthy in Ellis's shit production of *The Recruiting Officer* and wrote a musical with Ellis and Adam Cork (a brilliant and now Tony Award-winning composer) called *Stud* in which I also acted. (I didn't play the title role.) And in the panto that year, Rob and I were the leads, playing Dick Whittington and his cat respectively.

We didn't really know how to write our own two-man show, which, in retrospect, was a good thing. We didn't, for example, start writing self-contained two-man sketches, which would have led to a stop-start show with too many blackouts. Neither did we approach it in the sort of two-man stand-uppy way of which I'd seen a lot around that time – where the two men address the audience alternately along a theme such as 'A History of Love' or 'A Guide to Being a Dick'. We just sat down and started a silly story. It was about a Victorian inventor and a semi-alcoholic rustic programmer travelling through time to try and foil the apocalyptic ambitions of a crazed Welsh super-computer.

This was to be how all the stage shows of our early career were formatted. Pairs of characters would talk to each other, hopefully in a funny way, and then separate. Another pair of characters would do the same. Then maybe another. Then they'd start to mix pairings, in a way that was obviously limited by who was playing which character. Only by cheesy theatrical sleight of hand could anyone Rob played ever meet anyone else Rob played. We milked these limitations for laughs. As the show progressed and our stupid, often James Bond-style plot became dafter, any consequent slackening in audience interest could be made up for by the frequency, speed and desperation of our costume changes. The story didn't have to be gripping if they were entertained by the sight of us frantically trying to tell it with inadequate resources.

To put it another way, it's funny when people fuck up. That's what we learned in our first attempt – the *Innocent Millions* debacle. From memory, we *occasionally* got a laugh from a pre-written joke, but largely our desperate attempt to struggle through the story and be wearing the right costume at the right time was what the audience were enjoying. At the end, they clapped and cheered like they'd properly enjoyed it. It felt like we'd done something good.

We learned a lot that night, some of which did us good. We learned that we worked well together as performers – that we were somehow greater than the sum of our parts. We learned that an audience wants to hear jokes or be told a funny story by people they're enjoying watching and that not much else about a comedy show matters – that sometimes it's okay, as Mr Sleigh at New College School tried to tell me, for the giant rabbit to take its mittens off. And we learned that our approach to writing material was basically sound.

But some of the other lessons we took from that night were harmful. However often we told ourselves in the years to come that rehearsing wasn't just for pussies – and that this year, finally, we were going to take a slick and professional show up to Edinburgh – neither of us could quite shake our infatuation with winging it. We knew that hard work and professionalism were important in the career we'd chosen – and yet we couldn't forget the first night of *Innocent Millions* when we'd wandered on stage with only the barest clue of what we were doing and it had gone down brilliantly.

- 23 -

We Said We Wouldn't Look Back

I don't get pants in the end. I go in there. I negotiate my way through the massive shop, avoiding getting stuck like Father Ted in the lingerie section, and find the bit where men's pants are on sale – beside massive photos of toned stomachs above snow-white-panted wholesome genital shapes. But there are lots of people and a massive queue, so I leave again. I hope someone isn't murdered in there around now. I mean, I hope that in general, but I particularly hope it because there'll be CCTV of me 'behaving suspiciously' – in both senses of the phrase. The police would be suspicious of a man walking into a department store, hanging around watchfully for a few moments and then disappearing. In fact, I only left because I myself was suspicious – unsettled by my surroundings, worried that I might be observed or even laughed at as I attempted to obtain the wherewithal to conceal my balls from work colleagues. 'There's nothing suspicious about it,' I'd say. 'It's just that I was suspicious so I left.'

Now I'm walking west down the scuzzy end of Oxford Street towards Marble Arch. This is the route the condemned were taken when public executions were held at Tyburn Tree, more or less where Marble Arch is now. It's a cold corner, busy in a threatening way, like the parts of London round railway stations: there are burger joints and overflowing bins and bureaux de change, multi-lane traffic and a couple of monolithic hotels, the Cumberland and the Thistle which, though large, lack the opulence of the Park Lane hotels stretching to the south. Not happy places to stay – just hundreds of cubicles of necessity from which to look out on the ceaseless traffic.

Better that than the subways under Marble Arch, though – built to facilitate access between traffic islands, pavements, Hyde Park and the Tube station but, for decades now, an icy concrete home for the homeless. A place of mouldering mattresses and shifting piles of cloth in which the desperate are seeking rest.

As a child and teenager, this was my entry point to London, where the coach from Oxford let you out. It felt dangerous and hostile and it frightened me. London, it made me think, was a bad place. There were great things there – excitements, opportunities, theatres, museums – but it was no place to live.

My final year at Cambridge was over-shadowed by the prospect of London. That was where I had to go, I realised. That was where Rob had gone, and Jon Taylor and, after a few months working for a computer firm in Cambridge while trying to maintain his under-graduate lifestyle, Ellis too. They shared a flat in Swiss Cottage, to which I went for the occasional party. It felt very grown-up and sophisticated, appropriate for the president of Footlights, to be 'popping up to town' for parties with friends who were now profes-sional writer-performers. The reality, when I arrived, was less impressive. My friends were drinking cans of lager in a dump they could ill afford, their professional status largely being that they didn't have jobs. It was fun to go and visit them – and Rob and I had plans for another two-man show, which we would take to Edinburgh – but I was apprehensive about the future that awaited when the sluices of graduation released me from the small pond of Cambridge.

That's if I managed to graduate, for which I'd have to do well enough in my final exams to get a degree. This was touch-and-go to say the least. Not that it should have been a problem. I was supposedly there to learn about history, my favourite subject at school. In my year off several people had told me that you could get a very good degree just by doing four hours work a day and the rest of your time would be free for hobbies and socialising. 'Well I think I can manage a bit more work than *that*,' was my response, 'and still have lots more time for fun than I did at either school or OUP.'

We were all wrong. You can get a good degree in history from Cambridge if you do as little as *two* hours of work a day, if you really do it every day and then cram for exams. Four is for maniacs. One would probably suffice. Unfortunately, after the first few weeks, I was incapable of doing even that. I'd stopped handing in weekly essays, which is all you have to do to remain part of the history course at Cambridge – that and turn up for your weekly 'supervision'. I was squandering my privileged access to a renowned university's world-famous one-on-one teaching system. What I quickly learned, instead of the economics of medieval England, was that if you hadn't written an essay, you could ring up your supervisor and postpone, in some cases even cancel, the supervision. There was basically nothing they could do about that, other than express concern – which they wouldn't do for the first few weeks because they'd totally believe you, or be nice enough to pretend they totally believed you, about whatever excuse you'd given: being ill, depressed, having lost a fifth grandparent. (Saying that you were feeling 'down' or 'weird' made them back off PDQ – the poor sods were terrified of students bumping themselves off, because the press then have a field day about the demanding Oxbridge 'hothouse' atmosphere. I know it happens, but the idea of killing yourself at Cambridge due to pressure of academic work seems as unlikely to me as dying of a surfeit of fillet steak in a North Korean jail.)

None of this solved the problem of exams, however. Back at the end of my second year, as exam time approached, my college (which treasured its reputation for excellence in history) had sensed there was a crisis brewing. So Dr Adamson, a bye-fellow of Peterhouse, took it upon himself to give me special supervisions on my essay technique. This was a suggestion which I considered to be useless and offensive in equal measure. The technique with which I wrote essays was fine – it was their complete lack of factual content that was the problem. More infuriating still was the first supervision itself, in which he'd clearly decided to be incredibly rude in order to knock some sense into me. He took an essay which my supervisor and director of studies had considered to be perfectly adequate and discussed it as if it were a dirty protest.

I suppose I deserved it. I was letting the college down. I was wasting my chances of an education. But he didn't seem angry, hurt or concerned for my academic progress. He was just enjoying making me feel small and I resented the pleasure he took. 'One day,' I thought, 'I'll call this man a cunt in a book.' After the supervision, I wrote to thank him for his help and explain that I wouldn't be needing any more of it. I think I said something bullshitty like it 'doesn't fit in with my revision schedule', as if I had any such thing other than three weeks blanked out of my diary for panicking.

Those second-year exams – my Part I's, as they were known – could have gone worse: I got a 2:2 – a long way off a fail, but below the 2:1 which Peterhouse considered the minimum requirement for its historians. I was called to see my director of studies, Dr Lovatt. They couldn't throw me out of the university – I hadn't failed an exam – but they could make me swap to a different subject which the college cared less about and which could have meant having to study for a fourth year. This idea appalled me as it would mean Rob had two years out in the real world before I could join him. He'd have his own show on BBC Two by then, I thought. I'd be left behind.

As part of my dressing-down, Dr Lovatt mentioned my having written to Dr Adamson but, as he did so, I swear he smirked. I think he liked the fact that I'd done that. As he balanced up whether to let me carry on reading history, which he eventually did, I'm pretty sure that letter weighed in my favour. It's not uncommon for academics to be at each other's throats, and I have a feeling that even Gandhi himself would have made an exception for Dr Adamson.

People often ask me how much like my character from *Peep Show* I am. Well, this is a clear point of difference. Mark Corrigan is obsessed with history. At university, he dutifully read Business Studies, but he would have loved to do history and would, I'm sure, have cherished the opportunity. I can't claim to have a fraction of Mark's fascination and passion for the subject.

I do like to bang on about it, though. Any of the bits I'm keen on – late eighteenth-century British politics, the Napoleonic Wars, the Congress of Vienna, the Treaty of Versailles or the Second World War – are subjects on which I dearly love to hear the sound of my own voice. I will go on and on and on about it, often stopping to ask people whether I'm going on too long or being boring, and then, horror of horrors, *believing* their expressions of continued interest even though I know that politeness would prevent them saying anything else.

That's a point of similarity, I'm afraid. And I don't have as good an excuse as Mark – I'm not starved of any other outlet. The only thing that'll make me shut up when I'm busy explaining that the Treaty of Versailles was an inadequate fudge born out of weird and unsatisfactory circumstances, is fear of comparison with him. It raises the spectre that the piece of comic work for which I'm best known is not something that I've co-created, in which I'm deliberately funny, but just a context in which my risibility has been skilfully harnessed for the entertainment of others. Still, there are worse ways to make a living. Working as a loans manager, for example.

In order to convince Dr Lovatt that I shouldn't be dumped to Classics or Land Economy, I'd made a lot of promises about the third year. I didn't even believe them as I made them. I'd got a 2:2 after all. To work any harder would steal valuable time from my new dream job running Footlights.

When I took charge of the club in the autumn of 1995, there was a crisis. The money had run out. For many years Footlights had been generously sponsored by Holsten Pils: £15,000 a year and as much free beer as the students could be bothered to pick up from the factory. Student motivation can be inspiring in this sort of area, and so vans were hired and vast numbers of crates fetched. Sadly, the money of the good years had been wasted – the club operated at a loss which was exactly balanced out by the sponsorship, but not a penny had been saved. When the deal ended, the operating loss did not and the two intervening years had cleared out the club's reserves. That was the hidden significance to the phrase 'The lager's just run out' which had greeted my arrival at the Footlights squash back in October 1993. It was the last of the Holsten Pils. I arrived just as the booze and money tap had been turned off. That was now a problem which Matthew Holness and I had to solve.

We also had to write the pantomime, appoint a new committee and a director and production team for the panto, and organise a smoker, a stall for the freshers' fair, a squash, a membership recruitment drive and a 'virgin smoker' which was a special unthreatening beginners' show for which unthreatened beginners had to be found. The two of us were also appearing in the final run of the previous year's tour show, *Fall from Grace* (the tour always returned to the ADC for a sort of 'victory lap' in the Michaelmas Term). On top of all this, I was writing another musical with Ellis and Adam Cork called *Emergency Exit*, which I was also directing, and a weekly column for *Varsity*. In the previous two years I'd told myself I had no time for history. Now I really didn't.

I loved all this and clung to it all the more because of those two shadows: the real world and finals. When it came to problems that, in the overall scheme of things, didn't really matter – putting on a show for students, writing for the university newspaper, saving an undergraduate comedy club from penury – I had tremendous drive and application. I set about solving Footlights' money problems, cutting budgets and ramping up publicity with so much energy that you'd think my own financial future was secure. In fact I had no idea how I was going to set about earning a living when released back into the wild – no idea whether I'd even have a degree to 'fall back on' when my future of constant backwards pratfalls began. I was frightened of graduation and even more frightened of not being allowed to graduate at all, leaving university unqualified and disgraced.

I was helped with the latter problem by Dr Harry Porter. He was the longest-serving member of the Footlights committee, a Selwyn College don who'd been Senior Treasurer since the early 1960s, swapping to become Senior Archivist in the 1970s when the club's income was such that it was being investigated for Corporation Tax evasion and two Customs and Excise men turned up at Harry's house. He considered this beyond the call of duty and created the archivist job for himself, leaving the accountancy to others.

He'd retired from teaching by the time I knew him but remained an active link with Footlights' famous past. As president, I found him a tremendous support and a good friend. And he did me a very good turn by inviting my director of studies, no longer Dr Lovatt but a friend of Harry's and a very nice man called Dr Shepard, to come and see me play Jeffrey Bernard in *Jeffrey Bernard is Unwell* at the ADC.

Playing this part was an act of arrogant bravado similar to that of Ellis in accepting the role of Willy Loman two and a half years earlier. It's a very funny play but all it really consists of is the central character, Jeff, talking to the audience about his exciting, glamorous, romantic and pitiful life. A few other people wander in and out but it's very nearly a monologue. In deciding to play that part, I was conscious that it was the sort of ridiculous opportunity that would probably never be repeated, certainly not for decades.

I think I did a better job than most 21-year-olds would, which is not to say that I was any good, but it was the right sort of bitter-sweet show for Dr Shepard to come to – much better that than a revue full of *Day Today* rip-offs and swearing. Better still, after the show when I was having a drink with him and Harry, and he was saying he'd enjoyed it, a panic went round the bar because Dylan Moran, who had been booked to do an hour's stand-up as that evening's late show, failed to turn up. These late shows starring established comedians were organised by Footlights – they were part of the new money-making drive – so when Moran failed to arrive, with the auditorium full, it was the club's responsibility. We had to put on a smoker at ten minutes' notice and, as president, I was expected to compere it.

In truth, this was quite easy. There were plenty of performers around that evening, we all knew a few sketches and we could fill an hour's show without breaking sweat. But, to Dr Shepard, I think this looked quite impressive. It was like there'd been a fire and I'd put on a helmet and walked into the inferno. Thanks to Harry and Dylan Moran, he left feeling that, even if I ended up getting a poor class of degree, I hadn't entirely wasted my time at university. My last few months were spent largely unharassed by the college's academic authorities.

This felt more and more like an eerie silence as finals approached. The fact that I'd managed a 2:2 the previous year was ever scanter consolation as I reflected on how much less work I'd done this year, now that it mattered even more. So I tried not to think about it and to keep myself busy at the ADC and with Footlights. But gradually, distractions from study fell away. In the weeks leading up to university exams, no plays are put on and Footlights takes a break in the writing and rehearsing of the tour show. As even the most feckless of my fellow finalists started to buckle down, it became harder and harder for me to ignore reality and avoid getting started on what I was still calling 'revision'. But it wasn't revision because I'd hardly done any work all year so there was nothing for me to revise – no notes or essays for me to read through. The task ahead of me was to fake a year's worth of study in about four weeks. And I wasted most of the first week in the pub.

On the day of my last exam, I sat desperately reading in the rooms I shared at Peterhouse with my friend Paul Keane (who's now a Catholic priest, like Daniel Seward from my group at Abingdon – but I tell myself that's not a statistically significant enough sample from which to infer anything about me). I was urgently trying to cram information into my head in exactly the way that people who have properly prepared for an exam – and I knew this because I had once been such a person – pretend is useless.

'If you don't know it by now, you'll never know it' is what they say.

But no, I could still learn it. If I don't know it by now, I could learn it now! Shut up, leave me alone and let me learn it now!

The phone rang and I answered. It was Rob. Singing.

'Congratulations! And jubilations!'

This went on for what felt like a long time. I'd never taken him for a Cliff Richard fan but he seemed to know quite a few of the lyrics. I waited patiently, too stressed to be either annoyed or amused. Just terse. Super-terse. Densely terse, as he finally reached the end and I said: 'It's this afternoon.'

'I'm sorry. That was misjudged.'

My last memory of Cambridge is of walking through Jesus College in the June sunshine, with a huge hangover, swinging a tennis racket, deeply aware of looking like a stereotype of something that no longer really existed. It was the morning after the last night of the Cambridge run of the 1996 Footlights Revue, *The Rainbow Stranglers*, and I'd stayed on a friend's floor in Jesus because Peterhouse had chucked me out. Not because I'd failed – I'd got my 2:2 – but because I'd had my graduation ceremony the previous day and, after that, you had to vacate your room.

I was leaving. Jon Taylor, whose mother was giving us a lift to a party in Norfolk, was carrying my overnight bag because he said I looked too fragile. My parents had taken the rest of my stuff back to Oxford. I was left carrying only a tennis racket, meandering along, realising that I had to leave.

There was a garden party in full swing in the Fellows' Garden as I walked out of the college and I could hear a band playing 'Life is a Cabaret'. I hoped so.

- 24 -

The Lager's
Just Run Out

I spent the next two years in miserable poverty. And it wasn't even the sort of poverty where you lose weight – quite the reverse. The main thing I spent my meagre resources on, other than rent and the Tube, was beer and snacks.

I'm walking west along the Bayswater Road, past the Royal Lancaster Hotel. My dad always points out this hotel when we pass it in the car. He says that when it opened in the 1960s it was the first new hotel to be built since the war – the first time since then that the poor exhausted old country had summoned up enough spare energy for anything as frivolous as a hotel. In its flamboyant ugliness, I can imagine how it could have been inspiring – a gleaming modern block of lights, full of cocktails and miniskirts – to a city tired of a penurious existence eked out in mouldering, smoke-stained Victorian brick.

Under the hotel is a Tube station. When I first lived in London, I couldn't believe how expensive the Tube was. It's even more expensive now, and not a day goes by that I don't thank my lucky stars that I no longer care. Whether it's three, five, seven or ten pounds a day to use the Tube no longer matters to me and, having no aspirations to be a politician, I can relish that fact. I can forget the price of a loaf of bread and a pint of milk because I have no fondness for the memory of what it felt like to have to worry about them – and to get an extra two cans of Skol instead.

But in my days of being broke, at least it was possible to skip fares. I'd hate to be broke now, in the era of ubiquitous automatic gates and no one accepting cheques. I mean, I hated being broke then. But at least, while I had my chequebook and guarantee card, I could continue to borrow money from the bank without having to get their permission – or put my precious card into a lethal, balance-knowing machine.

I lived in Swiss Cottage, which wasn't as nice an area in 1996 as it is now. But my only paid work was in Hammersmith, where Robert Webb, Jon Taylor and I were ushers at the Lyric Theatre, so I spent a lot of time on the Tube. Rob and Jon, who'd been living in London for a year longer than I had, showed me the ropes.

Rob hadn't yet got his own series on BBC Two but, on the plus side, he had learned from Jon how to fare-dodge by walking past the ticket inspector holding up an old ticket with a finger strategically placed over the date. I tried this a couple of times and it worked perfectly. And it was hugely worth doing. Our fee for a night of ushering was £10 plus a percentage of the commission on programme and ice cream sales. Around Christmas, this could be as much as £2 a night but for most of the year it was about 50p. The Tube fare was £1.50 each way. So, if you paid the fare, you lost nearly 30 per cent of your wage in travel costs.

But, other than on a handful of occasions, I always bought a ticket. Not because I felt it would be terribly wrong not to, but because I couldn't take the stress of worrying that I'd be caught. I was willing to pay nearly a third of my income for peace of mind. I'm amazed I've never been scammed by an insurance company.

Ushering at the Lyric was a nice respectable holiday job for a teenager, which is what it had been for Jon when he'd started there, six or seven years earlier, when he was a schoolboy growing up in Chiswick. He'd returned to it because he wasn't getting any acting work, it was the only job he'd ever had and he felt, quite rightly, that if he got a 'proper job' that paid good money and actually had prospects, he might be lured into a career he didn't want. There's no risk, with ushering, that you get so used to all the money and perks that you forget to follow your dream.

Rob and I asked him to get us jobs there as well, because we didn't have any better ideas and because it was related to our chosen profession. But that fact only made it more soul-destroying. Not only were we doing teenagers' part-time jobs despite having Cambridge degrees, we also had to witness other people being properly employed as actors on a daily basis. We'd have been so much happier doing data-entry.

As ushers you got to watch, or as it felt at the time 'had to watch', the theatre's shows again and again. I don't remember thinking the standard was very high – but then I wasn't seeing these productions in their best light. I was usually watching for the umpteenth time, eyes watering from sour grapes: other people were on stage instead of me.

No one can spot an actor's flaws as quickly and as mercilessly as an out-of-work actor. 'I could do this!' Rob and I thought and said to each other. Having so recently left an environment where you could just roll your sleeves up and get involved, this was a very frustrating feeling.

But I used to enjoy watching the productions decline. The one I saw most often, because it was on at a time when I had absolutely nothing else to do with my life so I was ushering every shift I could get, was *Mrs Warren's Profession*. All I can now remember about that show, which at one point I could practically recite, is a moment when one character, a personable old duffer, meets a younger, more serious character. They shake hands. Early in the run, the old chap had done a very subtle movement or gesture to indicate that the younger man's handshake had been rather too firm. It was beautifully done and got a big laugh. I then had the pleasure of watching that moment deteriorate.

The actor's reaction got larger as the audience response got smaller. You could tell he was worrying about it between shows, fretting over how to recapture that comic moment from earlier in the run. Sadly for him he only ever came up with the same answer: he needed to do it *more*. He started to wince and exhale visibly. The laughs got quieter. He cheated his body round to project his apparent discomfort across the stalls. They got quieter still. 'Why aren't they noticing?' he must have wondered. By the end of the run he was desperately wrenching the tiniest titter from the crowd with a shameless piece of tremendous ham.

But such moments of schadenfreude were few and far between. Mainly I was wondering what the hell I was doing with my life and bitterly reflecting how I had left everything too late. Why didn't I have an agent? Because I hadn't really tried to get one – I hadn't written to any agents and then I hadn't rung them up and persuaded them to come and see shows at Cambridge or in Edinburgh. And now there wasn't anything for them to come and see. Maybe I was too shit to be an actor or comedian, I bitterly reflected to myself in bed every lunchtime, but I hadn't even checked.

I now know that persuading agents to attend student shows is like drawing teeth, so a concerted letter-writing and phone-call-making campaign might well have led to nothing. But still, as things were, I could hardly say I'd tried everything.

And actually, one agent did approach me early on. A good agent, Christian Hodell, who'd seen the Footlights show in Edinburgh, wrote and asked me to come meet him. I knew very little about agents, having been too useless an idiot to find anything out, but Robert Thorogood told me that this guy was proper. The agency he worked for represented Fry and Laurie, Robert told me.

I thought that sounded bloody promising. Unfortunately our meeting was at 11 in the morning, and getting myself into the centre of London at that early hour was pretty much beyond me during this period. I'm serious, it felt impossible. It meant getting up in single figures – the wrong sort of single figures. As a student, I had had no early mornings. My mean time of rising was 1pm. My whole constitution was used to a ten- or eleven-hour sleep from about 3am onwards. Breaking that cycle for a day took a tremendous act of will.

I nearly managed it and arrived at Christian Hodell's office, hair wet from the shower and armpits wet from the brisk hungover walk from the Tube, at about 11.13am, which I considered fairly respectable for an 11 o'clock meeting.

'Hello, how are you?' said Christian Hodell.

'Nice to meet you. Very well, thanks.'

'Well, I have a stye, so I've been better.'

Do you know what a stye is? It's like a spot on your eyelid. They can look a bit gruesome but they just go away – a bit like an aspirant comedian before lunchtime. This struck me as a very specific ailment for him to refer to. Not quite like saying piles but not like saying you've got a cold either. Like referring to a bad case of water on the knee. It made me slightly miss my conversational stride as I was checking in my head that a stye was what I thought it was, and that he hadn't made a more serious revelation to which my reaction may have been deemed inadequate. He was also American and quite camp, which further rocked my little provincial soul, trembling in the face of London's West End. But he was very nice about the show I'd been in and said he wasn't saying he'd represent me yet but that we should keep in touch.

'Great. Nice to meet you,' I said as I left.

He never heard from me again. Good move, eh, Mitchell? It's slightly embarrassing, having to ring people up and tell them what you're doing. So I didn't. Rob and I wrote and starred in a pantomime on the London Fringe over Christmas 1996, called *Oedipus the Pantomime*, in which I played Jocasta as a dame. It's difficult to get agents to fringe venues, but one who *specifically asked me to keep him up to speed with what I was doing* might have been prevailed upon to come. But I never mentioned it. Neither did I mention the production of *The Miser* that Rob and I were also both in at a pub theatre in Camden in the spring, nor the production of *Latin!*, a play written by his own client Stephen Fry, that we did in Edinburgh that year, or our own two-man show that was on in the same venue. I told him nothing. I maintained a dignified silence. At some point, he rang up and said he sadly wasn't able to represent me and suggested another couple of agents. I said that I understood. Looking back, he was lucky that I even took the bloody call.

Christian Hodell made one final attempt to help me. Later that year, after he'd let me down gently, I did send a photo and CV round to agents, including him. I got some serious-looking photographs taken by a friend and chose one to be blown up to 10x8 format and reproduced dozens of times. But the shop blew up the wrong photo. I didn't notice until I'd got it home. It was quite a bad photo with my mouth sort of half open, looking weird. It was more appropriate to a charity's website than the CV of an aspiring TV star. But the photos had cost me £70 and I didn't have another £70 spare. I suppose I could have gone back to the shop and complained but this was not a good patch for me, competence-wise. So I sent them round anyway and heard nothing back except standard rejections. Except from Christian. He sent a note, which read something like this:

'I hope you won't think it's not my place to say this but that is a TERRIBLE photo. Seriously. Don't send any more out. Burn all copies.'

He was right. It was good and kind advice. But it was too late. 'Well, looks like I've pretty much fucked up my whole life,' I thought. I went next door: 'Pub, anyone?'

Throughout that difficult time, what sustained me and distracted me, what helped me stick to my guns but also, for hours on end, leave my guns unattended, was the community of people I lived with in Swiss Cottage. Don't be put off by the word 'community' – this wasn't anything hippyish or communistic. It was three flats above the shops on Winchester Road (with entrances on Fellows Road), in a building that's since been demolished, full of friends from Cambridge.

The first flat, 169 Fellows Road, had initially been rented by Katie Breathwick and passed on to Rob, Jon and Ellis a year later. Jon then noticed, in the summer of 1996, that two more flats were up for rent and suggested that some of his friends who were graduating that summer might want to take them as they were quite cheap and spacious. We jumped at the chance and so 161 and 163 Fellows Road were added to the roster.

I lived in 163 with Leila Hackett, Rob's then girlfriend and a fellow Footlighter, and Sally Watson, Tom Hilton's partner these days. Back then, Tom and Sally were entering the second year of an incredibly slow-moving Beatrice and Benedick mutual spikiness scenario. They'd gone out for about 25 minutes in 1994, then fallen out, then become friends who were 'completely over each other', then fallen out in a way that friends who are 'completely over each other' never do, then become friends again – and by friends I mean two people who constantly bickered. This remained the situation for about another eight years before they finally got together, a few months after the last person who always said to them 'You two should get back together' had stopped bothering to do so.

Tom lived in 161 with Charles Dean, who'd handled the technical side of Footlights for many years, and an ever-changing third occupant. Matthew Holness was there for a while, as were Robert Thorogood, James Bachman, Mark Evans and my friend Ed Paleit from school.

Because there were so many of us, we became a sort of centre of gravity for people who'd recently left Cambridge and wanted to act, write or tell jokes. We had quite a few parties, since all that involved was announcing the intention and buying a bottle each. Even such niceties as crisps and dips we considered to be the preserve of a royal garden party. In a way that was basically awful, friends started to refer to us as 'Swiss College, Cambridge'.

It was like a sitcom. It really was. We were a bunch of fairly charismatic losers with lots of time on our hands. And funny things happened. Ellis came back from a long IT contract in France with case after case of cheap wine which turned out to be undrinkable, but we were so desperate to mobilise that alcohol resource that we spent more than the wine was worth on gallons of orange juice to mix it with, calling the resultant concoction Sangria. We invented a game called hand tennis, played on the roofs of the shop store-rooms below, which had special rules for when the ball went into the fetid piles of bin bags or the area of discarded pot plants outside the doors of 161 and 163. One night, Rob and Jon, after several bottles of wine, decided to put some posters in frames up on the walls of 169. They literally smashed 60 per cent of them. That all sounds funny, doesn't it? It felt it at the time. Maybe you had to be there.

I think we were a bit obsessed with its being like a sitcom, particularly those of us who aspired to write and/or be in a sitcom. The dream was to live glamorous and successful lives by being in funny shows about lovable failures. Instead we were broke, stuck in our flats watching *This Life*, a programme about glamorous, successful people our age. Everything seemed to be the wrong way round.

- 25 -

Real Comic Talent

I'm at the top of the Long Water, which is not a good place to be. I've dipped into Hyde Park to get away from the traffic noise, and of course this is a more attractive place to walk. It's the kind of place where people without bad backs might stroll anyway, for non-medicinal reasons. For the sheer hell of it. Laughing about their healthy spines as they go. Lovely. There are fountains here and everything. Unfortunately, my bladder seems to be able to hear them. Somehow it's been distracted by other thoughts since I swerved the public conveniences in Regent's Park, but now it's put its metaphorical hand to its metaphorical forehead and metaphorically said: 'I knew there was something!'

That reminds me of a night on stage – or rather an afternoon. The production of *The Miser* on the London fringe that I mentioned may sound like an unusual gig for me. You probably think that a play by Molière is a bit arty for a low comedian. The whole *Oedipus the Pantomime* thing sounds a bit poncy too, I dare say, though only in the clever-clever undergraduate way that you'd expect. But a straightforward production of a classic play? You may doubt my long-term passion for French literature.

Well, rat correctly smelt. The main reason Rob and I took part in a production of *The Miser* was that it could be paid for by a tour of independent schools, in a way an original comedy show featuring the word 'fuck' could not. You pick a play that's on the A-level syllabus, ring up a series of private schools, and say that you're touring a production of it, suitable for teenagers, and would they like to book you in for a performance? You also offer to throw in some 'theatre workshops'. Each school agrees to put us up for the night and pay a few hundred quid, which, if you get enough schools, covers production and transport costs, a bit of spending money for the cast and crew, and enough left over to hire the Etcetera Theatre, Camden, for a few weeks – so that we can invite agents along in the hope of using the production to kick-start our careers.

The Etcetera Theatre, Camden, I should add, is not a theatre. It's a room above the Oxford Arms pub from which you can hear the football match being watched by the regulars downstairs. Nevertheless it is, for some reason, on the London theatre map. Agents, casting directors and the like have heard of it and, in a quiet week, can be prevailed upon to go there.

This seemed like a workable scheme (and less financially flawed than *Oedipus the Pantomime*, which I had largely bankrolled using dead relations' bequests that had been in a Post Office savings account for my entire childhood, and for which hardly anyone had bought a ticket). Robert Thorogood was directing and he decided on a cast of four: Rob, who played Harpagon, the miser of the title; Thorogood himself, who played Cléante and Valère; Olivia Colman, who played Élise and Mariane; and me, who played everyone else. Let me tell you, this is not enough people to mount a production of *The Miser*.

Actually, though, I think we made a decent job of it. There was an ingenious set, built by Tom and Charles, which was easily trans-portable in a small van and looked like an old-fashioned pound note, but with lots of doors and flaps opening from it. All the doubling and costume changing added to the frenetic pace that Robert felt was crucial to the production. It wasn't an atmospheric *Miser*, it wasn't an insightful *Miser*, but it was quick and entertaining. It consciously borrowed the chaotic feeling which Rob's and my two-man shows tended to have in their closing stages.

It was certainly good enough for schools and its flippancy alone ensured it went down well with sixth-formers. We were a bit worried about the 'theatre workshops' we'd promised as we had no idea what such things involved. But we reckoned none of the kids coming to them would either. I suggested we could paint their faces like clowns and show them how to balance a hockey stick on one finger, but nobody could believe a school would stand for that kind of crap.

What became clear on the tour was that, at a lot of schools, we weren't the ones pulling a scam. That was the teachers who booked us; they could take the afternoon off while we minded the kids and then, in the evening, had a bunch of new people to talk to in the pub. At a lot of isolated boarding schools, the presence of a few unfamiliar and articulate graduates was warmly welcomed by staff and we were often under intense pressure to get pissed with them. Pressure to which we yielded.

But we had to do a lot of these shows and, being as unprofessional as we were unpaid, the production slid swiftly from slick and entertaining to lazy and gabbled-through and bored. At some schools, if we were warmly welcomed and there was a nice theatre, we kept our shit together. But when we found ourselves in a drab, unwelcoming institution, it became harder to concentrate, especially if we were in front of pupils who were following the play in their textbooks as it went along – or at a place where, when a bell went for the end of the lesson, the half of the audience for whom this didn't form part of a 'double period' would leave in the middle. Within a couple of minutes, they would be replaced with different kids, fresh from Maths or Geography, who were expected to watch the end of the play despite having no idea what was going on.

On days like that, our minds wandered and whole sections of the show would stall as some or all of us collapsed in fits of silent giggles. I remember the City of London School in particular because it had a pillar in the middle of the stage. The audience were just silent whatever we did. It was as if they were dead or getting on with other work. Once we started laughing there, in that eerie silence, it was really hard to stop. The tears came too – weird tears that were a mixture of crying with laughter and just crying. I remember a moment when Robert Thorogood was supposed to respond to some diatribe from Harpagon but couldn't and just stood there for minutes on end, wheezing and shaking and watering from the eyes, before muttering nonsensically, 'I'm as happy as Larry,' and exiting.

But the biggest nightly crisis for the show was just before the end. I had to come on in the last scene as a character who hadn't yet appeared in the play, Signior Anselme. He's the *deus ex machina* who miraculously solves everything at the end. This involved a complete costume change for me. Most of the parts I played were servants, but Signior Anselme is an authority figure so my costume was a rather nice cream suit and a silk bow-tie. Not a made-up bow-tie but one you had to tie.

I'm okay at doing that. It takes me a couple of minutes but I can fairly reliably make it into something bow-tie shaped. At the age of 22 I was still proud of my bow-tying skill and so, even when I realised that there wouldn't be a mirror in the wings where I'd be doing my quick change, I didn't suggest getting a clip-on as back-up. 'I can do it by feel,' I thought.

The problem was that I never knew the extent to which I was right about that, because I couldn't see the state of the object that was under my chin when I walked on stage. This was a very unfair position to put my already giggly fellow performers in, night after night. 'What will it be tonight?' they must have been wondering just before they turned to face me. 'What insane, lop-sided, unravelling knot, what weird lump or clod of cloth, will be lodged under David's chin unbeknownst to him as he comes on with the placid face of the character who's about to resolve the plot?'

Soon it didn't matter what the tie looked like – they'd still laugh. If it was a disaster, as misshapen as a *Generation Game* contestant's first attempt at a pretzel, that would be hilarious. If it was basically okay but a bit wrong on one side, that would be hilarious. If it was totally fine then that would be even more hilarious because it would make a mockery of all their giggling speculation about something disastrous: it would be a hilarious anticlimax. There was actually nothing funnier, they discovered, than me appearing placidly from the wings in a normal-looking tie. The moment had gone toxic.

The afternoon which my bladder has just reminded me about was at a very posh girls' school where we were performing in a brightly lit hall rather than a theatre. It was an uninspiring institution – clearly very focused on academe and discipline, to the extent that the spirit seemed to have been driven out of pupils and teachers alike. It was a joyless environment and so we were gigglier than ever.

I don't know what my bow-tie looked like when I walked on stage that day but Collie laughed so much she pissed herself. There and then. On the stage. Some muscle relaxed and wee was suddenly pouring down her legs into her shoes, which soon overflowed as her feet were already in them. The piss progressed speedily down the, we now realised, slightly raked stage. It's amazing how much piss there is when someone pisses themselves – in the same way, I suppose, that it's amazing how much water there is when you knock over a glass of water. Liquids really do cover a very large area when freed from restraining glasses or bladders. And, as she pissed, she continued laughing. We all continued laughing, in our bodies, mouths and face – but no longer our eyes, which had gone wide and desperate. All four of us were in a massed spasm of public humiliation from which we couldn't escape.

Collie was the first to recover herself – possibly as a result of finishing her wee. She promptly said her exit line and left to tidy herself up at just the moment that the puddle reached the lip of the stage and started dripping down in front of Row A's studious faces. Those pupils were so brainwashed, I don't even remember them reacting. We might as well have been touring North Korea.

I'm a comedian but that's the only time, to my knowledge, that I've ever made anyone piss themselves laughing. And it was not deliberate. After the show, we hastily left – aware that, as a company, we were now both taking and leaving the piss.

Our run at the Etcetera garnered a three-star review from *Time Out* from which we extracted the quotation: 'real comic talent'. The night after it was published our audience numbers leapt up into the low twenties. But they were soon back to the high single figures that guaranteed a feeling of embarrassment, of having made a mistake, among the people who'd come, but didn't justify cancelling the performance. For that, we felt, the audience had to be outnumbered.

Rob got an agent out of it, though: Michele Milburn, then of Amanda Howard Associates. I tried to be pleased for him – I made all the right congratulatory noises. And I salved my feelings of inadequacy with the thought that he'd been out in the world a year longer than me and he'd had the main part in the play. But it was a very unsettling feeling. An agent on the lookout for the likes of me had pointedly asked Rob but not me to be a client. Once again, I was convinced that he was about to be swept off to BBC Two, leaving me alone in the wilderness.

The news that a different agent had signed up both Robert Thorogood and Collie didn't improve my self-esteem. Maybe I was just talentless, I thought in dark moments. But then I'd turn on the television, watch a few minutes of primetime and remind myself that talentlessness was no barrier to success. So, maybe it was worse than that – maybe I was unlucky. Still, if my career was going badly, I had my absorbing hobbies and fulfilling love life to fall back on.

DO YOU SEE WHAT I DID THERE!? No, all I had to fall back or forwards on, all that I gleaned any self-esteem from, was my career/hobby. The supportive group of friends in Swiss Cottage were entirely derived from that, as was my key friendship with Rob. So it was either all going well or all going badly.

My parents were very supportive, as ever, but they didn't really know how to help and I didn't want to explain to them the feelings of foolishness and doubt I was labouring under. I wanted them to think I had things under control. Whenever I was in a show, they would come along and, knowing that we were desperate to sell tickets, they'd try and persuade their friends to come as well. For more than one London fringe show, they hired a minibus so that they could ferry over a dozen of their friends and colleagues from Oxford to the show and back again.

My parents were used to the edgy material and flaky production values of shows involving Rob and me. What their friends, more used to a professionally produced Ayckbourn at the Oxford Playhouse, must have thought, I dread to think. But the friends were universally enthusiastic, supportive and complimentary and I'm very grateful to them for coming – and even more so to my parents for jeopardising so many of their friendships in order to help me. But of course, this help was also a sign of worry. I remember them saying in Edinburgh one year, probably after I'd been foul to them and then asked to borrow money, that they'd completely support me if I decided the whole comedy thing wasn't working out and I wanted to 'change course'.

It made me laugh at the time because I knew they would. They're the most wonderful, unquestioningly loving people I know. I think they'd support me if I said I wanted to set up as a drug dealer. (At times, they may have thought that's what I was.) And the fact that they'd support me to try and do comedy meant that they'd *definitely* support me in a more prudent path. But it didn't take me long to realise that it was a very kind and gentle way of expressing concern, of intimating, in the face of my pride and brittleness, that they knew I had worries, wasn't altogether happy and was afraid about how things might turn out.

As I prepared for Edinburgh in 1997, failure felt both unthinkable and inevitable. There's a lot of crossover between those two qualities – probably because there's not much point in thinking about the inevitable. That's my view, at least – I would never have made much of a philosopher or priest.

I tried to suppress the panic I felt whenever Rob had to go off for an audition or a meeting or to have photos taken. Those trappings of an actor's career properly starting were terrifying, so best not contemplated. I just had to hope that something would come out of that year's Edinburgh Fringe, where we were doing two shows: a rewritten version of *Innocent Millions* and, as I mentioned before, a production of the Stephen Fry play, *Latin!* To save money, we didn't hire a flat of our own to stay in but slept on the floor of Rob's girlfriend Leila's brother's friend's living room.

Latin! was a success. I think it was a good production and Rob and I played our parts well, but most of the credit should go to Stephen Fry for the very funny script he'd written nearly two decades earlier and for the draw of his name. But we enjoyed good reviews, packed houses and, most excitingly of all, an answerphone message of support left on Christopher Richardson's voicemail by Fry himself. We were fucking thrilled. I know there is considerable televisual evidence that I have both met and worked with Stephen Fry lots of times, but that was all years ahead of me at this stage – so being in a show he knew about and was enthusiastic about was a crumb of affirmation on which I feasted.

The fact that *Latin!* was a hot ticket that year had surprisingly little knock-on effect on sales for *Innocent Millions*. But then the play-watching, Radio 4-listening Stephen Fry fans attracted by *Latin!* probably weren't in the market for new comedy from the unheard-of, especially when they'd already seen them in one show and were in the perfect place to watch new comedy by the very-much-heard-of. Rob and I, as history attests, weren't even soon-to-be-heard-of in 1997, unlike for example that year's Perrier Award winners, The League of Gentlemen.

The other thing *Latin!* audiences, and Edinburgh punters in general, weren't really in the market for was a show that started at 11 in the morning. Neither were we, of course, but it was the only slot the Pleasance offered us. And, we reckoned, peering for the bright side with the desperate super-luminosensitive eyes of deep-sea fish, we wouldn't be up against any of the big shows.

Well, that was certainly true. All we were up against were children's shows and the noise of cleaners hosing the previous night's beer and sick off the cobbles of the Pleasance courtyard. At the Edinburgh Fringe, 11am is like dawn. The early birds might see it as they're brushing their teeth but they're not out doing anything yet. Our venue seated up to 100. On the night – sorry, force of habit, morning – when the all-important *Scotsman* reviewer came, the audience numbered only two. And he was one of them.

Well, just like a Hollywood film, from the jaws of misery, failure and disappointment, through hard work alone, we were able to snatch a small, muted success. You've seen Hollywood films like that, yeah? Imagine the strapline: 'It could have been a disaster, but in fact it went okay.' The *Scotsman* review was a warm three-starrer, Rob's agent Michele Milburn liked my performance in the show and asked me to come in for a meeting in London after the Fringe, and two influential men came and saw the show.

Yes, it was Bernard Ingham and Gore Vidal! No. Perhaps 'influential men' is the wrong way of putting it. They were influential on our lives and they had a small measure of influence in the world that could help us. The first was Nick Jones, a TV director who 'was putting together a sketch show for the BBC'. It's a measure of how little we knew that we didn't know how little that meant. But he had some business cards with 'BBC' written on them. Unfortunately they didn't also have 'Nick Jones' written on them, which was disappointing. He was still waiting for his cards to be printed up, he explained, as he scribbled his name and number on one of the nameless ones.

Sounds like a confidence trickster, you're probably thinking. Our reasoning at the time was that a confidence trickster would have got cards properly printed up. But we couldn't deny the possibility that he was an inept confidence trickster. Still, since no one who had both the BBC's name *and* their own on a piece of card was showing any interest in conversing with us, we decided to send him some material and hope something came of it.

The other man was Gareth Edwards, who may have scored 20 fewer international tries than his rugby-playing namesake but was considerably better thought-of by the comedy department of London Weekend Television. Gareth's card had both 'LWT' and his name on it and he left it in our pigeon-hole at the Pleasance with a note on the back saying: 'I saw your show and laughed. Do give me a ring when you're back in London,' or something equally British and understated.

I'm glad that one of the first producers to show interest in our work was from LWT – it's like a link to the history of television. It was such a big and successful company for so many decades and now there's no trace of it. It's been absorbed into the shrinking giant that is ITV. But I'm glad to have been given a business card embossed and glinting with those three friendly letters, which for years used to assemble themselves from striped lines crawling across the TV screen. It felt proper, in a way a card from something like 'Lucky Vampire Productions' or 'Depressed Spaniel Pictures' would not have done.

In those days there were still only five TV channels in Britain. Counting the BBC as two, we'd now made contact with three of them. That was more than half! Surely our big TV breakthrough could only be months away? Just think how that would help with the rent.

- 26 -

Going Fishing

The most evil dog I've ever known is my friend Ed's mother's dachshund, Brock. He once savaged Ed's brother and lost his testicles. I should clarify: the dog lost his testicles, not Ed's brother. To clarify further: the testicles weren't lost in the skirmish but in a subsequent medico-punitive procedure. I don't want you to run away with the idea that Ed's brother is the sort of guy who, in extremis, could bite the balls off a dog. He isn't like that at all. He worked for the *Financial Times* for many years.

Continuing west through Kensington Gardens, I'm reminded of the canine down side to walking through a park. I don't hate dogs – I've encountered several good-natured examples in my time, which have given me some sense of the emotional upside there must be, to compensate for having to feel the warmth of another organism's excrement through a thin film of plastic every day. For example: the golden retriever of Mr Paine, a history teacher at Abingdon.

Mr Paine used occasionally to invite boys round to his family home to watch the Varsity rugby match (this was instead of a history lesson, hence the enthusiastic uptake). An entire A-level history set would pile into the living room and the dog would be pleasantly surprised. Boys would sit on and around him, shoving aside his pillows, blankets and chewable objects, but the most the dog would do was stay still with a slightly embarrassed expression, as if to say: 'This is awkward.'

But overall I'm not a massive fan of dogs because they're dangerously delusional. They think they're in a pack with you and your family, maybe also your friends, but probably not the postman. They think there's an important team thing going on; they are so convinced of it, they become blind to the evident boundaries of species. They think there is a bigger picture – the survival of this fictional pack – which is of more importance to them than a reliable supply of warmth, shelter and Chum.

This makes them dangerous. They are capable of self-sacrifice in the name of this fictional pack, this fictional greater good. Stories of dog bravery and dog savagery are both caused by this delusion. It is why dogs will attack strangers, why a small terrier will try and kill a postman. The terrier knows that, in the end, the postman is mightier and will almost certainly prevail, but perhaps it thinks that, if it can only slow the postman down, some of the pack may evade the deadly letters. These delusions make dogs trainable, employable for our purposes. They allow us to make them care about the safety of sheep despite having no use for knitwear. But they also mean that, if you are a stranger to a dog, you can't guarantee, however small it is, that it will not suddenly try its very best to destroy you.

I cannot keep this from my mind when I pass dogs in the park. I don't think they'll *probably* attack me, but I know that they might. Unlike passing a scruffy-looking youth in a dark alley, it's not rude to give them a wide berth. Their feelings won't be hurt, as the youth's are when he turns out to be a socially responsible *Guardian* reader rather than a flick-knife-wielding smackhead. But it's wearisome, when walking along, to be slightly aware of all the dogs. I'd rather be looking at the sunlight-dappled trees than following a King Charles Spaniel with my eyes, as assiduously as a toddler who's spotted a wasp.

I've never really felt the need of a pet myself. I did look after a goldfish once. For about twenty minutes. Then I left it on a petrol pump.

I was in a car on the A1 when I realised. I was furious. Why did I have to notice?! Or why did I have to notice so *soon*? We'd hardly gone any distance from the petrol station – my Hula Hoops were still unopened – and it was too easy to go back. 'Speak now,' I thought, 'or be a fish murderer, unmitigated by tartare sauce. But there are hundreds and hundreds of miles to go! All crammed in, with it sloshing around on my knee. It's panicked most of the twenty-odd miles so far. It'd surely never survive until London anyway. But still ...'

It had to be done.

'Emma. We've left the fish at that garage.'

'Oh my God, have we!?'

Immediate screeching U-turn. It was scarier than a pit bull in an FRP with a sparkler attached to its tail. For the sake of a fucking fish.

Rob and I were driving back from our successful *Latin!* stint in Edinburgh with Emma Stenning, a theatre producer with a Ford Fiesta. Princess Diana, we were slowly realising from the sombre tone of the radio DJ, had died the night before in an unrelated incident.

The car was crammed with props and costumes – the stuff that you should probably just throw away but, having spent a month with these objects as the key to your existence, it's almost impossible to accept how valueless they have immediately become. You can never forget how deeply, sincerely, all-consumingly you've wanted to find a hat, pair of glasses, telephone or other key prop in the darkness of a theatre wing – you're like Richard III inquiring about a horse. You have to be very unsentimental to let go of all those objects at the end, saying: 'Too late now.'

So I suppose it's understandable that Emma had been unwilling to dispose of the only prop with a heartbeat (as Bruce Forsyth was fondly referred to at the BBC before the final stage of his robotisation). The goldfish had been set dressing for a production of a play called *Fugue*. It was, I don't think Emma will mind me saying now, a pretentious play. The cast wore coloured boiler suits and talked archly. The only thing that I can remember happening in it was that the fish got fed.

When we pulled into the forecourt, it was still there on the petrol pump. The goldfish, unlike Princess Diana, did not die that day.

'That's lucky,' said Emma. Rob and I remained silent.

I tried to get myself comfy in the front seat, moved the nylon wig that was under one buttock, shifted the walking stick that was digging into my side and tried to flatten down the coloured boiler suits that were packed under my legs – and prepared a flat lap for the sparkly little vertebrate.

Edinburghs roll round rather like academic years – so, as I headed back south, I felt I was going back to Life for the start of my second year. I didn't have a degree from its University but I was doing a postgraduate course there. I still am. And you're reading the dissertation I had to hand in at the end of my sixteenth year.

My second year kicked off with two exciting meetings. One was with Michele Milburn who, as I would have expected from the way she spoke to me in Edinburgh if I weren't such an inveterate pessimist, offered to represent me. The meeting was in her office, somewhere between Hammersmith and Chiswick. This location was certainly a disappointment. Christian Hodell, and most of the agents I'd written to, were based in the West End. I was nervous of frauds, working out of their living rooms, pretending to be agents but with no way of getting their clients work, merely waiting to take a cut if actors found their own employment.

But the office seemed neat and prosperous – it felt like a proper business rather than some notepaper and promises. And Michele, rather disingenuously I think now, said, 'Of course you'll need time to think about it' and that I 'shouldn't say yes or no straight away'. I nodded sagely and figured that if I got home, went to the loo and then paused for forty seconds, that was about as long as I could wait before closing the deal and being able to say I had an agent

– being able to slip the words 'my agent' into conversation as if I were really an actor.

The sense of affirmation from being represented was immense. I wasn't expecting to get work out of it any time soon – possibly ever. But suddenly I was respectable. Michele Milburn, an adult who actually made a living, had announced that she thought that living could be improved by associating herself with me. She had looked at our flawed and faltering Fringe performances and seen promise – she had believed our hype and, consequently, made it so much more believable to us.

My other big meeting that September was with Gareth Edwards, the LWT producer who'd left us his card. So, maybe he'll ask us to make a comedy show for LWT, we thought. Maybe we'll be on LWT every Friday night starting next January? That's how little we understood television.

Gareth Edwards is quite tall and quite thin, with bright eyes. He looks almost elfin and his manner is academic. He wears suede jackets and leather shoes – he's bookish and reassuring. I don't think he made many hit comedies for the mainstream ITV audience. He is also, and this makes him very unusual and valuable in his profession, funny. He knows how to be funny – he knows how to write funny things – so he can tell when other people do it and he properly values that skill. (It is an irony that many of those comedy producers who have no idea how to be funny themselves are nevertheless rather dismissive of the ability, as if it were a clerical knack which can be learned on a course and is beneath their concern.)

We arrived punctually at the LWT building, 'London Television Centre' (not to be confused with BBC Television Centre, the iconic headquarters of the BBC), but didn't get beyond reception.

'I thought we might go for some lunch,' said Gareth after we'd all shaken hands.

It was a sunny September day and we wandered round the corner into Gabriel's Wharf, where there are lots of little cafés and restaurants with tables outside. This is more like it, I thought. This is modern, prosperous, entitled London. This isn't KFC on the Finchley Road or a Food and Wine selling taramasalata and cheap lager. I'm rejoining society.

We sat at an outside table and ate burgers and chips. Honestly, we might as well have been given jelly and paper hats. I remember the sunlight, I remember Gareth talking enthusiastically about our Edinburgh show and another script we'd sent him, and I remember Rob pouring sparkling mineral water all over his chips, somehow mistaking it for vinegar.

'Oh no, we've been discovered!' I thought. 'Nice one, Rob – now the nice producer knows we usually eat out of bins. He won't let us into comedy heaven now. We're busted.' I hadn't been so sad to see food ruined since John Wilkinson put pepper on my birthday cake.

But it was almost immediately funny. Gareth was so like a slightly older version of the kind of person we were used to working with in Footlights – not surprising really, considering he went to both Oxford and Cambridge. He's properly clever, is Gareth. He was going to be an academic but chose comedy instead. Whenever I hear comedy disparaged as an art form – for its silliness, its apparent superficiality, for the fact that people like it, or because unfunny things are less fun so must be more worthwhile – I wish Gareth was there to express the fact that being funny is one of the few things in life worth taking seriously.

Unfortunately – there being an increasing divide between people who make programmes and people who make decisions – clever, funny Gareth was not actually authorised to commission a TV show from us. Had he been able to, of course, he wouldn't have done. We had a lot to learn first. But he saw that we had promise and was talking to us, and developing ideas with us, years before an actual programme commissioner would even give us an appointment.

Nevertheless, that lunch with Gareth heralded a golden age of meetings for me and Rob. Thanks to Michele, over the next couple of years we were welcomed into dozens of offices by TV producers and production companies. Handshakes, teas, coffees and biscuits were lavished on us and we were even taken out for the occasional lunch. We would discuss the sort of comedy we liked and the sort of show we might one day want to make. They would discuss the sort of programme they were trying to pitch. Sometimes we'd say we'd send them some ideas or bits of script, sometimes not.

It took me a long time to realise how little was going on here. I naïvely thought that people in offices were busy – that if you worked in TV, you were constantly rushed off your feet making programmes or having meetings about programmes you were about to make. Occasionally, I thought, you might find time to squeeze in a chat with someone new, someone promising with no track record, but only in order to get them working on an idea that would, in time, become a TV programme.

The reality is that meeting new people and aimlessly chatting about ideas basically *is* the TV industry. Hundreds make their living in perpetually salaried 'development', seldom troubling a cameraman. Only under exceptional circumstances is a show actually made, at which point the key idea-developers, the ones who have meetings, often delegate that task to others. Our little chats with TV companies had only been about making contact, acknowledging each other's existence, as part of the vast, inefficient, meandering dance which the comparatively small amount of actual TV production manages to support.

I'm glad I didn't really understand any of that in our early days of getting meetings – because if I had they would have been less exciting and fun. As it was, the process seemed to show such promise, such cause for hope, that it was a long time before the absence of anything much coming from it made me concerned.

None of this constituted a full-time job, but I suppose it was a full-time obsession. I didn't think about much else. I was in my early twenties, living in London, so you might imagine I was always going to parties and hanging out in trendy bars. But no such thing.

I certainly didn't go on dates. In fact, until fairly recently, I didn't really believe that going on dates was something people did, except in stories and America. I thought it was like proms or spherical Christmas puddings. The fact that some people – probably most people – approach the absence of a romantic relationship from their life in such an ordered, almost clinical, way is something I've only cottoned on to in the last five or six years. In my twenties, I didn't have a clue. Sex was surely something that happened unexpectedly, occasionally and almost by accident, and 'going out with someone' was just a further happy accident that would follow if you didn't feel shit about yourself in the morning. The thought that you might actively try and meet women – at parties or bars, maybe by going along with male friends also looking for dates – and then get talking, exchange phone numbers and then, *horror of horrors*, ring up and ask them to join you for some sort of social event was ridiculous. That would be like just saying you fancied someone, to their face! Honestly!

And none of my friends seemed to go on dates – or, if they did, they didn't tell me. All of my friends were from Cambridge and some of them were going out with each other. In the absence of anyone in that group who I wanted to go out with and who wanted to go out with me, I was single. That just seemed to be one of the things about me, like brown eyes and a preference for tea over coffee. I tried not to think about it. I imagined that, one day, a supermodel with a rapier wit and a heart of gold would throw herself at me. And my friends didn't discuss it much either. Studenty conversations about crushes waned. In the real world, the crushes were fewer and further between – but the whole subject was somehow more serious. So I avoided it. I knew this sort of thing was important in the long run but, like eating enough fruit, it didn't feel like a pressing concern. I was perfectly happy single.

Besides, I seldom met anyone new, other than over a tea in a production company, discussing the difficulties of pitching a sitcom. Which, to be frank, worried me a lot more than the prospect of dying alone.

- 27 -

Causes of Celebration

A pink limo pulls over to the kerb a few yards in front of me. I doubt that it's local. It's not that sort of area. I'm back on the Bayswater Road now, having run out of park. The posh houses of Kensington Palace Gardens stretch down to my left. I'm not saying their owners are immune to vulgarity when it comes to choosing cars – they could probably be tempted to one of those slightly chavvy new two-door Bentleys – but this vehicle is full-on Vegas kitsch.

Various participants in a hen do, still fairly sober at this hour of the afternoon, get out to stretch their legs and finalise plans for their assault on the West End. They're all wearing devil horns and short skirts except for their two male friends who, for some reason, are dressed as pirates. I pity those men. The girls' devil outfits look perfectly sexy, while the two blokes are encumbered with cutlasses and parrots. When the paparazzi hope to glimpse a twat getting out of a limo, this isn't what they mean. What are these two doing there?

Maybe they're gay. A gay friend of mine was once invited on a hen do. He went along but couldn't quite get the rationale clear in his head. Surely, he thought, stag and hen nights have to be demarcated along the lines of the gender of the participants, not that of whom they aspire to fuck? Would a lesbian be made to join the stags?

Take that to its logical conclusion and loos, the gender division of which is presumably to preserve decency and avoid funny business, should actually not be for 'Ladies' and 'Gents' but for 'Gent-Fuckers' and 'Lady-fuckers'. So straight men and lesbians can happily pee in the same area, safe in the knowledge that mutual sexual attraction cannot occur – while the gay men are in with the straight women, happily talking about [insert sexist/homophobic generalisation of your choice here].

I really must stop thinking about loos. I stop briefly in Starbucks on Pembridge Road to relieve the problem. To clarify: I use the Starbucks loo. It's not an anti-capitalist demonstration.

Those poor pirates! I have awkward and mixed feelings about fancy dress. I'm very happy to dress in whatever stupid costume I'm given when appearing on TV. I won't be nude but any sort of ridiculous outfit, in a context where it's supposed to look funny, I'm fine with. That's probably because I can say I didn't choose to wear it, it's just my job (although that's a pretty flimsy excuse when it's a costume for a sketch I've written). But when a party invitation says 'fancy dress', it's different. I don't think it's right to turn up dressed normally, although people do and God knows that avoids hassle and embarrassment. I just think it's a bit rude and churlish. It's both failing to observe a clearly stated dress code and refusing to join in with the fun of a social event. Rather than that, I think one should probably just not go.

At the same time, though, a perfect, gleaming, hired costume would feel a bit OTT – a bit 'Look at me!' A friend of mine regularly has a Hallowe'en party for which some form of horror-inspiring outfit is required. Perhaps, to reflect what inspires horror in me, I should go as a party invitation requiring fancy dress. Instead, I make a lame nod towards compliance. The first year, I went to a 'party shop' and quickly bought a plastic vampire cloak and a wizard's hat and went wearing both. I felt this would do the job. It would be saying: 'Look, I'm joining in – clearly this is not how I'm normally attired.' The problem was that the first question everyone asks you at a do like that is, 'What have you come as?' and those two items don't really provide an answer. A vampiric wizard? A magic vampire? A wizard going to the opera?

The next year, I eschewed the hat but slicked my hair and said I was a vampire. A vampire with normal teeth. The year after that I thought I'd have to do better and so I cut up a furry hot water bottle and sewed bits of it to the backs of fingerless gloves and other bits to a T-shirt. No one got that I was a werewolf, even though I'd put fake blood round my mouth.

'You just look like a normal bloke who's trailing fluff everywhere,' someone said.

Why are the British so comfortable with this extroverted form of social event? What happens to our trademark repression when an accountant and his wife cheerfully get into a cab dressed as Sylvester and Tweetie Pie? What is it that makes an otherwise inoffensive man happy to go to a social event wearing round glasses, a false beard and sporting a stethoscope so that he can spend all night saying 'Yes, Shipman' in answer to appalled gazes?

And when did it start? To my eyes, before about 1950 most people were wearing fancy dress anyway. What on earth was a Restoration-era costume party like? Could a gentleman be persuaded to remove his ridiculous three-foot wig before donning the comparatively conservative horned Viking helmet? (I know, before you balk, that the Vikings didn't really have horns on their helmets, but I can't help feeling that's their mistake, not ours.)

What does the Queen go as, when she's asked to a fancy dress party? That must happen all the time – aristocrats love masked balls and other eccentric events that show breeding and conceal inbreeding. But she's got a problem. She's basically in fancy dress her whole life. She has to go to everything as the Queen. On a normal day, she'll be head to toe in canary yellow, salmon pink or frog green and, if she's opening Parliament, she'll be wearing a sparkly dress and a crown. Like me, she seems perfectly comfortable wearing weird outfits for work. But, if the footage of her from

Rob and me as Dick Whittington and his Cat in the 1994 Footlights pantomime. Gus Brown is playing the mysterious benefactor, Ben E Factor: 'Here is a blank cheque. I only wish it could be more.'

This is from the first photoshoot Rob and I ever did together – we were still young enough to think that irony can take the curse off gurning.

LEFT:
With James Bachman and Olivia Colman, just hanging out – the Bullingdon Club had nothing on us.

BELOW:
Jeffrey Bernard is 21.

Outside my parents' house when Footlights came to Oxford to do a gig at the
Playhouse. From left: Nick Nurock, me, Phil Radden, Robert Webb (seated),
Matthew Holness, Jon Taylor (seated), Charles Dean, Tom Hilton, Charlie Hartill
(seated), James Bachman, Claire Taylor and Sarah Moule. Not all of these people
have now gone bald.

At the Footlights garden party: John Oliver, Des O'Connor (sic), Richard Ayoade
and me. I am trying to pre-empt accusations of elitism by holding a champagne
bottle, wearing a T-shirt with a Latin motto on it and pulling that face.

With Collie, backstage on tour with *The Miser* (as we called the production manager). Seconds later, I was to place my entire head inside that shoe.

Neighbours has a miserly cast of eight

Amanda Blinkhorn

THEY SAY theatre runs in the blood, but in Swiss Cottage it's ingrained in the very bricks and mortar.

Most neighbours feud over the garden fence, this lot recite Molière. The six actors and two technicians who make up Juggling Fiends Theatre Company all live three doors from each other in Fellows Road, Swiss Cottage. Their director, Robert Thorogood, and the ninth member of the company, has wisely moved out to Clapham.

"It's very good for rehearsals because nobody is more than 30 seconds away – you just hang on the walls," said Mr Thorogood. "It's very nice for me because whenever I go round there's always someone there to have a cup of tea with or go for a drink with."

Spookily enough, the flats, though now privately owned, once belonged to the Central School of Music and Drama and the director Gordon Anderson once lived there. "They're definitely theatrical flats," said company manager Charles Dean, who moved in a year ago.

It all began, like so many luvvie friendships do, at the Cambridge Footlights. Tom Hilton, Ellis Sareen, Robert Thorogood, Charles Dean, Sarah Coleman, Robert Webb, David Mitchell and Jonathan Taylor were all from different colleges, but shared a love of fame and glory.

Graduations came and went and one by one they drifted to London. Jonathon and Robert were the first to arrive, lured by the link to the West End and jobs as ushers at the Lyric Theatre, Hammersmith. Ellis arrived shortly afterwards, followed, in the summer, by Charles and Tom who bagged a flat two doors down. When the flat next door became empty David Mitchell and fellow actors Sally Watson and Leila Hackett couldn't resist it.

Between them they founded a theatre company, Juggling Fiends, and, fuelled with irony and nerve, they put on a production of Molière's The Miser for their bank manager. He was so impressed he stopped bouncing their cheques and within weeks they'd sold their show to more than 20 schools all over the country.

That money helped them put on Molière's The Miser at the Etcetera Theatre above the Oxford Arms in Camden High Street where they opened on Tuesday night.

● Best friends and neighbours (from left): Ellis Sareen, Sarah Coleman, Charles Dean, Robert Webb, Robert Thorogood, Jonathon Taylor, and David Mitchell.

H&H SERIES
APRIL 11 1997

Swiss College, Cambridge, has since been demolished.

RIGHT:
Collie, backstage at the Comedy Awards. Or was it during a *Peep Show* shoot? I forget.

LEFT:
Only an anarchist would buy pants anywhere else.

RIGHT:
Mark and Jeremy are throwing a party.

LEFT:
'I find these inexplicable delays intensely depressing.' Waiting around with Matt King, who plays Super Hans.

ABOVE:
Dawn of the Bronze Age.

ABOVE:
Due to BBC cuts, Rob
and I are forced to
share a dress.

ABOVE:
Rob and I are disconcerted to be
photographed during what we call 'the
process'. (The man sitting down is Simon
Kane, who wrote the sketch we're about
to perform. It is about the Romans.)

ABOVE:
Context is all.

ABOVE:
mog schmog.

ABOVE:
Of course, it's an honour
just to be nominated.
Then again, fuck them.

LEFT:
Sam Bain, Jesse Armstrong,
Rob and me, at the Fort
Lauderdale International
Film Festival as usual.

A publicity shot from *Magicians*.

With Rob Brydon, Alan Davies, Stephen Fry and John Lloyd, for the special *QI*-themed edition of *The Unbelievable Truth*.

The end.

Millennium night, awkwardly holding hands with Tony Blair while singing 'Auld Lang Syne', is anything to go by, she finds it difficult to let her hair down at parties, which is also like me.

Where we differ, and where our Millennium nights differ, is that I didn't light a beacon, then cruise down the Thames to the sound of a 21-gun salute en route to a party at the Dome. I didn't watch 400 carnival performers do whatever carnival performers do (which is whinge about hamstring injuries and touch their parents for cash, I imagine; we may be a country that can cope with fancy dress, but the concept of 'carnival' is beyond us and I suspect that British carnival acts are the preserve of those intellectually sloppy but counter-culturally inclined children of the middle classes too lazy to train as homeopaths and too prudish for burlesque).

Me, I just had a few drinks in Swiss Cottage. We didn't even have a proper party because we thought any potential guests would have something better to do. So a handful of us got pissed and then walked up Primrose Hill to watch the fireworks on the Thames, which at that distance looked tiny. I somehow mistimed my drinking and got a headache that I couldn't shift.

It may have been a dull night but it was a fairly uplifting time for me professionally. For the last three years, everything had consistently got better. In 1998 Rob and I had met Phil Clarke, a BBC producer who had been given the thankless task of making a late-night sketch show for £29,000 an episode. That was the budget of the show, I hasten to clarify, not his fee. If it had been his fee, that would have been thanks enough. (You may think that £29,000 sounds quite a lot for half an hour's TV but, trust me, for a sketch show, with lots of cast, crew, locations and editing needed, it really isn't. A prime-time sketch show would have a budget ten times that.)

Phil cast us in it and so we got our first TV job. The show was called *Comedy Nation* and, if you look it up, maybe on IMDB, you'll see that it had a stellar cast including Sacha Baron Cohen, Ronni Ancona, Julia Davis, Kevin Eldon, Peter Serafinowicz, Sally Phillips and Phill Jupitus. Stephen Merchant was the runner.

Unfortunately Rob and I didn't meet any of those people, as all the different bits of the show were filmed separately. Also, it wasn't a very good programme. It consisted of sketches, written by the performers and then little more than camcordered by a tiny crew. For the first series, we had to provide our own costumes and props, and our sketches were filmed in an office at the BBC while its usual occupants were out at lunch.

But its artistic failings certainly weren't Phil Clarke's fault. For that budget it is basically a miracle there was a show at all. What felt equally miraculous to us was that, for our contribution (the writing and performing of half a dozen sketches) we were each paid literally hundreds of pounds.

Phil Clarke is another of those magic producers like Gareth Edwards who, having been comedians themselves, can come up with jokes without the help of writers or performers and who, consequently, get their best work. He is mildly spoken, calm in a crisis, accommodating to other people's views but very firm when he's convinced that he's in the right. But he picks his moments to speak out and is, in general, a civilising and humour-injecting influence in a stressful environment. I don't know if it's got anything to do with the strain of dealing with commissioning editors, but he's also a black-belt kick boxer.

Comedy Nation was a resistible viewing pleasure but, for Rob and me, it led to other work. Ash Atalla, who was later to produce *The Office*, had been *Comedy Nation*'s script editor and, when he was commissioned to produce a Radio 4 sketch show about disability issues, he asked us to contribute some material. So it was that *Yes Sir, I Can Boogie*, a show predicated on the flawed premise of being for the disabled what *Goodness Gracious Me* had been for Asians, became Rob's and my first Radio 4 writing credit.

Phil also put more work our way when he left the BBC and moved to Absolutely, the production company founded by the team of writer-performers behind the terrific late '80s/early '90s Channel 4 sketch show of the same name. They were making the second series of *Armstrong and Miller* and Phil asked us to join the writing team. This was a brilliant experience. Ben Miller and Alexander Armstrong were not only very funny, they were welcoming and enthusiastic to us and had an appealing, analytical approach to comedy. All of the writers would turn up with half-thought-through notions of what might make a sketch and then the group – Ben, Xander, Phil, George Jeffries and Bert Tyler-Moore were the other regulars – would discuss it, find the comic kernel and knock it into shape. It was like a more professional version of the Footlights system. Half-arsed ideas would be fitted with their second buttocks and everyone would leave the meeting with a list of coherent pieces of material to write up.

Armstrong and Miller was a massive turning point for me because that's when I started to make a living from comedy. For the first time, I didn't need to do anything else to supplement my income and I never have since. Fingers crossed, touch wood, turn around and touch the ground, etc., etc., etc. I was 24 years old and it was an enormous relief. I get asked a lot in interviews about 'break-through' moments in my career, presumably to elicit a glittering anecdote set in a revolving restaurant where a cigar-smoking producer screams, 'This kid's got something!' Instead I tell them about when the jobbing writing work started to cover the bills. That's when I properly became a professional comedian.

And I suddenly felt rich. Hundreds of pounds were entering my bank account every week and I hardly had any overheads. I seemed to have instantly gone from never having enough money to having more than I could imagine what to do with. This is not because I was very highly paid but because my spending imagination had atrophied through underuse. It felt beyond the dreams of avarice that, rent and bills taken care of, I was able to get my round in at the pub and occasionally go to Pizza Express. I couldn't think of much else to spend it on. In the same way that starting to get regular work was a bigger moment for me than the showier career successes that came later, those first regular arrivals of a few hundred quid felt like more money to me than any of the fatter fees

I've earned since. It turns out money *is* like a drug – to start with, it doesn't take much of it to get you high.

I was looking for ways to spend. And one night, I came up with the idea of going to one of those Angus Steakhouses (or possibly Aberdeen Steakhouses – they look identical) that were still dotted around central London. I'd long wondered about those places. The combination of their prominent (and therefore presumably expensive and sought-after) locations, their shabby '70s decor and the fact that they always seemed to be at least three-quarters empty had long baffled me. How did they survive? Outside, they gave a partial clue: a blackboard listing the unremarkable beef products they proposed to serve, alongside the prices. Those weren't '70s at all. In fact, they were positively futuristic. In the years of being broke, I would certainly never have set foot in such a place (if I was going to splash out on a restaurant, I'd go somewhere cheap where I knew what I was getting, i.e. a curry house) but now I had the chance to indulge my curiosity.

So one night, after a few pints in the pub, Rob, James Bachman, who was also finding solvency in comedy writing around this time, Tom Hilton and I decided to soak up the booze in an Angus/Aberdeen Steakhouse on Leicester Square. We wandered in and were favoured with a table in the window.

Our expectations were not high. We were basically going there because we thought it was funny. But I think we reckoned that we'd get competent steak and chips, for which we'd then be overcharged. Maybe slightly poor steak and chips but, as steak and chips is fundamentally nice, that would be okay – more than worth enduring for the adventure of going to one of those inexplicable restaurants. We were pretty determined to enjoy the experience: James ordered a side dish of Brussels sprouts purely because he was amused that they offered such a thing.

All seemed well when the food arrived: it looked funny. It reminded me of our very occasional trips to the Berni Inn when I was little. There were tomatoes in the garnish that had been sort of crinkle cut and all the food was served on enormous heaps of cress. I hadn't seen cress for years – which didn't bother me, it's a pointless food – but the reason for its disappearance was apparently that the Angus and Aberdeen Steakhouses had bought up the entire world's supply.

Then we tucked in, at which point the joke was on us. All of the food was terrible. Inedible. Burnt and unchewable. Apart from James's sprouts, which seemed to have undergone 40 per cent of the process of turning them into soup. The wine was expensive and like vinegar. We were sad. We'd wanted dinner.

'We should complain,' said James.

He was met with a cressy splutter from the rest of us.

'Typical American!' (James is half American) was our response. 'Why add the nightmare of embarrassment to the horrors of the meal itself?'

But he insisted. And, very gently and politely, he asked to see the manageress.

Well, she wasn't taking any shit. I think she was Russian. She was certainly cold and warlike. She wouldn't accept anything James said and, from the off, implied that we were only trying to avoid paying. At some point, I saw red. I hate complaining, I hate conflict – I'd rather nod and smile and then bitch behind people's backs. Or nod and smile and then ring my agent to get her to complain. But at one point James said something perfectly reasonable, and she interrupted and directly contradicted him.

This flew in the face of everything my parents had ever said about how you run restaurants and hotels. When people complain, you have at the very least to say sorry and accept that the complaint is sincere. So I sprang into action and gave this unpleasant woman what I remember as a devastating tongue-lashing. That is also how the others remember it, although it must be said that we were all a bit drunk.

I do know that I never raised my voice or swore. I merely contradicted the woman back and, when she tried to interrupt me, told her to be quiet and to listen to what I had to say – which was that she was running the worst restaurant I'd ever been in. To the last, she rejected all our complaints and refused to say sorry. Meanwhile, behind us, one of her staff started glumly hoovering.

We left feeling better for having had our say. But, ridiculously, we paid. In full. The manageress's technique of accusing us of trying to get a free meal tricked us out of the only action that could have hurt her. She didn't care about the argument or that we were unhappy, she had no hopes of repeat custom – that wasn't the business model. She needed only to get our money once. The next day, there'd be another bunch of dupes to fleece. Well, at least we didn't leave a tip. Still, we contributed to that miserable chain's survival. For evil to triumph, all that is necessary is for good men to go to the Angus Steakhouse once.

Writing on *Armstrong and Miller* led to other work. Ben and Xander asked us to help write their radio sitcom, *Children's Hour with Armstrong and Miller*, and Phil suggested us to the production team of *The Jack Docherty Show*, a Channel 5 chat show also made by Absolutely, as regular writers.

Meanwhile Nick Jones, the director we'd met in Edinburgh, had some excellent news. He'd finally got his name printed on his business cards. Also, he'd put together a BBC Two sketch show pilot called *Bruiser* with a producer and writer called David Tomlinson. Rob and I had written a fair bit of the material and Rob was cast as one of the performers. The BBC had sat on this tape for a few months before giving the green light to a full series. In February 1999, at the end of a writing day on *Jack Docherty*, David and Nick took us to the Hand and Racquet pub near Leicester Square to tell us about the commission, and to say that the only cast members they were planning to retain for the series were Rob and Mackenzie Crook (who subsequently dropped out to make the first series of *The 11 O'Clock Show* instead). They also said that they wanted me to join the cast and for Rob and me to head up the writing team. Suddenly, out of the blue, we had our own sketch show on BBC Two. Rob and I were so excited we immediately went to Pizza Express.

And we had yet another iron in the fire. Nick Symons, a producer at Carlton who'd seen our 1998 Edinburgh show, asked us to develop a sitcom with him. The idea was to pitch this to Channel 4 rather than ITV in the hope that it would initially be staged at the Channel 4 Sitcom Festival, where several promising sitcom scripts were staged as plays in front of an industry audience.

After years of indolence, suddenly we were extremely busy, writing sketches for *Bruiser, Armstrong and Miller* and *Yes Sir, I Can Boogie*, the sitcom pilot for Nick S (which we called *Daydream Believers* and featured Colin and Ray, characters who had been central to several of our Edinburgh shows) and a script for a new Edinburgh show which, in an act of brand simplification, we decided to call *The Mitchell and Webb Story*. No 'That' yet.

Then we had to perform all of those things, starting with the five-week *Bruiser* shoot which was my first experience of a concentrated period of filming. The *Bruiser* cast were almost all people we knew from Cambridge whom we'd introduced to Nick and David: Collie, Matthew Holness and Charlotte Hudson (who'd done a lot of acting at university but was best known professionally as a co-presenter of *Watchdog*). The only stranger in the cast was Martin Freeman, of whom we were consequently suspicious and whose naturalistic and charismatic performance style was immediately annoyingly entertaining.

Filming usually involves an early start in anyone's temporal currency. Even a farmer couldn't call you a slugabed during a location shoot. As an actor you have to be ready to film by 8am, which means, for a sketch show where you have to keep being made to look like different people, you start costume and make-up preparations at about 7am, by which time you need to have got to the unit base on the other side of London and eaten breakfast, so you're usually leaving the house at about 6. This prospect genuinely frightened me. As someone still accustomed to getting up at lunchtime, unless I had a pressing reason not to, setting an alarm for 5.30 seemed like a sick joke. Surely I just wouldn't hear it or would be unable to function? I was aware that other people got up early every day of their lives, but I was convinced that there was a significant metabolic difference between me and them. Clearly, tiredness didn't affect them as keenly. Maybe I had some mild form of ME.

One of the reasons I'd been attracted to showbusiness in the first place was that I thought, most of my experience so far having been of the theatre, that it was a profession that ring-fenced the lie-in. I didn't mind the idea of working in the evenings, maybe of rehearsing in the afternoons, but mornings, I felt, should be the preserve of sleep, tea and paracetamol. So the realisation that television, the medium I most wanted to work in, required such punishing early starts was a bitter blow. 'Don't lawyers only have to be in court at 10?' I thought. How had I made such a massive misjudgement?

What came as a surprise and a huge relief to me is that I loved location filming. The mornings were painful, vast amounts of the day were spent inexplicably waiting around because of unfathomable technical hitches, and the work itself was incredibly repetitive, involving performing the same shard of material again and again and again from different angles while everyone worried about light and sound and costume and make-up and practically ignored the performances. So most of the minutes and hours spent filming are stultifying. But the days are brilliant. The feeling of achievement at the end of each day is very satisfying. The camaraderie of a crew all working together to achieve the same unlikely and frivolous aim – the making of a funny show – is warm and inspiring. The breaks for lunch and tea, the relishing of comfort food, the ridiculous chats about nothing while waiting around with a cup of tea somewhere incongruous, are all great fun. When that five-week shoot ended I was deeply sad and desperately hoped that it wouldn't be the last such period of work I'd experience.

We then went straight into rehearsing *Daydream Believers* for the Channel 4 Sitcom Festival. The director was Gordon Anderson, who has since gone on to direct *The Catherine Tate Show* and *The Inbetweeners* but who, at the time, had mainly worked in theatre. He was great with our script. When he made an editing suggestion, it was concrete and achievable. His first was simple: swap the first and third scenes. It was an excellent note and meant the show started in the living room of Ray's disgusting house, with Colin recording an answerphone message:

COLIN: *(into answerphone)* Hello, you've reached Colin and Ray's house – well, Ray's house. Well you've reached Colin and Ray, or have you, because actually we can't make it to the phone at the moment, so if you want to leave a message, and we hope you do, then by all means do so. Excellent. So, we'll speak to you soon. Right. Cheerio. Bye bye. Hope that's okay. And – ooh it's after the tone. Oh erm … *(to Ray)* Shall I ask them to leave the date and the time? *(into answerphone)* Could you leave the date and the time and a number we can contact you on, unless we've got it, in which case don't bother. But, if in doubt – oh it's run out of tape, I think that was too long.

RAY: Colin, you should thank them for calling. It's rude otherwise. You should thank them and say sorry we're not in. It's just thanks, sorry, goodbye – it's like the end of the British Empire.

COLIN: No, I know, let's do a funny one – one, with music. No, no, just a funny one. Like I say, 'Leave a message or Ray gets it,' and you go *(muffled)* 'Mmm. Don't hurt me!' in the background.

RAY: We could do that, Colin. My only reservation is that we might then be mistaken for a couple of twats.

COLIN: Yeah, that's true. Okay, let's do a really cool one, really brief. Yeah I know. *(He presses the button and talks into the machine)* You know what to do. *(He lets go of the button with an air of cool finality)* That's it! I've done it! Although I'd better say who we are, in case it's a wrong number. *(into machine, very casual)* Hi, it's Colin and Ray, you know what to do – oh, I let go of the button. *(again, dismissive)* Hi, it's Colin and Ray, you know what to do. Oh, is that a bit arsey? You know, a bit 'you know where to stick it'.

RAY: What if they don't know what to do?

COLIN: *(again)* Hi, it's Colin and Ray. We assume you know what to do. If you don't, what it is is that we're out or we can't make it to the phone so do leave a bleh bleh bleh, oh this really is all just bollocks. I'll do it later. Ray, I'm doing it later. All right? I mean, if it's not all right then say. I just can't be fagged at the moment.

It's a very efficient, and hopefully amusing, introduction to the characters: what they're like and their circumstances. The show went down well and was, I think, the only one from that year's festival to be developed further: we were asked to write another couple of scripts with a view to making a pilot.

We went straight from the sitcom festival into rehearsing *The Mitchell and Webb Story* for Edinburgh, with James Bachman directing. As a publicity gimmick, our show that year was supposedly sponsored by a company called Künty Matches from Bremen, Germany. I expect you can see the joke. We even had thousands of little books of Künty Matches manufactured for distribution round Edinburgh (it's surprisingly cheap to have things printed on books of matches) and, with James, wrote an advertising jingle for them:

Künty Match, Künty Match,
Made one at a time and not in a batch.
From schoolboy to parson, for smoking and arson,
You're never alone with a Künty Maa-aaaaa-aaaa-aaaaa.
Maaaaaaatch!
Künty Match!
(-es).

In the show, Rob and I played the supposed representatives of this sponsor, unimaginatively named Gunther and Klaus. The opening scene included a joke by James Bachman, which may be my favourite of all the jokes I've ever performed on stage. Gunther and Klaus are performing sections of *Strike a Light – My Künty Career*, the autobiography of the matches' inventor Dr Hermann Künty, who was a well-connected German industrialist in the 1930s.

> *They take up a position.*
> KLAUS: Hello, Dr Künty.
> GUNTHER: Hello, Herr Hitler. I have heard so much about you.
> KLAUS: All good, I hope.

It was our most successful Edinburgh show ever, which isn't actually saying much, but it was well reviewed and sold out the whole run and, back in London, even more people wanted to give us cups of tea and talk about our ideas.

Among those who meant business were David Tyler and Geoff Posner. Geoff's first directing job had been *Not the Nine O'Clock News* and he'd worked with most British TV comedy stars who'd come to prominence since. David had cut his teeth on *Spitting*

Image and *Absolutely*. The pair's own company had recently made *Coogan's Run* and *Dinnerladies* and they wanted their next project to be with us. They quickly obtained a BBC commission for a TV script in the style of our Edinburgh shows – a silly story full of characters all of which were to be played by us. The idea was that, in a series, each episode would have a different context – the Middle Ages, Outer Space, Snooker in the 1970s, the Wild West – but the characters would recur, a bit like *The Goon Show*. The working title was *Extraordinary Tales of Exceptional Goodness*.

This was a very exciting prospect. It was only a script commission but David and Geoff weren't time-wasters. They were funny and successful, and the show, if we could get it made, might be relatively original. Original in TV terms – in that it would be a rip-off of a show that happened forty years before, rather than six months ago. It would also be the natural continuation of the stage shows Rob and I had been writing for years. If we could make this show for the BBC and *Daydream Believers* for Channel 4, maybe after a second series of *Bruiser*, we'd be well set-up men indeed.

And still more people wanted to have meetings with us, although they seemed less exciting now that we had so much proper work. As I surveyed the enviable position I found myself in at the start of the new millennium, as I looked proudly at my new BBC diary for the year 2000, I remembered that Rob and I had agreed to meet a couple of jobbing writers, Sam Bain and Jesse Armstrong, to talk about an idea they'd had. We'd met them on an ill-fated team-writing project organised by David Tomlinson, which attempted to make eight men committee-write a sitcom about squatters. Nothing came of it but we'd got on well with Sam and Jesse. We liked what they'd written and vice versa.

We've got a bit too much on, we thought. We're getting proper commissions now. But it would be rude to refuse to see them for a chat – we didn't want to seem grand. Still, we were experienced enough to know that nothing ever came of that sort of meeting.

- 28 -

The Magician

'Well, they've got a brand new cooker now, so we're having to shoot it all the other way.'

'How's that going to work?' I said. 'It's POV – the camera has to keep swinging round. How can two people have a conversation in a tiny kitchen without either of them catching a glimpse of the cooker?'

'It's going to be tricky.'

'Anyway, how come they're messing about, changing their kitchen? You've paid them a location fee.'

'That's how they bought the cooker.'

'Terrific.'

'We're also a bit worried about Rob's tan.'

'What about it?' asked Rob.

'Well, you haven't got it any more.'

'Yes, well it's February now –'

'It's March.'

'Shut up, David. So what do you want me to do – go to the solarium?'

'We haven't really got the budget for that.'

This is how I remember the conversation Rob and I had with the producer, Andrew O'Connor, in early 2002 as we returned to the tiny flat where, eight months earlier, we'd made a ten-minute 'taster tape' for Channel 4 of a programme called 'POV'. The channel had apparently enjoyed the taste – the way it was filmed from the two main characters' point of view was deemed to have worked and they'd liked the interior monologues – but not quite enough for a whole meal (or series – I'm going to abandon this metaphor with the parting image of *EastEnders* being a seemingly endless supply of gallon after gallon of gruel). Instead they'd asked us to show them the other half of the episode – the end of the story which had started in the taster tape. The only trouble was that we hadn't shot the other half so we were doing that now.

'This,' I couldn't stop thinking, 'is not the way television should be commissioned and made. We make a thing on the cheap, hoping against hope that its potential will show through the low production values. It takes us two days to shoot the ten minutes but, it seems, over half a year for the execs to watch it – and then they ask for the impossible.'

I wanted us to say: 'That's not the deal – you don't get to see the second half because you didn't pay us to make it. Make the call, commission a series – or even a proper pilot where we're not slipping a couple of flatmates a cooker's worth of cash on the quiet to make themselves scarce over a weekend. This is not how things should be organised!'

I have this feeling so often when making TV. With huge amounts of money at stake, stupid costs are cut and compromises made, causing crews on the ground, who are actually trying to make the programmes, huge logistical problems. I always angrily want the suits in offices who make arbitrary budgetary or policy decisions to come and answer for it at seven in the morning in a freezing field. Why was *Comedy Nation* made in a disused office while proper TV studios lay idle two floors below? Why do money constraints mean that sunny picnic scenes have to be shot in the pouring rain; that hundreds of man hours are wasted, when shooting at a cheap location near Heathrow, waiting for the tiny quieter intervals between planes passing overhead; that cutting back on vehicles means props and costumes get left at the previous location by tired, over-worked people, causing more hours to be wasted and costs to be incurred which are much higher than having an extra car on stand-by? These costs, which look cuttable on a balance sheet in an office, are slashed through with the pen of someone who doesn't have to live with the consequences of their actions. Meanwhile vast sums are thoughtlessly spent on public relations, rebranding, expensive advertisements, management consultants, etc. I'm not just talking about the BBC or Channel 4 but all of them, by the way – all broadcasters, all production companies, probably all large organisations. The consequences of bad decisions made by essentially unaccountable managers make me want to scream.

And yet, what do the TV crews do? They work round the problems. They wait for the missing prop and agree to work late. They listen uncomplainingly for the gap between planes. They make the show happen. This is a far nobler response than mine – and it keeps in mind the most important truth: that it's fun and a privilege to get to make TV shows, particularly comedy shows, and we should be grateful for any opportunity, however compromised by managerial incompetence, to do so.

This was very much the approach of the producer of 'POV'. Andrew O'Connor, whose fledgling company Objective Productions had made the taster tape, was of the opinion that we could work with all difficulties. We'd film round the cooker, we'd put a bit of fake tan on Rob, we'd make the second half of the taster tape like good boys and girls. Keep them sweet and we might just get a series.

Andrew O'Connor is one of the most interesting men I've ever met. A child actor, former Young Magician of the Year, impressionist and quiz show host, he was one of the last old-school non-alternative comedians. He became famous by the old route, having been a Pontin's Blue Coat. One of his best stories is of the time that Bruce Forsyth explained to him the technique for changing your trousers in the gents of a club without trailing any part of them on the inevitably piss-drizzled floor. The first stage, as I remember it, is to grip the end of one or both of the trouser legs between your teeth.

Unlike colleagues of his such as Gary Wilmot and Bobby Davro, Andrew saw which way the wind was blowing in the early '90s and, after stints in musicals and as a theatre director, he dramatically changed career paths and went into independent television production. When Rob and I first met him, over a coffee with Sam and Jesse in the memorable surroundings of the Royal Institute of British Architects building on Portland Place, he was charming, energetic and obviously intelligent. But could we trust him? His company had made no more than a couple of children's shows – certainly no comedy. I don't think there were even any permanent staff. Could we believe him when he said that he, a former star of *Copycats*, a conjurer, a song-and-dance man, aspired to make the kind of comedy that we were into? Was he the right man to bring a dark show about loneliness and self-doubt in an urban environment to the screen? I don't think any of us were sure he was – I don't think Channel 4 were either – but somehow, as we struggled with kitchen and sun tan discontinuity, we were all going along with it.

If we did get a series, it would be mainly thanks to Sam and Jesse for having written a terrific script. It felt like a long shot, though, and all four of us had higher hopes for the proper sitcom we were simultaneously pitching to the BBC. It was called *All Day Breakfast* (for reasons none of us ever quite understood) and it was also about two flatmates who didn't get on. A feckless layabout, played by Rob, and a dutiful dolt, by me. It was going to be a proper big studio sitcom; we'd done a reading of a pilot script only a couple of weeks earlier for the controllers of BBC Two and BBC Three, which seemed to have gone down very well except for the fact that the controller of BBC Three hadn't turned up.

The idea for *All Day Breakfast* had been hatched in the early weeks of the new millennium, as a result of the original meeting with Sam and Jesse that we'd squeezed in only to be polite. They'd treated us to tea and sandwiches at a little café between Wigmore Street and Oxford Street and basically said: 'How about the four of us try and do that team-writing thing properly? And, if the show gets off the ground, you two can star in it as far as we're concerned.'

Sam and Jesse are immediately engaging and entertaining people to spend time with – they're funny and interesting but they don't have the attention-grabbing megalomaniacal streak that compromises the personalities of most professional performers. We thought they were very talented and would be good people to work with. We were already involved in far too many other projects but we said yes to working with them mainly so as not to be rude. (You may begin to understand why we were involved in far too many other projects.) Nothing has ever made me gladder that I was brought up to be civil.

But by 2002 we were feeling a bit less busy anyway. We'd had a few knocks. *Bruiser* had been broadcast in February 2000 and no one had really noticed. We'd got the odd negative review but basically been ignored. And then we heard nothing. I don't think it was ever even axed. It was insufficiently important to warrant the meeting time for the bigwigs to decide not to order more. But it gradually became clear that it wasn't coming back.

Our pilot of *Daydream Believers* (broadcast as a *Comedy Lab* in 2001), in advance of which we'd written and agonised over four or five new scripts, had also been received with a rapturous silence. Though it was too painful for me to admit at the time, we hadn't made a very good job of it in the end. It came out as somehow just muted and odd. I realise now that it should have been an audience sitcom, like it had been in the Sitcom Festival. The characters were eccentric enough and the dialogue sufficiently cheesy and gag-bearing that it could sustain the sound of audience laughter – and indeed needed it. As well as Colin and Ray, Rob and I also played two characters in a parallel universe of Ray's creating. These were Info, a man pretending to be a robot, and an evil space villain called Baron Amstrad (this was nearly a decade before Alan Sugar's ennoblement). We thought it was funny but it was fairly wacky stuff. Shot single camera, in a supposedly realistic style, it seemed hollow.

Heartwarming Tales of Exceptional Goodness had also hit a brick wall. We'd written and rewritten a script of which we were really proud and the BBC had um'd and ah'd and then suggested a reading.

This is my second mention of a 'reading', so I should explain what I mean. It is the habit in television comedy not to trust decision-makers, whose main job is to read scripts and decide whether they're of sufficient quality to warrant production, to be able to do so. The received wisdom is that they need to be helped to imagine what it would be like if the words on the pages were spoken by actors in a funny way. So little half-rehearsed plays are put on for them, just in offices, with actors hired for the afternoon, holding scripts in their hands, miming the mimable stage directions (e.g. 'he takes a sip of water') while others are read out (e.g. 'a fireball rips through the ice cream parlour'). It's all an attempt to give a sense of how something might be televised.

This is another thing that makes me want to scream (maybe I just, in general, fancy a scream; it might do me good if I occasionally had one). Obviously reading a script and seeing its potential is a skill that not everyone possesses – but highly paid commissioning jobs in television should be the preserve of those who do. I feel that making a small, under-rehearsed, un-costumed attempt to make it seem exciting and televisual is a deeply flawed strategy: the commissioner sees something clunky and amateurish which cannot possibly live up to the production values of their imagination. Better, I always think, to refuse to do a reading and just provide a script. Then, if the decision-makers want to see that dialogue or action played out, they'll have to at least pay for a pilot to be made.

But readings were the vogue in the early 2000s and, with *Heartwarming Tales of Exceptional Goodness*, it was felt that extra effort would be needed to get commissioners to see its potential. So

David and Geoff decided to stage it. They hired a fringe theatre, the Latchmere in Battersea, for a couple of nights and put on a version of it, with Rob and me playing all the characters, and lots of the frenetic cross-dressing that had been the hallmark of our Edinburgh shows.

This was all planned considerably in advance and the BBC's comedy commissioner was due to come on the second night. Sadly, a few weeks before the show, she resigned and took a job at Channel 4, and her deputy was promoted to the job. This was bad news. When a commissioner leaves, all the projects they were developing are tainted in the eyes of their successor. 'I won't get any credit if that idea is a success – I need to be developing my own projects,' they usually think. So, if the commissioner who is your advocate, or even the person who's been giving you a sceptical hearing, changes jobs, there's a big chance your idea will be shelved. But we decided to go ahead as, if the deputy was enthused by the show, there was still a chance he'd feel 'ownership' of it and would push it forwards himself.

The show was well received on both nights. Afterwards, David, Geoff, Rob and I sat in the pub under the theatre to chat to the new commissioner. The first words said about the show were from his deputy: 'How on earth do you learn all those lines?'

Terrific, I thought. That's damning with faint praise if ever I heard it – and now I have to think of an answer more polite than: 'Because it's my job – how on earth do you remember to go to all those meetings?' They treated the show as an amusing entertainment they were coincidentally going to and had enjoyed – not a pitch that had been put on at their express request. They also said, and this made my already boiling blood create a weird 'haemovapour' which came out of my mouth in scarlet burps, that it seemed a bit too theatrical. Having just spent the past week converting a TV script for suitability to the stage, this was bitterly annoying. Two weeks after that show, the new commissioner left the BBC to join his former chief at Channel 4. *His* former deputy, the one who'd been impressed with the line learning, took the job and *Heartwarming Tales of Exceptional Goodness* was never heard of again.

The only show we were able to get off the ground in the first couple of years of what was becoming a frustrating millennium was for a cable channel, UK Play, which then rebranded to Play UK (for which change – and it is always important to remember this – someone was paid money) before closing down. One of the decisions it made on its journey towards unviability was to commission a six-part sketch show from Rob and me. This was almost as low budget as *Comedy Nation* but, as there were only two writers and performers involved, with occasional support from Olivia Colman, Gus Brown and Mark Evans, the money went a bit further. *The Mitchell and Webb Situation* (still no 'That') was a decent show, considering all the constraints on us, among which I include our limitations of time, experience and talent, but I think more people watched it round our various flats on video than saw it broadcast on Play UK. Still, it was a nice, if slightly tantalising, reminder of the fun we could have doing the job we aspired to do.

Meanwhile, Matthew Holness, together with his writing and performing partner Richard Ayoade, had won the fucking Perrier Award! Matt is a very good friend of mine – the kindest and most honourable of men – and his prodigious talent and hard work had created a brilliant show which was a rightful winner of the award. And how much better, I kept telling myself, that a good friend should win the award than a stranger? It's nice for your friend and even in cold, hard, mercenary, networking terms, better that the career leg-up should go to someone who you know than someone who you don't.

But no amount of that reasoning could soften the blow. As Gore Vidal apparently said: 'Whenever a friend succeeds, a little something in me dies.' I didn't want to be like that and I worked hard to conceal it, but I couldn't help feeling horribly envious. Matt and I had gone into comedy at the same time, I'd got the earlier breaks, but Matt had stuck to his guns, developed a character for the stage and created a show that was both brilliant and entirely 'him'. Meanwhile, I'd been messing around pitching compromise ideas to TV companies – and now he had an award and I'd just guzzled a lot of free tea. He was the toast of that year's Fringe, while Rob's and my show *The Mitchell and Webb Clones* (a 'That' wouldn't have really worked in this case) was languishing unnoticed.

So, as you can probably tell, the sheen had been rubbed off my early, excited experiences of television by the time we were shooting the second half of 'POV'. Everything seemed difficult and stressful and obstructed. My back kept playing up. I felt unhealthy, as if I was missing opportunities. And my private life was a mystery to me.

The reason I say that is, in autumn 2001, I'd briefly had a girl-friend. Within days of the relationship ending Ellis was already characterising my whole attitude to relationships as 'tried it, didn't like it, so I stopped'. I suppose that was a reasonable summary.

A very nice girl, a friend of friends, had come to see *The Mitchell and Webb Clones*. I don't know whether to tell you her name. It probably won't mean anything to most readers, which isn't to say she's not very successful at her job because she is, but it isn't one of the jobs that brings your name to prominence like pop star, chef or disgraced former chief constable. But obviously, for her and her friends, there it would suddenly be in a book, with me delicately implying I've had sex with her – which certainly isn't something she asked for (being in the book, that is – the sex was totally consensual; I'm an absolute stickler about that).

So I'm not going to tell you her name – I'm going to make up a name. So you can just imagine a girl, rather than anyone specific. Let's call her Meryl Streep.

I hope that doesn't make it difficult for you to not think of someone specific. My logic is that, if I call her Meryl Streep, anyone flicking through this in a bookshop might randomly open it around here and assume it's full of salacious Hollywood anecdotes. With me in them. Sleeping with film stars. A bit like *The Moon's a Balloon* but with Peter Sallis instead of David Niven.

So Meryl Streep was a bit flirty after the show and I liked it. I thought she was attractive and bright and entertaining. It didn't occur to me to do anything about it but I noticed. A few weeks later, I bumped into her at a play which a mutual friend was in. We chatted some more and the next day she sent me an e-mail asking me on a date.

Interesting, I thought. A date, eh? So they do happen! What should I do? Well, the first thing I noticed is that I was not in love or infatuated with her. I hadn't suddenly developed a crush – I was not preparing for her a pedestal in my heart. But I definitely liked her a lot and fancied her. And I was 27 and all my love life had consisted of was the occasional guilt-ridden one-night stand while I pined passively for someone else. At the time of meeting Meryl Streep, I was in one of the widening gaps between obsessive crushes. 'Isn't this exactly the sort of person I should be going out with?' I thought. 'People go out with people they're not in love with all the time – they like each other, fancy each other, enjoy each other's company and have a good time. Sometimes their feelings grow stronger, sometimes not. But either way, relationships like that are worth having when you're in your twenties, aren't they? Surely it's ridiculous of me to bloody-mindedly wait for the woman of my dreams to ask me out? Meryl Streep is lovely and seems to like me. I should give this a go,' I reasoned.

I know this is a fairly unromantic train of thought – but also probably a common one, although I suspect that earlier developers than me go through it in their teens rather than their late twenties.

So we went out for a while, Meryl Streep and I. But, while there were many aspects of the experience that I liked (I am now definitely sounding like a robot), I basically didn't take to it. We had fun, we had lots to talk about, it was brilliant having regular sex but, ultimately, being in a couple with someone I didn't have overwhelming feelings of love for felt wrong. Like a lie, even though I hadn't lied. I hadn't implied I was in love and neither had Meryl. But I wasn't comfortable with the physical closeness to someone I didn't feel sufficiently emotionally close to. I suppose that's a bit weird and repressed, and I felt terribly guilty when I had to say to her, apparently out of the blue, that the relationship wasn't working for me. And I had no satisfactory explanation of the situation other than Ellis's summary, which I felt wouldn't go down too well. But there it was.

So, in early 2002, my private life was a mystery to me. I was single and it was definitely my fault. I'd had the chance of a nice relationship and all I'd used it for was to hurt someone lovely. I really didn't know what I wanted.

Are You Sitting Down?

The landline rang in my living room. This wasn't as unusual in 2002 as it is now. Nowadays I'd assume it was a survey or someone trying to sell me something. If I answered it, I'd expect that suspicious pause after I said hello which tells you that it's from some poor sod in a call centre – a cold-call centre, in fact. Possibly a cold cold-call centre if it's in the North-East, or a humid cold-call centre if it's the subcontinent. The pause, I reckon, is because they've dialled a dozen, or a hundred, or maybe a thousand numbers at once, and it takes a beat for them to notice which ones have been answered. And of course it's an infuriating pause because, not only is someone about to waste your time, you're also expected to wait a few seconds until it's convenient for them to start wasting it. They require you to waste a bit of your own time for them first.

And then the battle begins. The battle, in my case, is to get off the phone politely and without having hung up on anyone. I feel that an element of my humanity will have been lost if I actually hang up while they're still speaking. I try, by adopting a firm and patronising voice, to put an end to the call in good order. Of course it never works. The techniques drilled into the staff of a cold-call centre presumably include never stopping talking and never saying, 'Okay, thanks, goodbye.' I'm a slightly obsessive 'goodbye' sayer – I come away from parties with an unsettled feeling because I haven't formally taken my leave of all the people I chatted to. I know that's fine and people don't expect it, but it feels like I've left lots of loose ends hanging.

All of which makes me easy prey for the cold-caller. My I'm-so-sorry-I'm-not-interesteds and thank-you-I-already-have-a-mobile-phones have no power over them and they can get through their full script. So they've won. Assuming that's their aim rather than selling anything. Because I certainly never buy anything and I can't imagine anyone would. If you're reading this and, when someone cold calls you, you actually consider buying what they're offering then please stop for all of our sakes. It's only the one in a million like you who actually pays attention to the unsolicited telephone bullshit that fuels this industry of time-wasting that's the scourge of us all – and would have led millions to abandon landlines altogether if the likes of Sky didn't perversely insist you have to have one. That's how far we've come in the last ten years: televisions used to work without telephone lines and now they don't. Well done everyone.

The other thing that was different ten years ago is that a lot of people still used landlines as their first way of getting hold of someone. Mobiles were a luxury for use in emergencies, like a mink life-ring or a fire extinguisher full of champagne. It was like my father's approach to the immersion heater at home.

Nowadays, of course, we've become too impatient not to use them all the time. The idea of calling a place not a person is insufficiently immediate for our increasingly self-important techno-civilisation. And you tell yourself that you've got lots of free calls to and from mobiles so it's all fine. No need to cross the room to either pick up or answer the phone – just use the one in your pocket that's slowly microwaving your upper femur.

Every month I pay about £60 to Orange. I think, if I managed my tariff choice as conscientiously as those with no real sense of the brevity of our time on earth say I should, I could probably get it down to about £30. That would still be £360 a year I'd pay – and for what? Being able to get hold of people and talk on the phone? No, that happened fine before mobiles. Being able to arrange to meet people? No, that happened fine before mobiles. To allow myself to be bombarded by text messages that require painstaking, thumb-arthritis-inducing answering and to indulge myself in sloppy meeting plans that have to be finessed at the last minute by phone? Yes, I get that. For hundreds of pounds a year. Well done everyone.

Anyway, back in 2002, I sometimes answered the landline.

'Hello?'

'Hi, it's Andrew. Are you sitting down?'

'What, er ... why? Do I sound sleepy? I haven't just woken up – I'm actually in my living room.'

'Are you sitting down?'

'No, well, sort of. I've got one knee on the arm of a sofa and I'm sort of leaning against a wall but I'm not really ... what?'

'Um, right. Yes, well, Channel 4 have commissioned a series of POV!'

'Oh that's brilliant news! Excellent!'

'Yes, isn't it?'

'Oh! Now, I see what you meant about sitting down – you were saying that it's, that it would be ...'

'Yes.'

'Sorry, I should've ... I didn't respond appropriately.'

'It's fine.'

'Good, thanks.'

'Anyway, all the details still have to be sorted out but I wanted to be the one to tell you first.'

'Thanks. Sam and Jesse mentioned it last week actually.'

'Did they?'

'They said it wasn't definite but that it was ...'

'Oh.'

'... likely, you know.'

'Ah. Anyway – it's good news.'

'It certainly is.'

'Bye then, talk soon.'

'Bye.'

At the time I was convinced that Andrew O'Connor, with his theatrical approach to life, had tried to express it in a way that might get into someone's memoir and that I'd ruined the moment. So, seeing as it was my fault, I feel duty bound to include it here.

And of course that was massive news for Rob and me. By the time of its commission, 'POV' was our last iron in the fire. Everything else that we'd been developing for years had ceased even to languish on television's giant and growing 'Maybe' pile. We'd also tasted the life of the jobbing TV daily writer, which was both moreish and somehow unsatisfying, like a Happy Meal.

I'd come to feel that this would be my career. I wouldn't have failed utterly – I'd be working in TV comedy, not as an on-screen writer-performer but a perfectly well-paid jobbing writer on other people's shows who would maybe, very occasionally, get a small part guesting in something as an actor.

Being a jobbing writer isn't like being a jobbing actor because it's much easier to make a living. There are far more good actors than there is work to go round. Even if casting was completely meritocratic, a lot of talented performers would be out of work a lot of the time. In the system we actually have, where plenty of useless, jammy and well-connected turns work constantly, it's even worse. But, while there are just as many injustices in the writing profession, the bottom line is that there's more work in TV for those who can write funny things than there are people who can do it. If you're funny and reliable and don't smell too much – and, let's be clear, you can smell a bit – you'll find work.

Rob and I discovered this. For example, we worked two days a week on the last series of *The 11 O'Clock Show* which Phil Clarke had been brought in to produce. As a project, it had completely run out of energy and Channel 4 were looking for an opportunity to axe it. Rob and I were part of the team which ended up providing it. Despite our efforts, that series was a mirthless and merit-free gap between the era when *The 11 O'Clock Show* was bringing stars like

Sacha Baron Cohen and Ricky Gervais to national attention and the point at which the show was cancelled. We insulated the channel against criticism – we ensured that the programme slipped away unmourned. But we were paid hundreds of pounds a day just to be there, scribbling down jokes for others to reject. It was good, civilised work – but it didn't feel like writing.

Daily jobbing writing on shows like that often involves no writing at all – no use of pen or keyboard. You sit in a room, supplied with too much caffeine and pastry and too little daylight and oxygen, and you pitch jokes and funny ideas, competitively, alongside other people. But you don't decide what gets written down. Some senior writer or producer does that. In my view, only he or she (to be honest, in TV comedy it's always been a he in my experience) could really be described as 'the writer'. Other sorts of writing, even other sorts of TV writing, where you're at home working on sketches or a sitcom script, don't work like this. You get to decide what gets put down. People might refuse to print, read or get actors to perform it – they might quibble with sections or suggest changes – but the piece of writing is yours to create and change. Nobody tries to grab the pen.

I'm now walking through Notting Hill and I pass one of those horrible modern office buildings that were put there in the '60s and '70s to make the adjacent Victorian stucco look even more beautiful than it is. In there, I remember, Rob and I had one of our most dispiriting experiences of jobbing writing, in the offices of a successful independent production company.

We'd been hired for two days to help develop an idea for a pilot for Ben Miller. I think Ben had kindly suggested us for the gig but he wasn't actually there and we were left to the tender mercies of some development producers. It was a panel show thing – I can't remember the actual premise but it was aspiring to be part of that spate of *Room 101* knock-offs, all essentially TV versions of *Desert Island Discs*, which were popular at the time. Popular with commissioners, that is. I don't think viewers ever expressed many feelings in their favour. So it was some sort of format in which Ben would talk to one guest for a whole half-hour show but the chat would be structured according to things they loved/hated, or movies, or bands, or historical characters, or types of cheese – that sort of thing. I can't remember which.

Let's say it's the last. So Rob and I turned up first thing in the morning and had the premise for Ben Miller's 'You've Made It to the Board!' explained to us by whichever hapless development monkey had been slaving away over it for the last few weeks, and were told that they wanted us to 'punch up the pitch' or 'develop the format' or something else meaningless. What I particularly remember about that job was the way the development people kept talking nervously about their bosses at the production company. They were referred to with trepidation throughout the day. This guy, Sebastian, kept being mentioned as if it should mean something to us.

'So yes, we need more thoughts for intros to run past Sebastian when we meet him at 5.'

'Okay, so Sebastian will be coming in at 5 and it would be great if we could pitch some more active rounds for the show to him then.'

'We hear Sebastian might be keen to hear if we could work a sketch into the format, so that would be great if you could get some of those together by 5 – for the Sebastian meeting.'

'Only forty minutes to go before Sebastian o'clock!'

They were terrified of Sebastian. After a few hours, I pretty much assumed it had to be Sebastian Coe. Either that or a massive Doberman. Sebastian, when he eventually arrived, was perfectly nice and reasonable and talked through the ideas like a sensible human for an hour. After he left, they were all: 'I think the Sebastian meeting went well' … 'Yeah, I feel Sebastian thought we've made some improvements,' etc. Maybe we were working with particularly anxious people, or maybe Sebastian was usually an ogre and we got him on valium day. Most likely, I think, it becomes psychologically necessary for some people to make elements of their life seem momentous – to inject a bit of 'Hey guys, this is TV – how badly do we want this!?' bullshit energy into a working environment to disguise the fact that, TV or not, the project under discussion is of no real interest to anyone involved, or indeed anyone else alive or dead.

All day, I wanted to say: 'Listen, I don't give a shit what Sebastian thinks as long as I get my £300 for the day.'

The real victim of work like that is the viewer. Good programmes are not made in the self-consciously cut-throat, 'results-orientated' environments which some production companies affect. It may be how you improve productivity in a factory but, in entertainment, it creates pap. There are too many programmes which nobody really cares about – as nobody really cared about this one (which never got made in the end). The format is developed by someone in format development who churns out a dozen such things a week; the star is attached because it looks like the right sort of show for them to be doing next; the company pitches it because it needs commissions to pay the rent; the channel commissions it because the idea ticks various boxes: it involves the right sort of name, or it's a kind of show people watch, or it's made in the regions, or a certain number of episodes can be churned out cheaply.

Now, all of these factors are rightly relevant to the decision about whether or not a programme should be made but, in my view, they aren't reason enough on their own. For a programme to justify its existence there should be someone involved who loves the idea – whose 'baby' it is; someone who has always thought, rightly or wrongly, that the concept is a properly good one. All really successful shows, as well as some terrible ones, have that. But even those terrible ones have integrity and fail nobly whilst actually trying something. 'You've Made It to the Board!' (that was not its title) would have had nothing noble about it because no one involved would have really cared. Far better to make shows for yourself than for Sebastian.

But it's quite a pleasant way to work really – it's hardly coal-mining. You sit and think of funny ideas while people bring you tea and sandwiches. As long as you don't mind the ideas subsequently being ruined and/or ignored, and if you can keep your terror of Sebastian under control, it's a pretty decent life and, if that sort of work were still the mainstay of my career, I hope I'd still count myself lucky.

My existence had become a little less studenty by this point, so regular income was a higher priority. The landlord of the Swiss Cottage flats had finally turfed us all out, saying that he wanted to redevelop the properties (in fact, they lay empty for the next seven years), and so most of us decided that the time had come to get mortgages. Financial pressures consequently forced our group's centre of gravity three Tube stops outwards from Swiss Cottage to Kilburn, where Sally, Ellis and I separately bought flats. Robbie Hudson (who was in *Go to Work on an Egg* with me at university and is now a novelist) became my flatmate in Kilburn, as he still is.

In a very nice way, the Swiss Cottage community has continued in mortgage-holding Kilburn. University was a bit distant for anyone to come up with a Cambridgey pun, but Robbie would occasionally refer to us in e-mails as 'The Kilburn Social Club' before appropriating that name for a book he was writing.

Satisfied though I'd probably have been with getting regular writing work, making regular mortgage payments and enjoying regular nights out in the pub with people I'd known for nearly a decade, the 'POV' series commission felt like a rescue. We'd had so many chances of getting our own show off the ground and some-how muffed all of them, but then, at the eleventh hour, the least likely of all the pitches we were associated with, the one which had been partly filmed with cameras on our heads, the one made by a company no one had heard of owned by one of the country's least fashionable comedians, had suddenly come off.

I think Sam and Jesse felt the same. They'd had a similar career trajectory to ours. Their equivalent of our *Bruiser* and *Daydream*

Believers failures was *Days Like These*, the British version of the American hit *That '70s Show* which they'd been commissioned to adapt for ITV. This had felt like a tremendously exciting opportunity, had been well paid and involved trips to Hollywood to meet important American producers. But it had not been a success. I imagine Sam and Jesse's comic instincts were defied by interfering executives from both sides of the Atlantic at almost every turn. They had little creative control over what was being done in their name. ITV, who were basically moving out of comedy at that point, dumped the show to a graveyard slot after disappointing ratings and reviews. So, for Sam and Jesse as well as us, 'POV' was a reprieve.

But that title had to go. Most people wouldn't get that it's an acronym of 'Point of View', we thought. And we couldn't call it 'Point of View' because of the BBC feedback show *Points of View*. We needed to think of a better name – preferably something classy.

- 30 -

Peep Show

'*Peep Show*?! They want to call it *Peep Show*.'

'Mmm,' said Rob.

'I don't like it,' I said.

'I think it's better than "POV".'

'I don't.'

'You always say it doesn't really matter what things are called.'

I do say that. Titles are difficult but I think, basically, they don't matter. Once a show is up and running, the title loses any significance. As long as it's not called *Some Wood and a Pie*, which is an extreme case. Usually, after a while, the title just refers to the show and carries with it the feelings or associations of that. You stop wondering if it's a good title in the same way that you never stop to think whether 'carrot' is a good name for a carrot. No one would ever say: 'Carrot, ooh I'm not sure – doesn't seem very carroty somehow. Doesn't say carrot to me. Wouldn't "splandeb" conjure up something orange and pointed more effectively?'

Actually maybe it would – maybe if carrots had been called splandebs, they'd have been 8 per cent more memorable or tasty-seeming over time and consequently 4 per cent more consumed. That's a vast increase in vegetable consumption over hundreds of years and billions of people. It would have saved lives. Hundreds of thousands, maybe even millions, may have died because no one ever thought to call a carrot a splandeb.

But I think that's unlikely. Even awful names for people don't matter post-playground – they just become a label. Of course the awful names – the Fifi-Trixiebelles, the Apples, the Peacheses (which are perfectly good names for an apple or some peaches, although dugnid and famp would be better) – will always end up referring to people who are scarred by having spent a childhood with an awful name (and growing up with the sort of parents who'd give them an awful name) so this is an experiment with no control. But what I'm saying is that should you, by some miracle, reach adulthood with a viable personality despite being called Moon-Unit, then Moon-Unit will cease to sound odd to your friends and just come to refer to the perfectly decent human you've miraculously found a way of becoming.

Have I Got News For You, for example, is an abysmal name. There's definitely an implied exclamation mark at the end. It's a weird rhetorical question – and the imagined poser of such a question is a total dick. 'Hey guys, have I got news for you! Margaret Thatcher's resigned! I wonder what idiot they'll pick next' … 'Listen, dudes, have I got news for you – you'll never believe this, the flat's full of asbestos!' But people don't think about that after a while; *Have I Got News For You* is just a noise denoting a great TV programme.

The only exception to my 'the name doesn't matter' rule is when a title is so bad, so misrepresentative or undermining, that it makes it impossible for a show, concept, chocolate bar or band to become successful in the first place. Whatever its merits, it can't get off the ground – like a perfume called 'You Smell of Poo'. Who's going to give it a go? That was why I thought 'POV' would be fine if we couldn't think of anything better. It might have been incomprehensible but it wouldn't be particularly off-putting.

Peep Show was different. It sounded licentious, which worried me. Surely that would put off some of the right people – those who might be up for a sitcom – and attract some of the wrong: those in the mood for a wank. Because, frankly, they were going to have to be *really* in the mood for a wank – the whole thing would basically have to be happening unaided anyway – for our show to do the job for them. The only really appreciative audience members would be those who, having been put off their masturbatory stride, found themselves in a receptive mood for comedy. That's a tiny demographic.

I know sex sells, but so do other things. And putting sex all over something that is, in fact, drain cleaner rather than sex is counter-productive. It just annoys sex-seekers and surrenders market share to more straightforward drain-cleaner promoters. I accepted that *Peep Show* wasn't totally dishonest – the title implied voyeurism which, as the show allowed you to look through people's eyes into the intimate parts of their lives, and to hear their even more intimate thoughts, was reasonable. But what it implied a lot more heavily was a peep show: a place where you squint through a hole at a stripper.

'Typical bloody Channel 4,' I grumbled. 'They're trying to make it sound all late night.'

'It is late night. It's on at 10.35,' said Rob.

'But, you know, all sexy. Why are they making me seem sexy? I don't like it. What do Sam and Jesse think?'

'It was their idea.'

At which point, I decided to stop moaning about the title. God knows, Sam and Jesse had written every other word in the scripts brilliantly – who was I to complain if I wasn't massively keen on the first two? And, like I said, titles don't really matter.

But it always annoys me when people call the programme *The Peep Show*. For me the distinction between *Peep Show* and *The Peep Show* is quite an important one. The former can be taken as a reference to the show's voyeuristic style, while the latter suggests it's a story about the day-to-day hilariousness of working at the low-rent end of the sex industry. Maybe people add a 'The' because of *The Office*, with which, in its early days, *Peep Show* was often either flatteringly or unfavourably compared.

Anyway, I'm getting ahead of myself. This decision about the show name was made a full year after 'POV' was commissioned. We'd made the whole series, not knowing what it was going to be called. So let's go back to the summer of 2002.

I was on holiday in France when my mobile rang.

I'm going to leave that sentence on its own because I found it all so impressive at the time. I was on holiday – a deliberate, organised period of sophisticated relaxation. In France: a foreign country which I had travelled to using my own money with no help from my parents and showing a valid passport which I'd managed to sort out for myself – I'd been to the post office and filled out the forms like a functional human. My mobile: yeah, sure, I had a mobile phone, I needed it for work, it was quite a small snazzy one if I remember rightly; I could pay the bills and stuff, that was never a problem. Rang: MY MOBILE WORKED IN FRANCE!

I answered and it was Phil Clarke – A TELEVISION PRODUCER CALLED MY MOBILE WHEN I WAS ON HOLIDAY IN FRANCE!!! I wasn't actually by the pool. It would have been better if I'd been actually by the pool. Phil said he'd been invited to have a chat with a bloke called Andrew O'Connor, who it seemed was some sort of magician-impressionist, to talk about a commission he'd got for a show where comedians wore cameras on their heads and he'd heard that I was involved. Would this be a good thing for him to produce or was it a nightmare being organised by a chancer?

I thought it probably *was* a nightmare being organised by a chancer but it was also a nightmare I'd already signed up to live through, with hilarious scripts, and the only opportunity on my horizon of actually getting on TV other than applying for *Big Brother*. Maybe, if it was a success, I'd have to field calls from more producers at even more exotic holiday locations. And Phil understood comedy as well as anyone I knew. I strongly encouraged him to go for the chat. After doing that, he took the job.

There were certainly times when I felt a little bit guilty. Phil had been working at Talkback, a production company with a great track record in comedy, while Objective was a company lacking a track record in anything other than filing accounts at Companies House (and I wouldn't be amazed to hear that it had dropped the ball once or twice where that was concerned).

And the 'POV' shoot was very tough indeed. We were shooting something in a style that hadn't been tried before – where every shot was looking through the eyes of one of the characters – and our first discovery was that it took much longer than normal filming. We hadn't realised this when making the taster tape because we hadn't really bothered with things like consistent lighting. But this was going on TV and had to look reasonably professional. And it turns out, when a camera is aping a person's movements, it has to keep turning round to look at another part of the room. This soon leaves you with hardly any parts of the room in which to put the lights, which are the main thing that stops TV from looking like someone's home movie.

If you haven't seen *Peep Show*, then I wouldn't be at all surprised. Few have. Televisually few; it would be a hell of a turn-out on the Edinburgh Fringe. But it's never been a ratings hit. It's been well reviewed and won a few awards, including a BAFTA, a couple of British Comedy Awards and a Golden Rose, and I feel enormously proud to be in it and lucky that Sam and Jesse have chosen to lavish such amazing writing on my weird voice. Still, if you feel the need to read the following description, I'll be neither surprised nor disappointed. Come to think of it, I won't even know.

It's about two young men (well, they were when we started) who share a flat, one of whom looks uncannily like me. They're called Mark and Jeremy and, looking through their eyes and hearing their voices, we're plunged into an intricate and comically heightened version of urban tedium. They're friends from university living disappointing lives, Mark as a pedantic, lonesome loans manager and Jeremy as a libidinous failed musician. Each feeds off the certainty, in the midst of all that baffles him about the world, that no one could be more wrong than his flatmate. Here's a typical exchange between the two of them from series 6. Jeremy has just fallen in love again and Mark has discovered that his computer is broken and he's lost everything on it despite being, as we hear his interior monologue say, 'exactly the kind of person who backs up':

JEREMY: Hey.

MARK: Bloody computer's dead.

JEREMY: Oh I'm so sorry! Oh that's really dreadful for you – oh, come here.

Jeremy hugs Mark.

MARK: *(Interior monologue)* Ugh, hugging?

JEREMY: Poor you!

MARK: Are you okay? Is this … Ecstasy? You're not getting into Ecstasy again, are you?

JEREMY: I'm in love, Mark. With amazing Elena. I don't want to tempt fate but I *think* everything's going to be totally great forever.

MARK: I'm pleased for you.

JEREMY: You don't understand, Mark. I've realised that everything's just a substitute for being in love. Reading, running in the Olympics, getting a job, being a doctor. And I don't need those substitutes any more. Elena is my one true soulmate.

MARK: It's remarkable, isn't it, that out of the three billion adult women in the world, your one true soulmate happens conveniently to live in the same block of flats as you. Rather than, say, in a village in Mozambique.

JEREMY: Who knows how these things happen? There are powers at work beyond our understanding.

MARK: No there aren't.

| JEREMY: | What was it that Shakespeare said? |
| MARK: | He said a lot of things, Jeremy. |

In the first series, we filmed everything with mini-cameras strapped to our heads. Unfortunately, the footage was so poor that a lot of it wasn't usable so we also filmed everything on a normal camera but with the actor whose POV the camera was aping reaching round the lens so that things could be picked up or put down or other characters' hands shaken. This was incredibly fiddly and took a lot of time. For series 2, we came to the conclusion that a lot of things didn't really need to be filmed on 'headcam' as well as by a normal camera. For series 3, the headcam was used, I think, once. We haven't used it since.

We filmed in a real flat, halfway up a tower block in Croydon, possibly the least convenient part of Greater London to get to from Kilburn. Croydon was chosen because the director of the first series liked the idea of setting a scene on a tram and Croydon is the only part of London with trams. Then Channel 4 told us not to set a scene on a tram as that would be weird because there are hardly any trams anywhere nowadays – mainly it's Croydon and Vienna. So the tram plan was dropped but somehow the Croydon plan wasn't, which was annoying. Sam and Jesse would have been just as happy setting it in Kilburn, which would have cumulatively saved me weeks in a car. Still, it wouldn't have helped in my struggle to differentiate myself from Mark Corrigan.

The flat was a fairly unpleasant working environment as, at any given moment, the whole crew had to be concealed in whichever room definitely wouldn't be visible in the scene we were shooting – which was often the smallest. Watching the show play out in a bland empty flat unfilled by Mark and Jeremy's bland empty lives, it's weird to contemplate that there are perpetually about twenty people just out of shot.

The scene in which Mark, very uncharacteristically, has sex with a seventeen-year-old he's picked up at a bowling alley is precisely such a moment. In that apparently intimate bedroom, there were six or seven burly men hiding just out of sight, behind the camera and under the bed as I did my valiant sex faces, and yet more people – make-up, costume, director, writers, producer, props and art department – lurking right outside the door. In fact, that made it less embarrassing, as the ambiance was vastly different from the one we were trying to portray.

I'd been dreading the sex scene. How much of my naked body would be on display? What if I got an erection? What if when I tried to look like I was having sex, everyone thought it was weird? How was I supposed to behave to this actress I hardly knew? Some of the crew discussed the scene as if I was supposed to be looking forward to it, as if pretending to have sex was a bit like actually having sex, and this made me more uncomfortable still. I wouldn't want to be rude to the actress by not looking keen, or rude to the actress by looking keen. It was a minefield.

Fortunately, the point-of-view filming style came to my rescue. It turned out that, through the eyes of the characters, viewers would only really see heads and shoulders – that, in this world at least, the characters did look at the mantelpiece while stoking the fire. So it involved very little nudity and very little rolling around in bed with a stranger in front of colleagues. Largely, I looked into a camera lens and pulled funny faces. I was helped here by my character who, in seven series, has hardly ever had good sex. So I was supposed to look uncomfortable and worried, which I can do. It would be mortifying to have to pull a confident, aroused face.

In that first series, I also had a love scene with Collie, who played Sophie, the object of Mark's desire. They don't have sex, they just roll around in bed for a bit before having to take Jeremy to hospital when he fakes an overdose. That was slightly less embarrassing as Collie and I knew each other well enough to frankly discuss how much we were both dreading the scene. We didn't have to behave professionally about it. We were singing from the same hymn sheet. And the hymn was: Oh Lord, let's get this over with as quickly as possible.

When the shoot ended, for Phil Clarke the greatest challenge began: making sense of the weird footage. In the edit, he discovered that parts of the show wouldn't cut together. The grammar of this new way of filming hadn't yet been fully worked out and Phil found himself desperately trying to make sentences without enough conjunctions or prepositions. The first editor was also a problem. I think he was a bit too arty and, according to Phil, the first cut of episode 1 was basically an indecipherable blur. He refused to show it to me or Rob as he thought we'd be too depressed.

So a new editor had to be found, reshoots organised, and the money to pay for them extracted from Channel 4; and in general Channel 4 had to be mollified and stopped from panicking. This was made easier by the fact that our commissioning editor was Iain Morris (who has since co-written the brilliant sitcom *The Inbetweeners*). He understood the show, he loved the scripts and was determined, in the face of all our difficulties, not to lose heart. This in turn heartened the rest of us as, in the nine-month gap between the end of the shoot and the first broadcast of the show, we had ample time to wonder whether anyone would like or get this weird thing we were bringing to the screen.

A lot of the time I wished that we could have done something more normal. I'd wanted to make an old-fashioned sitcom with a studio audience. I liked the 'POV' scripts very much but felt that the shooting style was a gimmick. Still, I reasoned, Rob and I were virtually unheard-of and so some sort of gimmick was needed as an excuse for giving us our own show.

And with the benefit of hindsight, I'm now pleased that *Peep Show* has a distinctive filming style. I think it's interesting, often helps the jokes and seldom hampers them. Basically though, I think the show succeeds in the same way as a conventional British sitcom. It's about two people, with whom the audience can identify, trapped in a situation with which the audience can also identify. Like all of us, they want love, money, success, security. But they probably end up pepper-spraying more acquaintances, urinating in more churches and burning more dogs than most of us:

JEREMY: There's a hell of a lot of steam.

MARK: Yeah. As it turns out, dogs do seem to be mostly water.

JEREMY: *(poking with a stick)* It's going a bit, just … not the legs.

MARK: Put the legs back on in the middle – maybe it'll burn better.

JEREMY: Oh right! I have to put the legs back on? If you hadn't refused to pay for firelighters it would have gone by now.

MARK: You shouldn't need firelighters to burn a dog, Jeremy!

JEREMY: How would you know? Shit – it's going out.

Jeremy bends down, starts blowing at it.

MARK: Look I've got to get my pitch sorted before I see Malcolm.

JEREMY: We'll have to bury it. Get the spade.

MARK: What spade?

JEREMY: You didn't bring a spade?

MARK: Do you think I'm some kind of freelance dog-murdering mafia man?

JEREMY: Oh, great. So we've got no fire, no spade … we'll just have to dig with our hands.

Jeremy tries pathetically to dig a hole in the earth with his fingers and a stick.

MARK: Jeremy. There are many things I would do to help you. But digging a hole in the wintry earth with my bare hands so that you can bury the corpse of a dog you killed is not one of them.

Mark and Jeremy are caught between jeopardy and opportunity in the same way as Steptoe and Son, Tony Hancock, the various incarnations of Blackadder, Gary and Tony from *Men Behaving Badly* and David Brent. In many ways it's a classic comedy masquerading as a ground-breaking one and, as a small 'c' conservative, I mean that as a compliment to the scripts, not a criticism.

The extended interior monologues, when you can hear the characters' thoughts, were a proper innovation in TV comedy and one that massively adds comic potential. Here are the thoughts that we hear going through Mark's mind as he attempts his first-ever jog:

MARK: *(interior monologue)* Hey, wow … I'm actually good at this. Maybe I'm a natural? Yeah, I'm a jogger! Of course, there had to be a sport for me! I just never realised – I'm a natural jogger! Feel the legs, like two great steam locomotives, pumping away. I'm Cram, I'm Ovett, I'm unstoppable, I'm – … Jesus, is that a stitch? I … fuck. I think I'm going to be sick. I've got to slow … I need to walk … Urgh. I think I'm going to puke. I am literally going to die. What an idiotic boob I was, back ten or eleven seconds ago.

If you only saw what Mark did and heard what he said out loud, he wouldn't be nearly so funny. He's such a model of conventionality that you'd have comparatively little (just the occasional desk-pissing or stationery-cupboard-ejaculating incident) from which to infer his inner turmoil. As it is, his thoughts can be funny even when his behaviour is meekly shy or just normal. Mark partly came out of the character I'd been chalked down to play in *All Day Breakfast* (the show that Sam, Jesse, Rob and I wrote together, which never got made) who was called Phil. We'd found him harder to make funny than Conrad, Rob's character on whom Jeremy was partly based, because he was so buttoned-up and controlled. But when you can hear the thoughts of such brittle pillars of the community as they begin to crumble inside, there's a lot more potential for comedy.

A world away from the concerns of two twenty-something men sharing a flat in Croydon was my home life: sharing a flat in Kilburn with another twenty-something man. In fact, one of the things that struck me when I first walked into Mark and Jeremy's flat for filming was that it was slightly nicer than mine. Certainly anyone stumbling into my Kilburn residence could have been forgiven for thinking that I was a method actor who'd taken things a bit far (if that's not a tautology).

But Robbie Hudson and I get along a lot better than Mark and Jeremy. I own the flat and am an inept landlord who doesn't know how to repair anything and finds even the process of contacting those who do very stressful. Things just go wrong in flats, it seems. All the time. It isn't just the doorbell. Things that used to work – washing machines, boilers, lavatories, lights – just stop doing so, for no reason. It's like a Microsoft application – except you can't just turn a blocked sink off and on again. And apparently, if you own the flat, it becomes your fault and you have to sort it out. Well, I'm not very good with that but, in compensation, I don't notice if the rent's a bit late. I'm not saying Robbie ever pays his rent late – just that, if he had, I wouldn't have noticed.

Of course we have our differences. He likes the place to be clean but doesn't mind a bit of clutter – whereas I'm not very fussy about cleanliness but do like things to be tidy. So we've compromised on neither of us getting his way.

But mainly we have lots of things in common: we drink a lot of tea; we work from home most of the time; we take any opportunity to be distracted from work by something stupid on the internet; we enjoy mocking daytime TV while avidly consuming it. And, most of all, we both believe that, if you're going to share a flat with someone for any significant length of time, you should never express annoyance. This principle, while it would hobble a sitcom, is vital to a calm life. It is so much easier to live with being annoyed by someone than to live with someone being annoyed by you: the first state is one of irritation, the second is a tyranny. So it's much better to suck it up and never get cross while, in return, all the maddening things about you are reciprocally overlooked.

We've had the occasional point of conflict, however. Robbie likes football, which I do not. During one international football tournament, he took to putting up England memorabilia around the flat. This was only to annoy me – he's not a moron. There were flags on the fridge, lions on the windows, bunting along the book-shelves, etc. He was clearly trying to wind me up, but I rose above it. And, as I rose, so did the tide of memorabilia. More and more household items were decorated with England-liveried plastic, including a large poster of one of the players on my bedroom door. The flat looked like we were celebrating a sort of nationalistic version of Christmas. But the more there was, the more determined I became never to mention it. I knew he was trying to provoke me and reasoned that the most annoying thing I could say was nothing. In a conflict, you should always do what your opponent wants least. One day, all of the memorabilia was suddenly gone. We have never spoken of it. In fact, only if he reads this book will he know for sure that I noticed.

And then there was the partial rent strike. It was over my failure to put in a shower. When we moved in, I promised I'd get a shower fitted and then did nothing about it as I had no idea where to begin. (Anyway, baths are fine.) Robbie would occasionally mention this. Then he would often mention this. I felt guilty. Then he said he was going to dock the rent he was paying until a shower materialised. I was very relieved by this strategy as it meant I no longer felt guilty. He wasn't paying for the shower any more, so I wasn't being unfair by not providing it. I was able to massively scale back my shower-procuring efforts.

I know what you're thinking: two eligible young men with their own pad in London's glittering Zone 2. What happened when one or other of us wanted to invite a young lady back? Well, it would be unfair of me to discuss the existence, extent or nature of Robbie's love life here but, on the rare occasions when I've had a one-night stand, and for the brief period when I was in a relationship, I avoided spending the night in the flat – but this was largely because, until 2007, I still had a single bed. Ridiculously monkish of me, I know. But for years, while single, I didn't like the thought of getting a double because it would feel like I was doing it in the expectation of starting to go out with someone or having more sex. There it would be: all big enough for two people, rebuking me as I lay there alone reading history books. And wanking.

It was my friend Benet Brandreth who finally made me snap out of this attitude, saying it was absurd not to have a double bed, whether I was alone or in a couple. He took me to John Lewis to choose one – which is (I'm sorry to disappoint some readers), without a doubt, the gayest thing I have ever done.

That's not been the only improvement to the flat over the years. I eventually got a shower and new carpets and even, under intense pressure from my parents, a new kitchen. We also got a cleaner. Robbie says 'she doesn't clean things properly'. I agree but counter that she's being paid so that we don't have to not clean things properly ourselves. I am heartened by the thought that this isn't an exchange Mark and Jeremy would have. Jeremy certainly wouldn't care how well the cleaner cleaned but would resent paying for her – and so wouldn't do it. Mark would both want a cleaner and worry that he was being fleeced. In fact, come to think of it, it's a conversation that Mark might have with himself, in his interior monologue. Oh God! Maybe Robbie's just in my head, like in *Fight Club*?

After filming that first series of *Peep Show*, there was a long wait for it to be broadcast. In the gap, Rob and I recorded our other new series: a radio sketch show, *That Mitchell and Webb Sound* (and there at last is the 'That'!). This was produced by Gareth Edwards

– six years after we'd met him, we were finally working together on something that was going to be broadcast. And it was just a normal sketch show, which was a very refreshing change. For years, since we were in Footlights in fact, Rob and I had been trying to come up with ways of dressing sketch shows up as other things – giving them 'themes'. Maybe all the characters know each other, or do the same job, or are related, or live in the same place? Maybe the end of one sketch leads into the start of another? Maybe there's a theme of 'modern life' or 'relationships' or 'food' or 'totalitarianism'?

For ages we'd bought into the notion that a sketch show needs something like this – something unifying to make audiences keep watching, like they do with a sitcom. But, by 2002, we'd realised that was nonsense. No sketch show theme can ever give it a through-line which will attract anything like the audience loyalty that you get for a sitcom. In a sitcom, you can properly get to know characters and follow their lives – a good one like *Cheers* inspires huge audience love and support. People will keep watching just to spend time with those characters, even in patches where the scripts aren't as good as they could be. In terms of repeat-viewing appeal, even the most heavily themed sketch show is hugely outgunned by the most lazily-plotted sitcom.

The only way a sketch show clings to viewers is by being funny and by providing variety – so, if an audience member dislikes one sketch, they'll have some faith that the next might be different and therefore preferable. An overarching theme hampers both of these potential strengths: it makes the show less varied and it precludes some jokes. In my experience, you've no sooner decided on your sketch show concept than you're frustrated by the discovery of a nugget of comedy gold that doesn't fit in.

So, if you want audience loyalty, write a sitcom. If you're doing a sketch show, accept the limitations of the form: you're only ever as funny as your last joke. To try and deny that truth is like putting on a ballet and complaining that all the performers have to dance the whole time. But, when discussing radio pitches with Gareth, we were almost shy to say that we wanted to do a straightforward, theme-less sketch show. But he was fine about it, saying the theme could be that 'every sketch has one of David Mitchell or Robert Webb in it and sometimes both'. That suited us, and theme-less it was. We could have a pair of snooker commentators, bemoaning the teetotal approach of modern players:

PETER: Look at John Parrott sitting there, staring mournfully at his water.

TED: Look at that. You could put a goldfish in that glass. And it wouldn't even die.

Some eager party hosts reminiscing about the tremendous fun they'd had hanging out with Hitler:

ROBERT: I love it when he goes off on one. It's so funny, and not a little persuasive.

DAVID: I know. But some of the things he was saying about Tube workers. I mean, we know him, so we know it's not racist, it's just very very clever irony.

Or an animal charity appeal:

Soft-spoken voiceover

For the price of a cataract operation which would restore this Sudanese woman's sight, you could fund months of trawling up and down motorways looking for kittens. For the £3 a month that could equip an Ethiopian farmer with seeds and tools, you could be providing a lifetime's doggie biscuits for this Labrador that wees itself every time it hears the Hoover.

After recording a pilot at the Edinburgh Fringe in 2002, Radio 4 commissioned a series.

In some ways this was more promising than *Peep Show*. As an opportunity, it had fewer possibilities but it was a more established, respectable achievement: our own comedy show on the old Home Service, rather than a late-night Channel 4 experiment that might disappear. It was a good thing for my parents to tell their friends about. Also, it was a show Rob and I were primarily writing ourselves. Getting laughs both for your material and your performance isn't just twice as good as one or the other. It is roughly 3.2 times as good. I have done the maths on this.

The recordings, held at the Drill Hall Theatre off Tottenham Court Road, were very exciting occasions for me. I invited everyone I had an e-mail address for – this was our chance to perform comedy professionally in front of friends who'd seen us monkey around for years as amateurs. The consequent atmosphere was warm and supportive, like a heated truss. Rob and I, together with Collie and James Bachman who made up the rest of the cast, had a lovely time. It felt like the first night of *Innocent Millions* – it had the same sense of excitement and possibility – but this time it was fine that we didn't know our lines because we were reading them off a script. That is one of the many things that makes working in radio so civilised.

Even though the radio show hadn't even been written when we shot *Peep Show*, it began transmitting first – in September 2003, with *Peep Show* starting four weeks later. We had a sketch show and a sitcom going out at once – surely the breakthrough that we'd expected at the time of *Bruiser* four years earlier was happening for us now?

31

Being Myself

The trendy, scuzzy expensiveness of Notting Hill Gate gives way suddenly to the leafy fashion-proof expensiveness of Holland Park. Whoever was spraying '60s buildings around wasn't allowed west of Ladbroke Terrace. From this point, until the end of Holland Park Avenue, the only interruptions to Victorian stucco and brick are elegant London plane trees.

One of the other things my dad talks about is how London plane trees were the only species of tree that could survive the Victorian smog. He's told me that several times. But that's okay – it's an excellent fact. London was so dense and polluted, such an unprecedented environment, that it had to find its own sort of super-tree that could survive it. Normal trees were too feeble for these circumstances in which millions of humans thrived. I also like the fact that, despite so many of the common decencies of life having been abandoned in order to make the brave new metropolis work – breathability of the air most notable among them – nobody considered tree-lined avenues to be surplus to requirements. The air was so poisonous that it *killed trees* (imagine how much weed-killer that would take), but the sheer quantity of airborne herbicide wasn't a matter of much concern, as long as they could find a tree which, like London, could take it. It's a perverse but somehow inspiring approach.

Soon after Holland Park Tube station, there's a pleasant-looking pub called The Castle around which a semi-circle of drinking, suited people, who have left offices early on this warm spring Friday, has developed. Why don't they go in? For years, I assumed that pubs with crowds around them must be jam-packed inside, but it's seldom the case. Some people, those who've spent all day sitting in stuffy offices, I suppose, prefer to stand outdoors and drink. It must seem a confusing choice to the tramps in the park.

The smoking ban has had an effect too. Rather than reducing the appeal of tobacco, it's given standing outdoors a new cachet. I've certainly smoked a lot more since the ban came in. I'm still only a cadger, who'll go days without one and then have two or three at a party, but for the couple of years before the ban I'd pretty much stopped entirely; I was down to a festive one or two on New Year's Eve. And I only smoked those for the benefit of nicotine addicts who were making resolutions, to rub their noses in my peculiar take-it-or-leave-it relationship with the drug.

Post-ban, I'm back up to about five a week – a lot of them smoked outside pubs in preference to staying inside looking after smokers' bags with the other non-smokers. I'm not saying smokers tend to be more interesting people – I'm sure that's a nicotine-induced illusion. I think the real appeal is the little trip, to break the monotony of pub drinking: 'Let's pop out for a cigarette.' It's like going for a quick swim when you're spending an afternoon sitting round a pool.

Maybe you can tell but I'm quite proud of my approach to smoking – that I can do it occasionally without getting hooked. You may think I'm a fool; after all, even a few cigarettes aren't exactly a health boost. But I reckon the amount I smoke is no more danger-ous than going for brisk walks along busy roads – although that doesn't quite answer the question of how I reckon I can get away with doing both. This is the smug and complacent position that many have been in on the eve of a forty-a-day habit – then again I've been adhering to the upper stretches of this slippery slope for years now, so I reckon I'm a sort of Spiderman figure in the world of this metaphor.

But in December 2004, I must have been outside the pub for reasons of space; this was two and a half years before indoor smoke was banned without an associated chimney.

'I've got to go in about half an hour,' I was saying to whoever would listen. 'I've agreed to do a try-out for a stupid pointless thing.'

This had been my sole topic of conversation all day. It was the afternoon of the BBC Radio Comedy Christmas party which I'd been massively looking forward to. The comparatively brief business of the lunchtime party having finished, everyone had now gone to the pub. In general things were going well for me. Both *Peep Show* and *That Mitchell and Webb Sound* had been given second series and so I reckoned I had a pretty viable career. I felt I was owed a nice relaxing Christmas, kicked off by an afternoon of heavy drinking at this most fun and least wanky of all media events.

It feels very much like the office party for a lot of people who don't have offices. Even those not invited to the do itself would wander along to one of the post-party pubs round the corner from Broadcasting House: the Yorkshire Grey or the Crown and Sceptre. I was outside the latter explaining to the umpteenth person that my 'end of term' piss-up was basically ruined.

'I've been nursing two beers for five hours,' I repeated sadly.

The 'try-out' that I'd said I'd go to was for a new Channel 4 panel show unappetisingly called 'FAQ U'. So, a bit like 'Fuck You'. Splendid. FAQ obviously stands for 'Frequently Asked Questions', and the 'U' for 'You' but, as the phrase 'Frequently Asked Questions You' makes no sense, it was impossible not to conclude that they'd wanted the show to be called 'Fuck You' – that they thought that would be good or funny. So I wasn't very hopeful about the project, but I also felt that refusing to go to a job audition because I'd earmarked that day for a nine-hour drinking session would be crossing some sort of Rubicon in a march away from professionalism.

Also, I wanted to do panel shows. Despite being in a genuinely award-winning sitcom and a well-reviewed Radio 4 show, Rob and

I didn't feel like we'd quite broken through. Maybe it was the fact that fewer people had seen *Peep Show* than read some of its complimentary reviews.

I really liked the thought of trying to be funny off-the-cuff as part of my job. I enjoyed the warm-up chats we always had with the audience at the beginning of radio recordings. I didn't want to do stand-up, but I wanted an arena in which I could try and just 'be funny' in public.

I'd had the occasional opportunity. I'd been a team captain in a show called *Fanorama* which had been broadcast on E4 in 2001 and 2002, long before E4 was a channel with an audience. The two series were hosted by Claudia Winkleman and Lauren Laverne respectively and the other team captain was Rhys Thomas. It was a show in which obsessive fans of bands, actors, celebrities or TV programmes competed to prove theirs was the deepest fanaticism. Rhys and I were supposed to keep it all light. We'd shoot three or four shows a day and get a series of twenty in the can in under a week.

It wasn't brilliant but I really enjoyed it and, as I'd hoped, it led to an invitation to appear on a proper panel show on a terrestrial channel. I'm afraid it might not be one of the ones you've heard of – in fact I've just checked and it doesn't even have its own Wikipedia page. Even *Bruiser* has its own Wikipedia page. It was called *Does Doug Know?*

You get asked a wide range of questions if you're on TV – particularly since the advent of Twitter – but no one has *ever* asked me if and when *Does Doug Know?* is coming back. Neither, to be fair, have they slagged it off. Or mentioned it at all. Most spookily of all, there's no trace of it on Dave.

I'm beginning to suspect that I dreamt *Does Doug Know?* It feels like a dream. I can't remember a lot of the details – the premise, for example – and there were odd and incongruous people from the telly there including both Jimmy and Alan Carr. I remember that it was on Channel 4, that I appeared on two episodes and that I wore a brown shirt for one of them.

The choice of shirt was my key creative decision on that show as I had very few shirts fit for national consumption. My non-folding policy had rendered most of my shirts unpresentable even if you tried to iron them. They were beyond ironing now – they'd gone feral. But I remembered with relief that my mother had recently given me this brown one so it was still in acceptable condition. What I didn't know, and have since learned, is that if you turn up to do a panel show looking like a dog's breakfast they give you a shirt anyway.

I don't remember *Does Doug Know?* being a huge humiliation, but it can't have been a triumph because I wasn't invited on another panel show for three and a half years. I hadn't had a single invitation between then and the pavement outside the Crown and Sceptre (which a lot of people call the 'Hat and Stick' to convey familiarity; you may find that that makes you want to be sick – it does me). And this try-out wasn't a proper invitation – it was just an audition for another new Channel 4 show with, if anything, an even less promising title than *Does Doug Know?* (which isn't very good but would, as discussed in the previous chapter, have been fine if people had liked, or indeed noticed, the programme – and in support of that, let me introduce *They Think It's All Over* and *Never Mind the Buzzcocks*, for fuck's sake, into evidence).

Yes, my *Does Doug Know?* performance must have been terrible. Panel shows are hungry beasts and always looking for fresh meat, more panellists – I know that now. But whatever I did on that show led the entire industry to conclude that such programmes were not for me, a conclusion that thankfully it subsequently revoked. Not mentioning any names, but just think of the most annoying person who keeps popping up endlessly on panel shows (apart from me). Think of the one you find most grating and annoying (which, actually, is unlikely to be me in your case unless you have a masochistic taste in books). The most awful witless twat whose continued employment you cannot understand. Done it? (I wonder if we're thinking of the same person?) Anyway, I must have been worse than him (and it *is* a him, let's be honest. Hardly any women are allowed on panel shows so the ones that break through tend to be pretty good).

I'd had the occasional invitation from clip shows, usually with Rob – to appear on the *I Love 1987* style of programme and affect nostalgia for Sodastreams – and I'd jumped at them until Rob said he hated doing them so we largely stopped. And he was quite right; they're a shit form of television and contributors seldom come across well. The context is too unflattering: you simultaneously look like a cheap rentaquote and someone sufficiently arrogant to think their opinions are fascinating. Oddly, a panel show doesn't carry the same implications, probably because there's usually a nominal game being played to conceal the fact that it's really some people behind a desk pontificating. Give *Loose Women* some sort of quiz structure and I reckon it would only be about half as annoying – although that is still very annoying.

So the *FAQ U* try-out sounded enough like it might be a reprieve for that foundering side of my career for me to forgo seven pints of beer. At 7 o'clock I stumped miserably away from the pub towards another pub, the Bricklayers Arms, in the upstairs room of which the audition was taking place. I got the job.

FAQ U was to be a nightly comedy discussion show, on at about 11 or 12, even later than *Peep Show*. I think Channel 4 was trying to recapture the success that they'd misremembered *The 11 O'Clock Show* as being – but with a simpler format. Some young comedians talk about vaguely topical stuff while sitting on sofas in front of an audience. The show had a three-week pilot run and they wanted to try out a new host for each of the weeks. I was given the job for week 2.

This show was not a success and did not get a series after this trial run. But not only did I hugely enjoy doing it, somehow it put me on the panel show map. Within a week of its first transmission in May 2005, Objective was developing a late-night show for me to host on More 4, and I'd been invited on *Have I Got News for You* and *QI*. Just like that, I was on the list. I didn't have to work my way up via *8 Out of 10 Cats* and *Mock the Week* – I went straight in at the level of the two premier panel shows. I don't know what it was I'd said on *FAQ U* – I mean, I felt it had gone well but not amazingly – but before it I'd only ever been asked on *Does Doug Know?* and after it I was asked on *everything*. Not getting pissed at the radio party had been the right call.

It's difficult to describe the combination of feelings that my first appearance on *Have I Got News for You* evoked in me. That programme started in 1990 when I was 16 and at the height of my comedy fandom. I think most people are at the height of whatever fandom they tend towards at about that age and I wasn't into music or even films particularly. I was into clever, wordy comedy. And *HIGNFY* was a new, clever, wordy comedy show that was suddenly part of the national conversation, leading the satirical assault at a time when Thatcher was falling from power. I watched it avidly every week with my version of the fanaticism that led some women to throw their underwear at the Beatles.

Doing TV comedy in general has always been all the more exciting for me because it's informed by nostalgia for those feelings of teenage enthusiasm. But with *HIGNFY* it was on another level because this was *exactly the same show as I'd watched when I was at school*. The set was the same, the team captains were the same – the only major difference was the presence of Des Lynam in the host's chair rather than Angus Deayton – but apart from that, it was literally a teenage dream come true. My unformed brain, only six years after it stopped aspiring to a career as a Time Lord or wizard, had looked at that show and said to itself: 'I want to be there.' So, as I sat in that studio and the lights darkened and the signature tune played, and those boards at the back of the set turned round like I'd seen on hundreds of occasions for the last fourteen years, it felt like I was flying the TARDIS: amazing and impossible and terrifying. Ancient childhood synapses were re-firing and I just wanted to soak it all up – but I simultaneously realised that this was no time to enjoy the atmosphere. I had somehow to give a decent account of myself. I was the newbie and I could sense the audience's fear.

That's the main battle with an audience – to help them deal with their nerves. They're seldom hostile to a new performer (and I have always carefully avoided performing in places where they might be) but they're often fearful for you: nervous that you're nervous and consequently won't be funny. In that mood, they can't properly laugh because they're on their guard. You need to put them at their ease quickly – say something confident and funny which gives them the impression, however dishonestly, that you're not nervous. Making reference to the unnerving nature of the situation can be a good way of doing this. In a TV panel show, if you say something that dies – totally fails to get a laugh even though it was clearly meant to – the consequent audience tension can often be defused with something as simple as: 'Blimey, I fucked that up!' You've got to be careful, though. If nerves creep into your voice at that point, you'll only make matters worse.

The bravest and most successful example of this approach that I ever saw was when I went to watch Ken Dodd's show in Oxford aged 15. He'd packed out the Apollo Theatre and the show was going fine, if mutedly, in front of the rather staid Oxford audience. Clearly this wasn't good enough for Doddy, who was used to more appreciative northern crowds. So, after a few minutes of respectable but not massive laughs, he put his old, knobbly hands together on either side of the microphone as if in prayer and looked upwards to the heavens.

'Please God, make me funny!' he said.

It got a massive laugh – the biggest of the night. All tension immediately dissipated as we all realised we were in the presence of a performer who was so supremely confident, he felt able to refer to the ultimate elephant in the room: the fact that he was supposed to be making us laugh more than he was. It was amazing, and I often think of it when I see comedians say outrageous, edgy things that 'other people are thinking but won't say'. But would they have said *that*? Ken Dodd was willing to go to a more frightening place than any Frankie Boyle or Jerry Sadowitz routine when making reference, as a technique for warming an audience up, to the fact that he wasn't being funny enough.

I wasn't quite up to that level of confidence on my first *HIGNFY* but I managed to give the false impression that I was expecting to be funny, which meant that I was able to get some laughs. And, to my surprise, I hugely enjoyed the experience. The honour, the excitement and then the terror all fell away quickly and soon I was quite straightforwardly having a good time.

This probably makes me a pervert. Having to appear and/or speak in public always comes high up people's list of worst night-mares – the sort of list which tells you that farmers always kill themselves and moving house is more upsetting than divorce. And to do so on TV while having to get laughs would presumably make the prospect even worse for most people.

I'm not completely unfamiliar with the feeling. When I first went on *QI*, a couple of weeks after *HIGNFY*, I found it much harder. It was a terribly pleasant, civilised environment. The producer John Lloyd, a brilliant and kind man, told me just to chat as if it was an interesting dinner party, and Stephen Fry and the panellists (who, as well as Alan Davies, were Phill Jupitus and Bill Bailey) were welcoming and inclusive. But I wasn't sure exactly what I was supposed to say. Without the focus of 'trying to be funny about the news' I got a bit lost and went quiet.

It's like vertigo. You sit there, listening to other panellists chat-ting easily and getting laughs, thinking, 'I haven't said anything for ages! Why aren't I saying anything?!' Then you think, 'Whatever I say next had better get a big laugh!' That's not much of an incentive to open your mouth. I snapped out of it, and did okay, but it was a nasty few moments. I've never felt like that on *QI* again. I'm comfortable enough to babble on about anything nowadays, reasoning that enough usable stuff will tumble out of my mouth in a 90-minute recording.

I don't worry about that vertigo moment recurring because I know it will if I do. I've enjoyed every panel show I've done since then. As a physical coward, I'm heartened by the fact that I regularly do something that would make some mountain climbers, bear wrestlers or fire-breathing snowboarders quake in their appropriate footwear. I don't really think that makes me brave, though – they're just getting things out of proportion.

A recurrent interview question for me is: 'Why do you do so many panel shows?' It implies, probably fairly, that I do too many – that I've become over-exposed, that I've become a serial invader of people's living rooms with my nasal whining on subjects that don't really concern me. The answer to the question is that it's because I love doing them. The money is nice and the exposure has helped my career, but I've also done them when the money's shit and I don't need it, and when my level of exposure is too high – when the canny career choice would have been to try and create some scarcity in the market for my services. Recently I've started saying no a bit more often. But, ultimately, when I'm asked on a panel show my first reaction is that I want to do it because it's fun.

There's no doubt that this was all a bit of a career breakthrough for me. At the time of *FAQ U* and my first panel shows, I wasn't that busy. *Peep Show* kept coming around again, although it was always a marginal recommission because audience numbers remained stubbornly unimpressive, and we had our radio show but, other than that, I just did the occasional incongruous acting job: the BBC Shakespeare reworking of *The Taming of the Shrew*; a pilot sketch show for Channel 4 called *Blunder*; an ITV comedy drama called *All About George*; and, most surprisingly of all, a straight-to-video Michelle Pfeiffer film for which I briefly had to go to LA. But Rob was busier, in particular because he played the lead in another TV sitcom, *The Smoking Room*.

So when the panel shows started calling, and then other people started wanting to develop new panel shows with me as a regular team captain or even host, I had time to get really stuck in and Dave viewers have been bearing the brunt ever since. As well as cropping up regularly on *HIGNFY*, *QI* and *Mock the Week*, I made a series called *Best of the Worst* for Channel 4 and a pilot called *Pants on Fire* for the BBC, which title was thankfully commuted to *Would I Lie to You?* by the time a series was commissioned.

Perhaps more excitingly, in early 2006 I received a letter, dated 14 February, from Jon Naismith, the long-serving producer of Radio 4's 'antidote to panel games' *I'm Sorry I Haven't a Clue*. It wasn't a love letter, although it was the nearest I got to such things at the time. Jon and Graeme Garden, one of the wittiest men alive, had devised a new format for a radio panel show which, like *Would I Lie to You?*, involved lying, albeit in a very different way. Panellists would come on and read out lectures full of humorous nonsense from which their competitors would have to spot the occasional nugget of unlikely truth. They wanted me to chair it.

Jon's pitch to me, basically, was that while radio panel shows don't have the same impact as their TV equivalents or pay anything like as well, when they succeed they can run for decades. This could be your retirement plan, he was saying. And you don't even have to shave before you turn up. Well, five years after the pilot was broadcast, *The Unbelievable Truth* is now on its tenth series, so the plan seems to be working so far. With luck, I'll still be doing that show long after I've stopped being able to hear the buzzers.

Panel shows changed the public perception of me enormously because before I did them there *wasn't* really any public perception of me. People who were into comedy might have known the name of the guy who played Mark in *Peep Show* but wouldn't have had any sense of what he was like. When I started doing panel shows, people began to know a bit about me – obviously only the side of my personality that I projected when appearing in public, but that's still very different from playing a character, or it is in my case. People now seem to be slightly interested in me and want to know what I think about things. They want me to rant on subjects that annoy or concern me. They think my presence will make a programme potentially more entertaining. This is something for which I am tremendously grateful and which, to be honest, massively appeals to my vanity.

So, even though I set out with Rob to make character comedy, to be a writer-performer, to avoid stand-up at all costs, my career has taken a very different turn and, like a stand-up, I spend a lot of my time trying to be amusing as myself. I write a weekly column in the *Observer*, I do a series of online comedy-opinion pieces called *David Mitchell's Soapbox*, I've hosted shows which comment on the news, initially More4's *The Last Word* then *The Bubble* and *10 O'Clock Live*. No one would have thought of me for that kind of work as I stood outside the Crown and Sceptre ranting about the pointlessness of TV try-outs and how I'd been duped into starting my own Christmas late. I wouldn't even have deemed it possible myself.

I sometimes worry that I've strayed too far from comic acting and from writing sketches or sitcom scripts for TV. I don't want to lose that side of my career and I certainly don't want to stop working with Rob. But I now value my 'panel show persona', and all the opportunities for showing off on screen, in print and online that come with it, equally highly.

32

Lovely Spam, Wonderful Spam

It stops being Holland Park Avenue very suddenly. It's like the credit crunch – there's no real warning. In hindsight, there were signs. There was something slightly low rent about that Hilton hotel on the left and just a suggestion of flaky paint on Royal Crescent to the right, but nothing to prepare the casual pedestrian for what happens next. The tree-lined avenue of stucco houses ends abruptly and a bleak and vast plain of tarmac is revealed: a huge and alienating roundabout that forms a barrier between leafy Holland Park and affordable Shepherd's Bush.

I stop and wait at a pelican crossing and, unable to endure a moment's inactivity somewhere so unpleasant, get my phone out to check for messages. No texts and no voicemails but, because this is an iPhone, I can check for e-mails as well and I establish the slightly stressful fact that I've got two new ones before the lights change and I have to start moving.

Marvellous. Now I'm wondering what those e-mails can be. All the little issues of background stress – the people I haven't got back to, the decisions that broadcasters have yet to make that affect me, even potential family crises, crowd into my head in a way they wouldn't if I didn't know I had messages. That's the trap – I check them in the hope of the reassuring feeling that no one's tried to be in touch – but that doesn't work if someone has. For years I resisted a smartphone because e-mail, I felt, was something that should always be able to keep until I got home. If it's urgent, let people ring or text. An e-mail is like a letter – people shouldn't expect a response in less than a day or two. But, if they get wind of the fact that you can receive e-mails 24/7, the timescale on which they expect a response suddenly shortens. A 24-hour delay becomes discourteous. Great, another massive boon from the monthly bill.

I'm not in fact a Luddite. They actually destroyed machines rather than just moaning about them. But I'm not even a Luddite in the modern sense of someone who rails against technological advance. A lot of people assume that I am, but I've basically got all the stuff – a big desktop computer and a tiny laptop, a digital camera, an iPhone and a Kindle. I love my Kindle, in particular. I genuinely think it's nearly as good as reading a book and it fits neatly in a jacket pocket. Paperbacks used to fit neatly into a jacket pocket before publishers collectively decided this was a design advantage of their product that was unfair on the rest of the market and decided to make books annoyingly slightly bigger to give TV and video games a look-in. Very sporting. But the makers of Kindles have cleverly borrowed that feature from the old sort of paperback and combined it with the ability to contain a whole library of reading. They've even solved the problem of making the screen visible in bright light. It's a terrific machine.

Of course I hate myself for liking it. I want to prefer books in the same way that, as a child, I wanted to like porridge. It seems to fit my image better – the slightly tweedy person with strong views. Liking a Kindle is neither tweedy nor a strong view. You can't get strident about it. I suppose I could get strident about all the people who idiotically hate Kindles – except I don't think that's idiotic. I think it's born out of fear that reading and books, cornerstones of our civilisation, are under threat. I totally get that – I just happen to think the Kindle's a neat little device.

The other way to go, and there's a lot of pressure on men to be like this, would be to become a gadget fanatic. That's another thing that some people assume I am: if not a Luddite then a geek who would love technology to a slightly weird degree. It seems I don't come across as someone with much of a sense of proportion.

Or maybe that's just the culture. We're not interested in moderation. You get that with TV all the time – every new show is on a knife-edge. If it falls one way, it's a massive hit; if it goes the other, it's a humiliating flop. The whole industry and its critical scrutineers seem blind to all the things that are kind of fine. But I'd say that was the feeling you get from most of what's on television: 'This is okay – I might keep watching for a bit but I'll happily watch something else if it comes along or indeed turn away when the microwave pings.' TV assaults us with wave after wave of acceptable, mildly diverting mediocrity. Yet, to see it reviewed or hear it discussed by those that make it, you'd think it was a weird alternating barrage of unprecedented brilliance and inexcusable garbage. That's just not how it seems to me – maybe I need to adjust my set.

So I feel slightly ashamed to neither despise nor adore all these new machines that are changing the world. My plodding, not particularly adept, reluctant but not resistant attempts to vaguely and half-heartedly sort of get to grips with some of these things is disappointing for people. I get it with cricket as well. I quite like watching cricket, as a result of which people assume that I'm a huge cricket fan. 'I know you're obsessed with cricket,' people say, as if to be able to stand cricket at all must mean that I can't get enough of it. But I just quite like it. I don't want to be painted a fanatic, or real fanatics will think I'm a fraud. Or a moron who, despite apparently being obsessed with the sport, can't remember who last year's county champions were. By saying I like to go to the cricket, it feels like I've misrepresented myself as someone who can think of nothing else. 'Not everything is like Marmite!' I want to scream. 'Including, I suspect, Marmite!' Never has a product more successfully concealed the truth of its mediocrity merely by conceding the fact that some people find it disgusting.

Maybe men are supposed to have fanatical hobbies – that seems to be a thing. 'Men are from Mars, they like to go in their cave and make model ships or play fantasy war games or tinker with vintage cars.' That's the current off-the-shelf analysis. My lack of a real hobby or obsession on which to lavish all my spare time is probably a sign of a want of masculinity, a lack of testosterone.

Certainly, if you read men's magazines, it's made very clear that men are supposed to be massively into watches and gadgets and yachts and possibly golf clubs. It's odd that the magazines push traditional masculine traits so hard – you'd think that would be counter-productive to their aims. One thing I'd have thought was definitely part of an old-school golf-watches-guns-and-cars view of men is that they shouldn't buy magazines. Magazines, under that system, are surely for women. As are novels. Men should read the *Financial Times* or pornography. Of course many men's magazines are fairly close to pornography but are trying to present themselves as something else. Or maybe it's the other way round? Maybe it's the pornographical element that makes men feel it's okay for them to buy a magazine. The veneer of tits allows them to indulge their secret effeminate interests in jewellery and scent.

It annoys me to be living in an era where one of the few tradi-tional male attributes that I naturally possess – an aversion to grooming, pampering and perfume – is no longer valued. Indeed, for transparent marketing reasons, it's positively discouraged. My attitude that hair should be neatly cut, washed in shampoo but not conditioned or gunked up with 'product' is almost frowned upon now, as if displaying a want of personal hygiene. Answering the question 'How would you like to smell?' by saying 'I'd rather I didn't' is also no longer acceptable. It's not playing the game. Men are expected to put some cash into the cosmetic pot too – it's seen as almost un-feminist not to. What a uniquely capitalist response to that gender inequality: women have been forced by convention for generations – millennia – to spend money on expensive clothes and agonising shoes, to daub themselves with reality-concealing slap, to smell expensively inhuman, to self-mutilate in pursuit of eternal youth; and this, quite rightly, has come to be deemed unfair.

But how do we end this hell? We make men do it too. Well done everyone.

I only feel like this because I have a slightly perverse approach to my own appearance. I'm desperate never to be accused of vanity – which is a vanity in itself. I hate the thought that anyone could point to any aspect of my appearance and say, 'You think that looks nice. You've chosen that in an attempt to stand out in a good way.' That's why, although I was pleased to become fitter from all this walking, and secretly a bit pleased to look it, the down side is feeling self-conscious about how often it's triggered the question, 'Have you been dieting?' All I ever want is for my clothing, weight, haircut and smell to go unremarked on. I don't think I'm particularly handsome or particularly ugly – if I'm to be deemed acceptable, or even likeable, it won't be because of my appearance. So my aim is that my appearance should in no way be noteworthy. But then again, not so un-noteworthy as to be in itself noteworthy.

That's how I ended up with this haircut. I was issued with it as a child. I used to have a standard kid's 'bowl cut' and then, at some point, it was combed into a parting – and I've stuck with it. Not because I like it, or hate it, but because to change it at any point would have provoked comment and, even if it was kindly meant, that would have made me cringe.

But now the fact that I've never changed it and it looks so old-fashioned (or indeed Hitlerian, as some people say) itself provokes comment. So I'd probably have evaded more total comment in my life if I'd bitten the bullet ten years ago and changed to something less self-consciously unstylish. And all of this means that I've spent more time thinking about my hair than I either want to or consider consonant with being a man.

This is no good. I'm going to have to stop again and see who those e-mails are from. I pause in a slightly stressful bustling bit of pavement outside the West 12 shopping centre, which now looks across nervously with its '80s shabbiness at the gleaming modernity of the new Westfield. Or maybe with pride: perhaps West 12 was the vanguard, and now here comes Westfield, the mother ship.

Hooray! They're spam! Too much spam can be annoying but a little bit, every so often, can give such a welcome reprieve. You think you're going to have to reply or in some way leap into action but you can just ignore them – lovely. I mainly get spam from malt whisky websites as a result of my habit of buying my grandfather a bottle every Christmas for most of his nineties. I also get regular correspondence from the Islington Folk Club where I once went to a 'Ukelele Orchestra of Great Britain' concert. Yes, I'd got the hang of dating at last. No, Robert Thorogood had organised a trip as research for a screenplay he was writing about a Hawaiian guitarist. (I think this is a guitarist with a ham and pineapple topping.) It was one of those places where, for reasons of their licence, you have nominally to join the club in order to be admitted once. They must have asked for an e-mail address. I hope the updates I'm ignoring aren't draining their resources too much. I pocket my phone and continue towards Shepherd's Bush Green.

Magic though the iPhone patently is (albeit a dark magic performed by thousands of exhausted Chinese fingers), Rob and I have reason to resent it. I'm pretty sure it's what put paid to our Apple advertising contract. We were hired to make the British version of their 'I'm a Mac, I'm a PC' online campaign to raise awareness of their computers' merits. But, when the iPhone came out, all focus swivelled to that. Computers and differentiation from PCs became a sideshow. They didn't seem to want us to do an 'I'm an Apple, I'm a Blackberry' series of ads, which is a shame as the costumes might have been funny.

Rob and I got quite a lot of shit for doing that campaign, which genuinely surprised us. We thought adverts were just something that actors and comedians did to subsidise their income. You shouldn't advertise something immoral, we thought, but everything else, whether you used the product or not, was fair game. And actually we did use Apple products – we'd both always had Macs, although I was nervous saying that in our defence because I wanted to make clear that I would have equally happily advertised Microsoft; it's an honest company and I'm an actor for hire.

I was annoyed when people accused us of 'selling out' because I felt they were projecting onto us anti-capitalist views that we'd never held or expressed. At the same time, I felt guilty, partly because we'd been well paid and partly because I always feel a *bit* guilty – I think feeling guiltless is somehow impolite.

And there's no doubt there's an anti-corporate feeling abroad, which comedy fans are particularly susceptible to. A general suspicion of the motives of companies is very healthy. I like the fact that comedy enthusiasts have a tendency towards cynicism. But it's a shame when the cynicism becomes unquestioning and automatic. Even though companies are self-interested, amoral organisations, the world wouldn't be better off without them. They should be better regulated and more highly taxed, but they should exist and should be encouraged to trade. If you'd buy something from a company, as I would and have from Apple, it stands to reason that you would also be willing to sell them something. I don't think that means my soul is forfeit.

Nevertheless, the reaction has had an effect on me. When I get offered adverts nowadays, which happens fairly often, I don't just think: 'Would this be a reasonable gig? Can I justify it?' I also think: 'How much crap is going to get hurled at me for this? How long am I going to have to spend justifying it?' If the answer to that question is 'several years', then the ad might not be paying such an astronomical hourly rate as it initially seemed.

- 33 -

The Work-Work Balance

The Apple campaign came in the middle of 2006, a ridiculously hectic year for me and Rob. It had started with our filming a TV pilot of our radio sketch show which, with a very environmentally friendly approach to ideas, we'd called *That Mitchell and Webb Look*. It was immediately commissioned for a series, which we had to start writing straight away in order to shoot in June and July. We were thrilled with this commission. At last we had our own sketch show on BBC Two. That is literally what I'd most wanted to happen to me in the world as I sat watching *Monty Python's Flying Circus* on VHS as a teenager.

The way we landed the commission taught me something about the TV business. In the autumn of 2005 Channel 4 was dragging its feet over recommissioning *Peep Show* after a predictably poor ratings showing for series 3. Someone at 4 got wind of the fact that the BBC had asked us to make a TV pilot and they panicked. They felt they were 'losing us' to the competition. They'd been seriously considering deliberately losing us but, if it looked like the BBC had poached us, then they'd have egg on their faces, they felt. (Unpoached egg. We'd be nicely poached, they'd be covered in raw egg. They'd go golden if baked. This sounds delicious.) Consequently Channel 4 immediately offered Rob and me a full sketch show series, as well as a golden handcuffs deal (where they pay you money for doing nothing – for literally doing nothing, as in refusing to work for the competition) and two 'one-off specials' for *Peep Show*.

This put us in a dilemma. Clearly *Peep Show* was dead in the water – Channel 4 didn't want another series and were just offering two longer episodes as a sop to stop us, as they saw it, defecting to the BBC. But they were offering what we wanted: a full sketch show series. All the BBC were guaranteeing at that time was a pilot. That all pointed towards taking the Channel 4 offer.

But, to set against that, we'd made two series of the radio show with the BBC; they owned the rights to the characters, some of whom we wanted to bring to TV, and would be mightily pissed off if we suddenly (as *they* would have seen it) defected to Channel 4. And they'd have been fairly justified in that feeling as we would have been abandoning a pilot at the eleventh hour. On top of that, we wouldn't be able to make the Channel 4 show with Gareth Edwards because he was a BBC staff member. Channel 4 wanted to slip us into a sketch project which Phil and Objective were already developing – it wouldn't be 'our show' in the way the TV version of our existing radio programme, made by Gareth our long-time sketch show collaborator, would have been (and indeed proved to be).

After much agonising, we decided to stick to plan A and take the BBC pilot, hoping against hope that it would get a series – and resigned ourselves to the axing of *Peep Show* and Channel 4 being a bit pissed off with us for a couple of years. We felt this was the only honest course of action.

Well, it worked out so much better than we could have hoped. The BBC pilot did go on to be a series, and Channel 4, in order not to look like we'd jumped ship, promptly recommissioned *Peep Show* for a fourth time – a proper six-parter with no talk of 'one-off specials'. It was the last sticky recommission that show had and this year we're making series 8. Rob and I had only meant to be honest but somehow we'd also pulled off a Machiavellian coup.

That sketch show was the first of three big projects that we squeezed into 2006, as well as the Apple campaign. Next we shot a film, *Magicians*, in which we played childhood friends who fall out when their magic act is compromised by some shagging and beheading, written by Sam and Jesse. It was directed by Andrew O'Connor who, having been the man who had unconvincingly told me he was going to get a sitcom starring me onto television, had equally unbelievably gone on to say 'I'm going to direct a film with you in the lead' and been proved right again – he truly can pull rabbits out of hats. And lastly we were going on a national tour with a show, which we had to write (or at least compile from things we had already written) and rehearse.

On top of that, I'd taken a regular part in a new comedy-drama called *Jam and Jerusalem*. I didn't really have time for this as well: it involved getting late-night cars across the country after live shows with Rob in order to catch four hours' sleep, spend the next day filming at Shepperton and then be driven back to another theatre venue. It was exhausting – but I couldn't bear to turn down that series. It was written by Jennifer Saunders and, as well as Saunders herself, the cast included Dawn French, Joanna Lumley, Sue Johnston, Maggie Steed, Pauline McLynn, Sally Phillips and Patrick Barlow (star of *The National Theatre of Brent*, a brilliant two-man comedy troupe). I was hugely flattered to be in such company and, when we'd made the pilot, they'd all been so nice and so jolly. The atmosphere on that show, exhausted though I usually was when we filmed it, was uplifting.

The *Magicians* filming started straight after we'd finished the sketch show and just before we had to start rehearsing the tour. It fitted in perfectly, in just the same way as a night job fits in perfectly around a day job. It went well but it was exhausting; it had longer working days and longer working weeks than anything else I've ever filmed. That's because, in Britain, film-making is sort of a hobby: the occasional script will manage to cobble together funding and get itself made by calling in favours and making people work against the clock on minimum wage. It's odd how British film reviewers, who presumably know how this little cottage industry works, take the snooty approach of basically saying, 'Welcome to the big league – are you ready for the big screen? It's a much more demanding medium.' They seem to sneer at people who work in television, which is an *incredibly* similar medium and is actually solvent.

All of which is just a roundabout way of saying that, when *Magicians* came out, it got bad reviews, but I think it's quite a good film. Not amazing but certainly not shit. I think, if you like comedy, you'd find it an entertaining thing to watch over popcorn.

And then the tour. How had we got ourselves into this? We had to start rehearsing a week after the *Magicians* shoot ended, a week which I spent in Devon shooting exterior scenes for *Jam and Jerusalem*. When I got back, we had a week before our first preview at Pleasance London and a fortnight before our opening night at the Brighton Dome, which seats 1,500. Our last live comedy gig for a paying audience had been in front of 30 people, five years before, on the last night of the 2001 Fringe. We were seriously out of our depth, but were too busy to think this through at the time, which is lucky because I think we would have panicked.

At least the script, thank God, was written. The other factor militating against panic was our director, Lee Simpson, and supporting cast, James Bachman and Abigail Burdess, who was by this point engaged to Rob. They all behaved as if getting everything ready and putting on a storming show was an eminently achievable goal in the 'over a dozen' days that stretched out before us. And, in the end, it was fine. The first night in Brighton was a bit glitchy, to say the least, but the audience laughed a lot and Rob and I were so worried about quick costume changes that we barely gave our performances a moment's thought, which is often a good thing.

It's bizarre how things that seem impossible early on in the run of a theatre show – usually things to do with changing shoes or jackets in minuscule pockets of time – after a couple of weeks are ludicrously straightforward. You develop skills and aptitudes for them, dozens of useful knacks that allow you to transform your appearance at an almost magical speed – like Bruce Forsyth getting his trousers on and off in the gents of a comedy club with the aid of his teeth. It's so easy to forget, in professions like mine which involve doing lots of different things, how, if you do the same thing over and over again, your brain can make you properly good at it.

Extrapolate from this and you get a tiny glimpse of what it must be like to be a craftsman – to do those things that seem miraculous to outsiders but are quite routine to the skilled, whether it's putting in a hip replacement or a new shower, navigating the Bosphorus or a company database. Humans have the ability to do incredible things – more amazing even than gluing on a false moustache with one hand while tying a bow-tie with the other – if they put in enough time and practice. Actors, writers, journalists and politicians are apt to forget this and to think that, if intelligent people like them can't master something in a week and a half, then it must be impossible for those poor dullards who can't cut it in the media.

I saw a funny example of this on BBC News during the build-up to a recent London marathon. The journalist and newsreader Sophie Raworth was going to run the marathon and the news was doing a feature on it because, I think, only a handful of people had been shot in Syria that day. In preparation, she was televised doing a training session with a British Olympic runner. She ran along with her for a bit, at the athlete's warm-up pace, and then they stopped. Raworth was exhausted and said something like: 'That's amazing! I'm totally destroyed and you're not out of breath at all!'

Now, I'm sure Raworth meant well with this remark, and was largely trying to illustrate the situation to viewers, but that fact really is *not* amazing. She should expect the runner to be immensely better at running because her job is to run. She runs and runs and runs every single day. But Raworth, like a typical journalist, seemed to imply that there wasn't much to professional-standard running other than not having a beer gut and pushing for the burn. She probably wouldn't beat this runner in a race, she will have thought, but there's no reason to assume that she'd fall massively behind. She was amazed by how much better the runner was at running because she didn't really believe in skills. It's the whole 'It's not rocket science' refrain. Well, many things, while not being rocket science, simply cannot be picked up on the hoof.

Maybe I'm particularly aware of the power of a skill because I can't drive. Sitting in the passenger seat while someone makes a car go along, navigating junctions, changing lanes, stopping at lights while simultaneously chatting, fiddling with the radio and eating a sandwich leaves me as amazed as Raworth. But clearly it's the most routine of aptitudes – most people I know possess it.

I'd probably be less amazed if I'd never tried to do it myself. I'd assume it was easy. As it is, I've tried to just the wrong extent. Twice I've started, then given up at the point when my head was swimming with things to remember – mirrors, brakes, windows, indicators, coordinating feet and hands for gear changes, reversing round corners, finding the fucking biting point.

The first time was when I was seventeen, the age you're supposed to learn. You're used to learning things at that time of life – you've been doing it since before you can remember. Seventeen solid years, from sitting up, through talking and toilet training, reading and writing, autumn, basic maths, autumn, capital cities, autumn, all the way up to calculus, historiography and autumn. The prospect of those driving lessons and tests is a lot less intimidating in the context of so many other lessons and tests.

I had a nice instructor – he seemed kind and responsible. He was an ex-policeman. He told me I was doing quite well. I believed him. Then he said something quite strange: 'Left here. So, the weirdest thing happened to me last night – watch your speed. I woke up at about 3am and there were these lights outside. Down to second, it's a hill. Flashing lights – don't flash your lights. Yeah, flashing lights. So I went to the window and looked out and – have you seen the cyclist? Aliens! There was this alien ship hovering over next door's garden. Careful, it's a mini-roundabout …'

I didn't have any more lessons after that. Not for fifteen years, at which point I went on an intensive driving course in Norwich with Mark Evans. Mark had promised his girlfriend that he'd learn and suggested he and I get back on that metaphorical horse together. Norwich was chosen on the basis that when Mark googled 'intensive driving course', or possibly even 'crash course', a Norwich driving school came up first.

My new instructor showed no signs of having recently undergone an alien epiphany. He was a slight young chap called Eddie who smoked roll-ups and coughed a lot. He was a bit like a Dickensian waif – but more of a stickler for checking your mirrors.

On day one, ten minutes into my first lesson, I was tentatively driving around some suburban streets with Eddie when I stopped at a junction. Slightly abruptly. I hadn't yet got the feel of the brakes and, I suppose, I was erring on the side of caution. Eddie screamed.

'Aaaaaaaahhhhhhhh! What did you do that for?'

'Sorry, I was just stopping.'

'Christ that hurts! Jesus, careful!'

'Sorry.'

'It's okay. I dislocated my shoulder last night.'

'Right.'

'It's right where the seatbelt digs in.'

'I see.'

'Why did you stop so suddenly?'

I wanted to say: 'Because I can't drive a car, you moron! What the hell did you expect!? When has anyone ever got in this car with you and known how to drive!?'

It was a weird week. Every day, Mark and I would go out with our instructors, meeting up every couple of hours at a lorry drivers' caff on the ring road. On the first morning, Eddie ordered teacakes. A large plate duly arrived. Eddie smiled:

'Massive plate of teacakes. And that's only three quid. Pretty good, eh?'

To be fair, it was exactly what I was thinking.

In the evenings, Mark and I would go to the pub and discuss both Eddie and Mark's instructor, whose name escapes me but who had a shiny nut-brown head, which was entirely hairless but for a magnificent moustache. He ran the company and Eddie looked up to him like a god. During the day, I would undergo hours of stressful tuition which would make me sweat profusely. It was January but, unless we kept the car windows wound down, they'd steam up within minutes. At the end of the course Mark passed and I failed. I blame Eddie.

So, when Rob and I were touring around the country in 2006, I still couldn't drive. But that didn't matter because the producers had hired a massive gold tour bus for us to travel around in. This was quite the ego boost, even if thoughts of rock bands on the road made us nervous about inspecting the upholstery.

Even more of an ego boost was the warmth of crowds that had specifically paid to see us. These weren't Edinburgh audiences wandering in because they'd read a review or merely failed to get into the more successful show in the venue next door. These were 'Mitchell and Webb fans' – a new type of human whom the power of television had called into being. Consequently the show always went down well and was a huge pleasure to perform. Except in St Albans – that was a shit night. I don't know what those guys were expecting but they sat there in baffled silence throughout. Maybe they'd seen a dog get run over on their way in or something.

I worried most in advance about our visit to Liverpool. You hear a lot, usually from Liverpudlians, about what a warm and lovely and naturally witty and comedic place Liverpool is. It's as though you can't fully understand humour if you're not from there. To those of us with no real connection to the city but who still aspire to amuse, it's an irritating claim. Being all kind and sentimental and northern doesn't give you the monopoly on jokes, we want to say. I'm all southern and buttoned up and I don't cry at weddings or give a single solitary shit about football but I still think I can make a reasonable stab at raising a laugh. I don't want to accept that there's this place, where I'm a stranger, in possession of the warm beating heart of mirth. I considered mentioning that my father's from Liverpool in the opening sketch, but that would be cheating because I'd never been there before myself. The audience would only see a repressed public schoolboy and might be sceptical about his comic powers. Rob isn't a repressed public schoolboy – he's from a working-class family, he's from Lincolnshire, and he went to a state school – but, damn him, nobody can tell. Thanks, Rob – way to suppress your fashionable underprivileged regional roots!

So we were a bit apprehensive about the night we were to play Liverpool's Royal Court Theatre and weren't much enthused when we arrived. It is a beautiful theatre but, in 2006 at least, it was in a terrible state of repair. Everywhere, doors were blocked and signs warned of asbestos. The seats had been ripped out of the stalls and replaced with cabaret tables and there was a bar at the back – actually in the same room as the stage. This gave the place a discomfiting, cabaret, chair-throwing feel.

Nevertheless, the show had sold out and, half an hour before it was due to start, a long, chatty queue had developed round the block. It was a cold night and the theatre had no bar other than the one in the stalls, so the audience would have to remain shivering outdoors until the house opened. And there was a problem. Our technicians had discovered that the main lighting bar over the stalls – the large piece of metal from which other large, sharp, hot and electric pieces of metal were suspended – was only held up by a few flakes of paint and plaster. It was terribly unsafe and we couldn't open the house with it in that state.

It was one of those problems that kept developing. Initially, it looked like the bar needed screwing in some more; then it transpired that the thing it was being screwed into needed screwing in; then some bits of ceiling came away in someone's hand. This all made things much worse where the audience was concerned because the theatre management wouldn't just say: 'The show will be delayed an hour,' at the outset. That would have allowed people to go off to the pub or ask for their money back, not just be left there shivering. Instead, the hour's delay came in increments of ten minutes each. I know what that would have done to my mood if I were part of that queue round the block.

Soon Rob and I were desperately hoping that the lighting bar couldn't be fixed and we'd have to cancel the performance. It would be a big blow to ticket sales but at least we wouldn't get bottled off stage. So, when all was fixed and the audience came shivering in an hour late, we were extremely nervous. At the start of the show we went on and explained the situation and apologised. We were met with such an atmosphere of warmth from those freezing people that we were immediately ashamed for having expected them to be angry. It was a wonderful audience. Noisy, enthusiastic and determined to have a good time – every joke was relished. I'd been determined to leave Liverpool with something negative to say about that city's attitude to comedy, but not only was I denied that, this audience gave such a positive demonstration of everything Liverpudlians claim for their city and its comic heart that I'm absolutely duty bound to mention it here. Grrr. Still, that building was in a shocking state.

Throughout this tour Rob and I were powerfully sick of the sight of one another. We'd been working closely together for years – and that year, more closely than ever. Also, we were no longer desperate or poor so the fear that drew us together, that need for mutual reassurance, had lessened. We remained good friends – we knew that objectively – we just didn't want to be in the same room for a second more than was necessary. I suppose we'd been thrown together into a situation as intense and stressful as marriage – but we didn't fancy each other and we weren't in love.

I wouldn't want you to think, though, that we ever argued. Rob and I have virtually never exchanged a cross word. Neither of us likes confrontation or believes that it's healthy to 'have it all out' (Rob learned that filming *Confetti*) and we're both quite self-indulgent when it comes to rhetoric. I think we instinctively know that if we had a row, and particularly if we'd had one during that frantic and stress-charged year, we'd both have said TERRIBLE things. Unforgettable, dark truths about each other would have been slung around in a way that neither of us would ever be able to forget even if we managed to forgive. So, for months, we interacted with thin-lipped smiles – all icy politeness, passive aggression and significant pauses. It's a feeling I'm determined to remember in case we ever play a gay couple in a film.

I certainly obsessed about all the things I was doing in the show, and for our act in general, that I felt Rob didn't contribute equally to, and I'm sure he must have done the same. I would tell myself I didn't need him and that, if he suggested we should stop working together, I'd agree in a flash. But I never seriously considered suggesting that myself. Other, wiser and nicer parts of my brain were counselling caution, reminding me of how far we'd come together and how foolish it would be to imperil this double act, the cornerstone of both of our dream careers, in a fit of pique. So I restricted myself to bitching to James Bachman.

On the tour, it got to the point when, in any sketch, we'd each be trying to upstage the other. Literally. I'm not talking about hamming things up or changing the performance at all, but just trying to be standing further upstage so that more of your face is visible to the audience and more of the back of the other performer's head. (It may sound counter-intuitive to move away from an audience to get more attention but, unless you're enough of a performance-whore to entirely dispense with the notion of looking at the other person on stage who you're supposedly talking to, and neither Rob nor I is that bad, the best way for your performance to be more visible and better communicated to people watching is to stand further away so, while talking to the other person on stage, you're the one facing the crowd.) I didn't mean to do this unfairly, and I'm sure neither did Rob. I just wanted to make sure *I* wasn't upstaged and was erring on the side of caution. But, as a result, in the many sketches where we were both talking to each other on stage, a small, almost imperceptible, dance away from the audience would commence.

I could no longer imagine Rob just as a friend. For all his good qualities, the thought of him was inseparable from the burden and stress of work and, I suppose, from this entity 'Mitchell and Webb' which had started to feel like a denial of my own individuality – whereas panel shows were an expression of it. On his side, I was pretty sure he'd started to hate me.

Just before Christmas that year, only a few days after the tour ended and a few days before the fourth series of *Peep Show* started filming, Rob and Abbie got married. Rob asked me to be his best man.

Oh God, I thought, I'm such a cunt. This is, basically, my best friend. And I'm so lucky to have been working with him for ten years. I haven't 'lost my individuality', I'm just a bit knackered.

Obviously I was honoured by the best man thing. Obviously I was touched. Obviously I was annoyed. Those are always the chief feelings at such times: you've been asked to be part of a close friend's special day – that's in the plus column – and the terrifying prospect of making a speech will ruin it for you as a result – that's in the minus. But I was just going to have to pretend, for one day, that I wasn't a total cunt.

And in the end, it was easy. At the wedding, a wonderful Christmassy occasion on an ice-cold foggy London day, I actually went a bit 'method' and forgot I was a cunt at all. I thought about how much Rob had made me laugh at that first audition in Cambridge, despite his scandalous haircut and his ear jewellery, and how much he'd made me laugh since. I thought about the frantic first night of *Innocent Millions*, and all the other shows we'd done together when there was no money in it, only fun and possibility. Once again, I could feel our friendship rather than just remember it. And I felt properly happy for him, not just that I ought to feel happy for him. Having got to know Abbie better by then, as a result of the tour, certainly helped. She usually understands what I find annoying about Rob – she can see what I've spotted and will often commiserate. But she always sees beyond that in a way that I sometimes failed to, and certainly had done for most of 2006.

It's always weird to see someone you've known for ages, a contemporary, get married – or at least I always find it so. Throughout the time that I'd worked with Rob there'd been something else going on in his head, something more important than performing or his career, or even his friendships, for all that he valued those things very highly. I realised, as I listened to his tearful speech about Abbie, and her tearful one about him, that he'd remembered and prioritised the attitudes and feelings that all loved children experience before anything else. Through all his ambition, failure and success, he'd kept a sense of perspective, while I had not.

As Abbie sat down, in floods of tears and to rapturous applause, I stood up to make some jokes.

The End of
the Beginning

I'd met Victoria before, I was certain of that – briefly, at some after-show drinks years earlier. I could tell she hadn't remembered. This meeting was different, though. Last time, I hadn't fallen in love with her.

This was a very posh party. It was a film premiere party – the reward for having been to a film premiere (which, I'd just discovered, is quite a distracting way to watch a film). It was 2007 and I was starting to get invited to this sort of thing but usually I was filming or doing a panel show or my back hurt too much. But my back was on the mend, thanks to all the walking, and I'd been personally invited to this, rather than just getting an e-mail through my agent, so here I was. I was immensely glad.

There were lots of famous people there, some of whom had introduced themselves to me and said nice things. They thought I was famous too, it seemed, so there was a sort of implied acquaintanceship between us. I liked this, but it also made me queasy.

Then she'd been introduced to me – and I'd said we'd once met, just out of pedantry really, and she had neither denied nor remembered it. She was all chatty and sparky and gossipy and interesting and it seems ridiculous that I can't remember a single thing she said, though I can still see her face looking up at me when I close my eyes.

After a while, the little chatting group developed and widened. She was a couple of yards away from me now and I was talking to a middle-aged woman who had some theory about comedy. I wasn't interested but I still considered parties like this to be basically hostile environments so I was also grateful to the middle-aged woman for paying me the attention. But then she was back, in my eyeline again, interrupting the woman.

'Do you smoke?' She was gesturing towards the door.

I'm a moron. 'No,' I said. I was just answering the question. I hadn't had a cigarette for about six months so I felt like I didn't really smoke. I only ever have a bit. I didn't want to lie to her. Amused irritation flashed noticeably across her face. Irritation, though, not disappointment. I suspect she already knew.

She went off for a cigarette – she kind of had to now – but was back quite soon, if not quite soon enough. She wasn't trying to mingle. I was pretty sure she was flirting but was unwilling to believe my instincts as that seemed too good to be true.

We talked for a long time. I think the main topic of conversation was how awkward parties like this were and how some people seemed so adult and adept about working their way round them, but how we found that difficult and didn't know how you were supposed to break into other conversations. We. I hoped she didn't really want to break into another conversation because I certainly didn't. I wanted to stay in this one forever. The pessimist in me said that she was just what she said she was – a bad mingler, someone shy at parties who didn't know how to break away from someone else shy at parties.

Eventually she did: 'I really should go and say hello to …' I can't remember who she said, I was suddenly too depressed to care. 'Maybe see you in a bit?' She walked away and I got the first wave of a sensation that would become familiar to me: missing her.

I date the current phase of my life from that party. I changed then. Everything that happened to me after that moment, even incidental things, are in a different context, a new world where different things matter.

We went on a few dates – I clumsily managed to organise that, self-consciously booking a restaurant for a time and a place and then feeling amazed, touched and flattered when she actually turned up – this beautiful, exciting woman, just to see me, wearing clothes that she'd picked out while thinking of me.

But it didn't work out. She e-mailed me and explained, carefully, lovingly really, why it wasn't a good time for her and how she felt something, in fact had strong feelings for me, but didn't think it could work at the moment. But can't one always get over that? Timing can't be crucial – not outside the context of a joke? And she said she'd met someone else as well. Ah. She didn't know what would come of that and who knows, maybe in six months or so …? But it was a bad time. A very bad time. Her father had just died. Everything was wrong.

It may sound strange but I treasured that e-mail. It was such a reluctant brush-off – I felt it was almost a sign of achievement for me. Part of me was amazed, overjoyed even, that I'd got so close so quickly to someone I'd fallen for. Because I knew I could only be with someone I'd fallen for and I wasn't falling for people very often any more. And it had never been quite like this.

'Close but no cigar,' as Ellis says. Well that's all right, I thought. Give it another 34 years and you'll meet someone else nice.

I did not think that.

I didn't blame her – she'd been clear, honest and fair and I loved her – but I didn't really know how to cope. Being single had never made me lonely before – now the feeling was crippling. There were couples everywhere, it seemed. Everyone had someone. I wanted someone more than I'd ever done before at precisely the same moment that I realised that only one person would do.

Never was I more bitterly aware that I didn't have three wishes. But what if I'd already had a wish? What if I'd used it up? I'd wanted my career success so much and for so long. Had I wasted my luck, my wish on that, something that seemed so trivial now? My career, acting, comedy which, at the time of every other crush, had been a consolation and a distraction, this time felt like a rebuke. That's the cold, selfish glittery object of my desire that I get. Instead of her. Try and console yourself with that, sneers the genie.

Shepherd's Bush Green is not a nice place to walk, I think to myself as I cross it diagonally northwestwards, weaving between bench-focused gatherings of chatting tramps. It's noisy and ugly, but I'm used to walking in drab, boring, featureless places. For years, from the end of 2007, it didn't matter where I walked. I wasn't looking at the view. I started walking for my back, I kept going because of her. It made thinking about her more bearable. If I got more miserable, I could just speed up.

Drinking helped too. I'd always liked getting drunk in the pub or at parties – now I had a real use for it. At the end of a miserable day you could use it to speed up time – almost like cutting to the next morning's hangover. So I did that a lot.

A few times, when drunk, I'd get off with someone. The booze allowed me to tell myself that it might make me feel better. Maybe I'll manage to fall in love with this person instead, I always wondered. It seems that it can happen very quickly. And surely I should be doing something to shake myself out of my obsession with a woman who's going out with someone else.

One of those pissed late-night snogs was captured by a paparazzo and printed in *Heat* magazine. That felt pretty humiliating. What a fool I'd been, I thought. I had no personal life to speak of, not even much experience of how to meet women and form relationships, and yet I'd already become famous. If I was ever to work any of this out, relationships, women, life, as I probably should have done as a teenager, I'd have to do it sneaking around because the press might be interested. I was snogging a girl outside a bar, for God's sake – that is a normal thing to do, something I should have done more often, and now thousands of people will have seen. No one, I thought bitterly, can have had a higher percentage of their life's snogs appear in the papers than me. I wasn't ashamed of what I'd done but I was embarrassed for it to be shown to the world – as if someone had taken a picture of me washing my balls or having a shit.

It dawned on me gradually that quite a lot of people who I didn't know were interested in my private life, or my apparent lack of one. My profile had grown slowly – initially *Peep Show* had barely been noticed but, as more series aired, more people became aware of it. Then some became aware of the sketch show. Others started to see me crop up on panel shows. Gradually the likelihood of a stranger knowing who I was had grown.

And, as it grew, I was interviewed more often by newspapers, and the nature of the questions I was asked in those interviews changed. They were fishing for details of my private life. I suppose that's natural – people are always interested in that sort of thing, and my character in *Peep Show* has his private life very much to the fore. They wanted to know how mine compared. And I'd certainly implied in panel shows, as a way of getting a laugh and developing a persona that people could get a handle on, that I was a lonely, dysfunctional, OCD loser.

For years, I was very happy with this image. People found it funny, and when I wasn't that well known they didn't want to dig any deeper. The language of lonely self-loathing gets a lot of laughs when bluntly used in a comic context – it's like doing a sketch about the Samaritans. But, in an interview, the context becomes more serious. They weren't letting me paint a stereotypical, broad-brush picture of an isolated wanker – they wanted details. And, because I was broken-hearted, it was a joke that was getting a bit too edgy for me anyway. It made me sad to describe myself as so sad.

'Is that what you're really like?' interviewers wanted to know. 'Lots of women find you attractive, you know – just look at the internet.'

It was absolutely true that, by googling my name, I could find lots of examples of people saying that they fancied me, usually (they added) to their surprise. But then some people will fancy anyone who's on telly. That just turns them on. As, sometimes, does being funny. As does being unattainable. As does not being there 'in real life', all wrong/normal/unglamorous/unhilarious/hairy/human like people are when you actually know them. I get it a lot on Twitter – people saying they fancy me or asking their friends if it's 'wrong' that they fancy me, which is definitely a backhanded compliment, or possibly a backhanded insult. It's all a bit of an ego boost, I suppose. But I think that moment of saying they fancied me would always be the high point of the relationship, so there's no need to take it any further. Even in my memories of my racy encounter with the girl at Cambridge who was keen to bed a Footlights president, it's only the initial realisation that's an exciting memory – after that it fades to drunkenness and guilt.

I suppose, if you do decide to shag groupies – and I'm not saying those who do are necessarily wrong as I'm sure it can be done in a fun and mutually satisfying way – you have to deal, as soon as it becomes clear that you're up for it, with your sudden lowering in the groupie's estimation. It's like what I get when someone realises I'm not the novelist. Suddenly you've become attainable to the groupie – the excitement of fancying a star from afar evaporates and they have to deal with the reality of a stranger's body – usually an older man's.

There were lots of things about my life that seemed to baffle interviewers. Why did I still live in an ex-council flat in Kilburn? was a very common question. Why did I show no interest in some of the trappings of fame: expensive cars or clothes or giant TVs? Perhaps I came across as some sort of weird ascetic or the kind of person who 'keeps himself to himself' and is later discovered to be dwelling on a pit of human bones.

I think people thought I had something to hide. Maybe he's gay and can't admit it, they may have thought. Or spends all his money on morphine. Or, as the *Heat* photo might have suggested, he's as promiscuous as Russell Brand but is somehow managing to do it on the quiet. *What is his secret?* was the implied question I feared. So I tried to be honest, when I went on *Desert Island Discs* at least, about the bare facts of my life and how I felt – that I was single and unhappy.

I resented the interest. I didn't think – I don't think – that the specifics of my private life were anyone's business. I was just a purveyor of comedy. If people liked it, they could keep watching. If not, they should stop. I didn't want to encourage people to buy in too much to 'what I was really like'. They couldn't know me personally and I didn't want to be trapped into creating the illusion that they could – an illusion that might subsequently be shattered if I was caught on film strangling a cat.

But mainly I resented it because I *was* hiding something. I couldn't stop thinking about Victoria. I was hopelessly in love in a way that wouldn't go away. That's why I had no private life to speak of – because I didn't want one, couldn't face one without her. I told no one about it. Never mind interviewers, I didn't tell my closest friends or my parents of the enormous sadness that over-shadowed my life. I didn't tell them because I was ashamed and I knew what they'd say. 'Stop indulging yourself in these hopeless feelings. Snap out of it. She doesn't want to go out with you – she said so. She's going out with someone else. It's not the end of the world – it happens to people all the time. It's happened to you before. Deal with it.'

They would probably have put it more gently than that. But I'm sure that's what they'd have said I should do. So, if I already knew that, what was the point in telling them? It was stupid to have such an all-consuming crush at my age. So I couldn't talk about it – and without doing so, I couldn't adequately explain my life.

I didn't want to move from Kilburn, partly because my friends lived there but mainly because it would be a sign of my life moving on without her. I didn't want to change any major aspect of my exist-ence on my own – I wanted to do it as part of my future with her. I couldn't let go of that hope even when I told myself that I should.

And my career just went from strength to strength, as if taking the piss. I had a successful sitcom and sketch show on the go at once, I was a sought-after guest for panel shows, I was a praised columnist in a fine newspaper, everyone wanted to make a programme with me, everyone seemed to be saying I was the next Stephen Fry. And, because of the walking coupled with the appetite-suppressant effect of a broken heart, I'd lost some weight. I was looking healthier and more attractive. *Every* wish had come true except the one that mattered.

The 'six months or so' came and went. I'd occasionally see her at panel show recordings. If there was a *Peep Show* screening party, I'd invite her. She'd come and we'd chat and it would be lovely but I was never left in any doubt about her status: she had a boyfriend. That was that.

I waited for three years. Isn't that weird? Aren't I odd? I can't explain it other than to say that I couldn't do anything else. She's not only too wonderful, she's too right for me. Any sane straight man would find her attractive but she's funny, bright, sexy, nervous and confident in ways that could have been meant for me. I suppose that's why I waited. I couldn't shake the cheesy thought that it was 'meant to be'.

Three years after we met at that party (met for the *second* time I bloody-mindedly can't not say) she became single again. And we went on some dates again. It was different this time. We started gradually – secretly really. But each week, we spent more time together than the last.

I switched over from feeling cursed, as if the world had been constructed to spite me, to feeling so much luckier than I believed I could ever deserve. If only I'd known I just had to wait three years, I kept thinking. That was nothing – I would have gladly suffered ten times as much, as long as I'd known it would work out and we'd have our chance. *We.*

It's so much easier to talk about what makes you unhappy than what makes you happy, I'm now discovering. And I am happy now, I can't deny it. And I am happy because of Victoria. All my priorities are different now, and better.

In March I asked her to marry me and she said yes. In fact, to my unsurpassable delight, she said 'Of course.' Of course we're getting married. It's obvious. Perhaps I should have asked her at that party.

There's a down side to all this – and I don't mean not being able to drink beer in the bath or scratch my balls during dinner, because she insists on both. Neither do I mean the fact that we won't be living in Kilburn, although I'll miss it. But Harlesden it has to be – she insists.

The down side is the fear. The fear of something happening to her, the pressure of there being two bodies in the world that I want to keep from harm and only being able to watchfully inhabit one of them. I wonder if you know what I mean. I hope you do, for your sake.

It's a worry I'll have to learn to live with because I'm definitely out of wishes. And whatever happens from now on, I want to concentrate on being grateful. I thought I was too old to change – someone once told me that anything you haven't done by the age of 28, you'll probably never do. And by my mid-thirties I'd never formed a long-term relationship, never moved in with anyone, hardly ever got off with the same woman twice. Now I've met someone who I can't live without – and I don't have to.

So I'm inexpressibly grateful, to her and to fate, for this change, this miracle. It would have been an incomplete life, one not properly lived, if I'd never fully loved or had the amazing feeling of it being reciprocated.

- 35 -

Centred

I cross Uxbridge Road opposite the Defectors Weld pub. Now there's a name! No apostrophe so we can't be sure that the weld – the joining of two metal parts together – belongs to the defector or defectors. But, as apostrophes are often omitted in names of businesses (Waterstones, where you may well have bought this book, have dispensed with theirs) we can't be sure that it doesn't either. Maybe it's a statement: that's what defectors do – perhaps metaphorically. Is it a refutation of the argument that suggests defectors, those who desert or leave a country, company, cause or civilisation, are divisive figures? On the contrary, the pub is saying, defectors weld: they join together nations and ideas, their very act of treachery a sign that people are not so different. Somehow. Or is it just a reference to a Soviet émigré's bodged bit of metalwork?

I like quirky pub names and I think it's always a shame when one is lost and turned into an All Bar One or Slug and Lettuce, horrible chains that roll out their dismal puns nationwide. But my pleasure here is marred because I'm pretty sure Defectors Weld was an Edwards Wine Bar ten years ago. Maybe this is a reversion to an older name? I hope so but I suspect that 'Defectors Weld' is a recent attempt at quirkiness which I slightly despise. Although, full marks for weirdness – and I suppose for confirming my theory that it doesn't much matter what things are called.

I continue past the pub up Wood Lane. I'm nearly there. I'm tired now and, as I drag myself along the side of the giant retail cuboid that is the Westfield shopping centre, I feel like an ant doggedly crawling across a tile. Or antedly perhaps. This place where things are sold was built in a massive 'brown field site' where, a hundred years ago, things were made. Not many things are made in London now. I'm going to one of the few places where they still are. Although not for long.

I pass a multi-storey car park, continuing under a railway bridge and past the new Wood Lane Tube station, on the site of the derelict remains of the old Wood Lane Tube station. I carry on a little further without looking to my left yet. I want to get to the point where I can see it all properly, before turning. To catch that famous, familiar, ugly, lovely sight all in one go.

I turn and read the words written across the bland brick of Studio One: 'BBC Television Centre'. There's no visible 'For Sale' sign.

I've worked here a lot. I still do, although at the moment I'm making a Channel 4 show, *10 O'Clock Live*, here. We did the studio recordings of our sketch show in TV Centre. We shot our first *Comedy Nation* sketch in an office here. So many excited *Bruiser*, *All Day Breakfast* and *That Mitchell and Webb Look* meetings happened here, so many panel show recordings, so many drunken after-show drinks dos in the dingy basement green rooms.

I'd been heading here for years, really. Since I first saw it on TV – this was the place the programmes came from, we were given to understand. This was where the *Blue Peter* garden was, where *Not Only … But Also* and *Monty Python's Flying Circus* were dreamt up, as well as *Morecambe and Wise*, *The Two Ronnies*, *Dad's Army*, *Fawlty Towers*, *The Fall and Rise of Reginald Perrin*. Yes, this was a place where the British still made things.

They're closing it, selling it. Everything's moving either to Portland Place or up to the new 'Media Village' in Salford. 'It would cost more to update it than it would to knock it down,' some people say. Although it's listed so they're not allowed to knock it down. Anyway they're leaving and I only just got here. It seems, when I left Oxford, I took the M40 in the wrong direction.

I'm not from London, but I came here because it's the capital. It seemed logical to me that this would be where most of the TV comes from – just as it's where most of the theatre and film happens. I thought that was the system, so that's why I made the journey. I didn't think it was unfairly advantageous to Londoners because London, I thought, was everyone's, was the world's. That's what Sherlock Holmes thought too. So it's galling to see that system suddenly change, apparently for the benefit of people in other regions whose desire to get into broadcasting isn't sufficiently strong to make them willing to move house.

I'm confused. Confused that the thing I've been travelling towards is closing just as I arrive. I don't just mean the BBC, I mean the whole old media. Television, radio, publishing and newspapers, these grand old thriving British traditions that I grew up with and dreamt of being part of, are all now foundering and changing. They're retreating in the face of technological developments that threaten to render them obsolete, or at least undermine their ability to pay people for their work.

Opportunities, excitements, technological revolutions abound – we're living in a heyday for entrepreneurs. But I don't want to be an entrepreneur or a businessman. I don't want to try and guess the future and make money from it. I want to make normal programmes within established parameters. I feel like a painter who's been handed a video camera.

For years, I was driven on by ambition. And also by the absence of a private life – a nagging unhappiness like the burn of sciatica which can suddenly rear up into crippling pain. I had to keep moving to walk it off.

There was this brilliant exciting job called 'TV comedian' that I knew a very few lucky souls could get. I was determined to be one of them. And now I am and I love it. I don't want to do anything else. I don't want to move on – I just want to carry on. And that's an increasingly unacceptable aspiration in our age. People say, 'If you're not moving forwards, you're moving backwards.'

Well, I'm not moving forwards any more. For the first time in a long while I'm standing still.